Religion, Education and Society

This volume presents findings from recent research focusing on young people and the way they relate to religion in their education and upbringing. The chapters are diverse and multidisciplinary – in terms of the religions they discuss (including Christianity, Islam and Sikhism); the settings where young people reflect on religion (the classroom, youth club, peer group, families, respective religious communities and wider society); the different perspectives which relate to religious education and socialisation (the teaching of RE, the role of teachers in pupils' lives, the way teachers' personal lives shape their approach to teaching, school ethos and social context, and the place and rationale of RE); the contexts within which the authors work (different national settings and various academic disciplines); and the methodology used (qualitative, quantitative and mixed-method approaches).

The authors make important contributions to the debate about the role of religious education in the curriculum. They demonstrate the crucially important formative influence of religious education in young people's lives which reaches well into their adulthood, shaping religious and other identities, and attitudes towards the 'other' – whatever that 'other' may be.

This book was originally published as a special issue of the *Journal of Beliefs & Values*.

Elisabeth Arweck is Senior Research Fellow in the Warwick Religions and Education Research Unit (WRERU), Institute of Education, University of Warwick, UK, and the Editor of the *Journal of Contemporary Religion*. Her recent research has focused on young people's attitudes to religious diversity and the religious socialisation and nurture of young people. She is author of *Researching new religious movements in the West* (2007).

Robert Jackson is Professor of Education at the University of Warwick, UK, the former Director of Warwick Religions and Education Research Unit (WRERU), and Professor of Religious Diversity and Education at the Council of Europe-related European Wergeland Centre in Oslo. He was Editor of the *British Journal of Religious Education*.

Religion, Education and Society

Edited by
Elisabeth Arweck and Robert Jackson

Routledge
Taylor & Francis Group
LONDON AND NEW YORK

First published 2014
by Routledge

2 Park Square, Milton Park, Abingdon, Oxfordshire OX14 4RN
711 Third Avenue, New York, NY 10017

Routledge is an imprint of the Taylor & Francis Group, an informa business

First issued in paperback 2018

Copyright © 2014 Taylor & Francis

All rights reserved. No part of this book may be reprinted or reproduced or utilised in any form or by any electronic, mechanical, or other means, now known or hereafter invented, including photocopying and recording, or in any information storage or retrieval system, without permission in writing from the publishers.

Notice:
Product or corporate names may be trademarks or registered trademarks, and are used only for identification and explanation without intent to infringe.

British Library Cataloguing in Publication Data
A catalogue record for this book is available from the British Library

ISBN 13: 978-0-415-82472-9 (hbk)
ISBN 13: 978-1-138-37771-4 (pbk)

Typeset in Times New Roman
by Taylor & Francis Books

Publisher's Note
The publisher accepts responsibility for any inconsistencies that may have arisen during the conversion of this book from journal articles to book chapters, namely the possible inclusion of journal terminology.

Disclaimer
Every effort has been made to contact copyright holders for their permission to reprint material in this book. The publishers would be grateful to hear from any copyright holder who is not here acknowledged and will undertake to rectify any errors or omissions in future editions of this book.

Contents

2 Park Square, Milton Park, Abingdon, Oxfordshire OX14 4RN
711 Third Avenue, New York, NY 10017

Routledge is an imprint of the Taylor & Francis Group, an informa business

Citation Information	vii
Notes on Contributors	ix
Preface *Linda Woodhead*	1
Introduction: Religion in education: findings from the Religion and Society Programme *Elisabeth Arweck and Robert Jackson*	5
1. Relationships between local patterns of religious practice and young people's attitudes to the religiosity of their peers *Julia Ipgrave*	13
2. Contextuality of young people's attitudes and its implications for research on religion: a response to Julia Ipgrave *Olga Schihalejev*	27
3. Young people's attitudes to religious diversity: quantitative approaches from social psychology and empirical theology *Leslie J. Francis, Jennifer S. Croft, Alice Pyke and Mandy Robbins*	31
4. Religious diversity, empathy, and God images: perspectives from the psychology of religion shaping a study among adolescents in the UK *Leslie J. Francis, Jennifer S. Croft and Alice Pyke*	45
5. Failures of meaning in religious education *James C. Conroy, David Lundie and Vivienne Baumfield*	61
6. More purpose than meaning in RE: a response to James Conroy, David Lundie, and Vivienne Baumfield *Christina Osbeck*	77
7. Seeing and seeing through: forum theatre approaches to ethnographic evidence *David Lundie and James C. Conroy*	81
8. 'We're all in this together, the kids and me': beginning teachers' use of their personal life knowledge in the Religious Education classroom *Judith Everington*	95

CONTENTS

9. Teachers only stand behind parents and God in the eyes of Muslim pupils
   Jenny Berglund — 109

10. Keeping the faith: reflections on religious nurture among young British Sikhs
    Jasjit Singh — 119

11. Christian youth work: teaching faith, filling churches or response to social need?
    Naomi Stanton — 133

12. Religious young adults recounting the past: narrating sexual and religious cultures in school
    Sarah-Jane Page and Andrew Kam-Tuck Yip — 151

Index — 163

Citation Information

The chapters in this book were originally published in the *Journal of Beliefs & Values*, volume 33, issue 3 (December 2012). When citing this material, please use the original page numbering for each article, as follows:

Preface
Preface
Linda Woodhead
Journal of Beliefs & Values, volume 33, issue 3 (December 2012) pp. 249–251

Introduction
Religion in education: findings from the Religion and Society Programme
Elisabeth Arweck and Robert Jackson
Journal of Beliefs & Values, volume 33, issue 3 (December 2012) pp. 253–259

Chapter 1
Relationships between local patterns of religious practice and young people's attitudes to the religiosity of their peers
Julia Ipgrave
Journal of Beliefs & Values, volume 33, issue 3 (December 2012) pp. 261–274

Chapter 2
Contextuality of young people's attitudes and its implications for research on religion: a response to Julia Ipgrave
Olga Schihalejev
Journal of Beliefs & Values, volume 33, issue 3 (December 2012) pp. 275–278

Chapter 3
Young people's attitudes to religious diversity: quantitative approaches from social psychology and empirical theology
Leslie J. Francis, Jennifer S. Croft, Alice Pyke and Mandy Robbins
Journal of Beliefs & Values, volume 33, issue 3 (December 2012) pp. 279–292

Chapter 4
Religious diversity, empathy, and God images: perspectives from the psychology of religion shaping a study among adolescents in the UK
Leslie J. Francis, Jennifer S. Croft and Alice Pyke
Journal of Beliefs & Values, volume 33, issue 3 (December 2012) pp. 293–307

CITATION INFORMATION

Chapter 5
Failures of meaning in religious education
James C. Conroy, David Lundie and Vivienne Baumfield
Journal of Beliefs & Values, volume 33, issue 3 (December 2012) pp. 309–323

Chapter 6
More purpose than meaning in RE: a response to James Conroy, David Lundie, and Vivienne Baumfield
Christina Osbeck
Journal of Beliefs & Values, volume 33, issue 3 (December 2012) pp. 325–328

Chapter 7
Seeing and seeing through: forum theatre approaches to ethnographic evidence
David Lundie and James C. Conroy
Journal of Beliefs & Values, volume 33, issue 3 (December 2012) pp. 329–342

Chapter 8
'We're all in this together, the kids and me': beginning teachers' use of their personal life knowledge in the Religious Education classroom
Judith Everington
Journal of Beliefs & Values, volume 33, issue 3 (December 2012) pp. 343–355

Chapter 9
Teachers only stand behind parents and God in the eyes of Muslim pupils
Jenny Berglund
Journal of Beliefs & Values, volume 33, issue 3 (December 2012) pp. 357–367

Chapter 10
Keeping the faith: reflections on religious nurture among young British Sikhs
Jasjit Singh
Journal of Beliefs & Values, volume 33, issue 3 (December 2012) pp. 369–383

Chapter 11
Christian youth work: teaching faith, filling churches or response to social need?
Naomi Stanton
Journal of Beliefs & Values, volume 33, issue 3 (December 2012) pp. 385–403

Chapter 12
Religious young adults recounting the past: narrating sexual and religious cultures in school
Sarah-Jane Page and Andrew Kam-Tuck Yip
Journal of Beliefs & Values, volume 33, issue 3 (December 2012) pp. 405–415

Notes on Contributors

Vivienne Baumfield is Professor of Pedagogy, Policy and Innovation in the School of Education, University of Glasgow, UK, and works with practitioners and policy-makers in education both in the UK and overseas. She is the Editor of the *British Religious Education Journal* and the International Dean for South Asia and Eurasia at the University of Glasgow.

Jenny Berglund is Senior Lecturer and researcher in the Department of the Study of Religions at Södertörn University in Stockholm, Sweden. Her particular area of interest concerns the matter of Islam and religious education. This is reflected in her 2009 dissertation *Teaching Islam, Islamic Religious Education at Muslim Schools in Sweden* (Waxmann), which examined the formation of Islamic Religious Education (IRE) as a confessional subject under the jurisdiction of the Swedish school system. Since earning her PhD, Jenny has collaborated on the editing of several Swedish books, in which her own contributions have generally dealt with Islam in Sweden. She is also working with the project 'Religion as a Resource', which concerns the lives, values, relations, leisure time activities, and religious interests of Sweden's youth populations. More recently, Jenny has become involved in TRATEBB (Teaching Religion and Thinking Education at the Baltic-Barent Brim), a research project designed to study religious education at four sets of 'twin-schools' located on either side of four state boundaries in the Baltic-Barent region. Jenny is a committee member of EASR (European Association for the Study of Religion) and actively involved in the organisation's working group on religious education. She has initiated (and participates in) a teacher exchange programme with the Centre for Women's Studies at the University of Jordan.

James C. Conroy is Professor of Religious and Philosophical Education and Head of Internationalisation in the College of Social Sciences at the University of Glasgow, UK. He has written and taught widely on issues of religion and education, leadership and philosophy concerning parenting and childhood. He was the Principal Investigator of the project 'Does Religious Education Work?'.

Jennifer S. Croft was (until September 2012) Senior Research Fellow in the Warwick Religions and Education Research Unit (WRERU) in the Institute of Education at the University of Warwick, UK. Her research interests consist of implicit religion, monitoring religious attitudes, personality and religion, and mental health and spirituality.

NOTES ON CONTRIBUTORS

Judith Everington is an Associate Professor and researcher in the Warwick Religions and Education Research Unit (WRERU) in the Institute of Education at the University of Warwick, UK. Spanning two decades, her research and publications have focused on the relationship between the personal and professional lives of beginning teachers of RE and the implications for teacher education and development. Her current research is concerned with the lives of RE teachers from minority ethnic backgrounds. Her publications include articles in the *British Journal of Religious Education* and chapters in several volumes of the Religious Diversity and Education in Europe series.

Leslie J. Francis is Professor of Religions and Education in and Director of the Warwick Religions and Education Research Unit (WRERU) in the Institute of Education at the University of Warwick, UK. His research interests include the fields of religious education, practical theology, empirical theology, and the psychology of religion.

Julia Ipgrave is Senior Research Fellow in the Warwick Religions and Education Research Unit (WRERU) at the University of Warwick, UK. Her research interests include young people's understanding of religion and religious plurality, inter-faith dialogue between school children, and the place of religion in school.

David Lundie completed his PhD in Religious Education as part of the project 'Does RE Work?' and conducted postdoctoral study at Cornell University, USA. He is currently Lecturer in the Philosophy of Education at Liverpool Hope University, UK. He has carried out a range of projects tracing the diverse processes by which educational policy is mediated into practice.

Christina Osbeck was, until recently, Associate Professor of Religious Education at Karlstad University and is now at the University of Gothenburg in Sweden. Her major ongoing research project is about knowledge of RE as language, looking at how pupils are expanding their linguistic repertoires of religions, societies and life in relation to lessons in RE.

Sarah-Jane Page is a Lecturer at Aston University, Birmingham, UK. She was a Research Fellow in the AHRC/ESRC-funded project 'Religion, Youth and Sexuality: A Multi-faith Exploration'. Her research interests include sexuality, gender, embodiment and religious identities.

Alice Pyke completed her PhD thesis as part of the AHRC/ESRC project on 'Young People's Attitudes towards Religious Diversity'. Her research interests include young people's attitudes towards religious diversity and materials used in schools to teach religious education.

Mandy Robbins (CPsychol) is Senior Lecturer in Psychology at Glyndŵr University, UK, and Research Associate in the Warwick Religions and Education Research Unit (WRERU) in the Institute of Education at the University of Warwick, UK. Her research interests are in the field of practical theology and the psychology of religion.

Olga Schihalejev is a researcher and Lecturer at Tartu University, Estonia. She has worked as a teacher of religious education and has written teaching and learning resources for students in Estonia. Her research interests include the perception of religion by young people in a secular context and by different ethnic groups in Estonia.

Jasjit Singh was a doctoral student at the University of Leeds, UK, working on an AHRC/ESRC Religion and Society Programme studentship 'Keeping the Faith: The Transmission of Sikhism among Young British Sikhs (18–30)', in collaboration with BECAS (Bradford Educational and Cultural Association of Sikhs). His research investigated why young British Sikhs wish to learn about Sikhism and how they go about it.

Naomi Stanton is a Lecturer in Youth Work at the YMCA George Williams College in London, UK. Her chapter is based on research undertaken as part of her PhD thesis at The Open University, which explores young people's engagement with organised Christianity. She has a background of working in various community and youth work settings.

Andrew Kam-Tuck Yip is Professor of Sociology in the School of Sociology and Social Policy at the University of Nottingham, UK. He was Principal Investigator of the 'Religion, Youth and Sexuality' project. His research interests include contemporary sexual, religious/spiritual, and ethnic identities, human rights and citizenship, youth identity and culture, and same-sex relationships.

PREFACE

This collection makes sense in relation to several wider contexts. The first is that of the Religion and Society Programme from which most of the research presented here is derived. This initiative was launched in 2007 by two research councils – the Arts and Humanities Research Council (AHRC) and the Economic and Social Research Council (ESRC). Its generous funding of £12 million and its long duration – more than five years – recognized the urgent need to strengthen research on religion in UK higher education institutions. The imperative arose from the internal secularisation of great portions of arts, humanities, and social sciences which had taken place in preceding decades. The Programme was designed both to commission new research across these disciplines and to train a new generation of researchers competent in the study of religion.

Research in the Programme was commissioned by way of an open call to submit applications for funding. In the end, 75 projects were funded, selected by a multidisciplinary panel solely on the basis of their research quality. From my perspective as Director of the Programme, this meant that the overall shape of the research, and its areas of concentration, were dependent on the subject and quality of the bids received. We were tied to a free-market model of research funding, with no room for central planning. The huge benefit was that we were not trapped in our own agendas but open to proposals from any academic – or academic team – in UK higher education, irrespective of discipline.

The results were interesting. Clusters of research concentration did result, not necessarily in the areas we had anticipated. One of the largest was in religious education in the broadest sense of this term. A number of the projects in this area are represented here. Some looked at the religious socialisation of young children, some at religion in higher education institutions, some at educational initiatives for adults. Others, like most of those represented here, looked at Religious Education (RE) in schools.[1]

In aggregate, this set of research offers a very significant advance in knowledge about RE in Britain. For the first time we have a considerable body of evidence, which provides more than partial glimpses of: how RE is taught in secondary schools in England, Wales, Scotland, and Northern Ireland; how religion is handled in both the formal and informal curricula; how resources are distributed; what impact RE has on pupil knowledge and attitudes; what seems to be working well or failing.

The findings do not make for very happy reading. The word crisis comes to mind as one reads many of the pieces in this collection. This is in no way to denigrate the efforts and achievements of large numbers of educational professionals, whose skill and dedication often in very challenging situations are equally evident in the research. The problems are much wider.

Consideration of these problems leads to a second context in relation to which this collection should be read: the current situation of RE in the state education system in Britain. The last three decades have seen the slow dismantling and de-regulation of the relatively unified educational system which developed after 1944. In a desire to improve standards in schools, both the New Labour government and the current Conservative–Liberal Democrat coalition government have loosened the control of Local Authorities (LAs) over schools and introduced a series of measures which give individual schools greater autonomy. While there are significant opportunities for RE in this situation, resources on which RE has long depended at local level – like special advisors and Standing Advisory Councils for Religious Education (SACRE), composed of representatives of the LA, the different local faith communities, and school staff, who, among other things, advise on the local syllabuses for RE) – can no longer play their accustomed roles.

A related part of the problem has to do with the curriculum and the anomalous place of RE within it, especially in comparison with other core subjects. Although RE is a statutory subject in schools (one which all pupils must be taught), there exists no national curriculum as there does for other subjects of similar standing. Non-statutory guidance for RE, in the form of a National Framework for the subject, was introduced under New Labour, but never became statutory, and RE syllabuses are still shaped and agreed at local level and subject to considerable variation across the country. The status of the subject has also been degraded under the coalition government by virtue of being excluded from the new English Baccalaureate.

In addition, there is a crisis in the understanding of the nature and purpose of RE. On the one hand there have long been those who wish to affirm the objective, scientific, and academically rigorous nature of RE. From their perspective, religion is a central phenomenon of human life and society and the study of its history, beliefs, practices, and development is just as serious and demanding as the study of history or literature or sociology – perhaps even more so since it combines elements of all of them. On this account, RE is chiefly a matter of learning about religion – and that is as rigorous and objective a 'science' as any other. On the other hand, there are those who point out that religion is essentially about meaning making and fundamental commitments. Its subjective dimensions cannot be evaded. It is a diminution to study it without regard to questions of truth and value and without allowing room for serious and perhaps heated debate and discussion. In this respect, RE is more like philosophy or ethics and one of the few areas in the curriculum where students can engage seriously and critically with questions about the nature of life and how to live it. What is central here is not just learning about, but learning from, religion.

All this has resulted in confusion about the nature and purpose of RE. It has also been a factor in the way in which the subject has become overburdened with a vast range of often conflicting aims and demands. As research reported in this collection sets out in detail, RE teachers are often asked to deal with a range of subjects, which includes personal and social education (including sex education), pastoral issues, and other bits and pieces that other teachers refuse to cover. Further, there is the question of assemblies or acts of collective worship, which are compulsory for state schools and must include a Christian element and which RE teachers are regularly asked to organise. The result is a dilution of RE and a widespread perception that it is not a 'proper', rigorous, academic subject. Related to this is the problem of resourcing. This is tied up with the ambivalence about RE which simultaneously affirms its centrality and freights it with an impossible burden of duty and significance, while failing to give it the same status or resource as other core subjects.

A final context in relation to which this collection must be read is that of wider religious and social change. Religion in Britain today is vastly different from the way it was in 1944, when the historic churches were still dominant. It is different, too, from the way things were in 1988, by which time it had become common to think in terms of six major 'world religions' and equivalent 'religious communities' in Britain. Since then we have seen the continued decline of the historic churches relative to other forms of religion and spirituality, the growth of numbers identifying as having 'no religion' and of a (much smaller) aggressive secularism, and the rapid disaggregation of religion into a plethora of different identities and 'communities', many of the latter linked by real and virtual networks which cross national boundaries. These changes undermine an approach which presents religion in terms of a small number of traditions sharing relatively homogenous beliefs and practices. Religious and secular identities have become more varied, more complex, and more individualised as Britain has become a 'super-diverse' society as never before.

Thus RE today faces very significant challenges. The research reported here greatly aids our understanding of what they are, draws attention to areas of success which can be built upon, and makes interesting suggestions about where we might go from here – all of which is a vital first step in responding to the crisis which is identified. The next step, taken at Programme level, has been to bring these findings to the attention of the public and policymakers through a high-profile debate (as part of the Westminster Faith Debates held in 2012, see http://www.religionandsociety.org.uk/faith_debates/faith_in_schools). The next priority is to formulate clear policy recommendations which can help place the subject on the new footing which is urgently needed. Nothing less than a new settlement as radical as that made in 1944 seems to be called for, one which consolidates the piecemeal change which has taken place over the years and which meets the challenges identified here. Good research not only allows us to see things as they are, but helps us to see how they can be improved. This collection is testament to that and its importance will be evident in what happens to RE in Britain in the years to come.

Note

1. Other projects in this area not included in this collection include Mark Pike's project looking at conservative Christian academies in the north-west of England and Alison Mahwinney's project looking at the operation of the right to opt out of RE in schools in Ireland. For information on these and other projects funded by the Programme, see http://www.religionandsociety.org.uk

Linda Woodhead
Lancaster University, UK

INTRODUCTION

Religion in education: findings from the Religion and Society Programme

Religion, education, and society

This collection includes a selection of the papers presented to the conference 'Religion in Education: Findings from the Religion and Society Programme', which was held at the University of Warwick in July 2011. The conference was hosted by the Warwick Religions and Education Research Unit (WRERU) as part of the Religion and Society Programme (jointly funded by the Arts and Humanities Research Council – AHRC – and the Economic and Social Research Council – ESRC), at the behest of the Director of the Programme Professor Linda Woodhead.[1] The main aim of the conference was to offer a forum for the dissemination of (in some cases initial) findings from the various education projects in the Programme. The conference was held under the *aegis* of the Religion and Society Programme, the largest cluster of research projects on Religion and Society so far to have been conducted in the United Kingdom.[2]

The conference was designed to place the two large projects – 'Does Religious Education Work?' (located at the University of Glasgow, under the direction of Professor James Conroy), and 'Young People's Attitudes to Religious Diversity' (located in the Warwick Religions and Education Research Unit – WRERU – at the University of Warwick, under the direction of Professor Robert Jackson) – at the centre of the programme and to invite all the research teams within the Programme whose projects were related to education and/or young people to present at the conference. Inevitably, some of projects teams were not able to accept the invitation. However, many of the speakers were deeply involved with projects focusing on religion and education and religion and youth.

This also applied to the invited audience at the conference, which included a range of professionals concerned with education and young people in various contexts. Conference delegates also represented many kinds of potential users of the education and youth research from the Religion and Society Programme. They included: members of the Religious Education Council of England and Wales (including, at national level, representatives of different religious traditions and secular humanism), members of key professional associations concerned with religious education, editors of key publications in the RE world, advisers from local authorities and religious bodies, representatives of charities concerned with religious education and dialogue (including the Tony Blair Faith Foundation), representatives of academic associations (including the Association of University Lecturers in Religious Education – AULRE – and the British Association for the Study of Religions – BASR), teachers and representatives of teachers' organisations (including the National Association of Teachers of Religious Education – NATRE), and MA and PhD students from the University of Warwick and other universities in the UK.

Delegates also represented various geographical areas, both within and outside the UK, with participants from England, Scotland, Northern Ireland, and Wales as well as from European countries (including Sweden, Norway, Finland, and Estonia).

The conference coincided with news about the tragic events which were sending shock waves through Norway – the bomb which had been detonated in Oslo and the deaths of many young people attending a youth camp on the island of Utøya. This news highlighted the various ways in which our personal and professional relationships are interconnected and how the impact of such news is felt beyond distance and national borders, as we become conscious of how easily colleagues face unexpected turns of events: for example, the bomb in Oslo caused destruction in the vicinity of the new offices of the European Wergeland Centre, with which WRERU has close ties – colleagues from the Centre and other parts of Norway were present at the conference, all visibly shaken by the violent acts aimed at the whole nation.

Why study religions in publicly funded schools?

The question might be asked why religion(s) should be studied in publicly funded schools at this point in time. There are both 'intrinsic' and 'instrumental' reasons for studying religion(s) in publicly funded schools. Underlying the former is the argument that a liberal education should cover all distinctive areas of human experience or 'realms of meaning', while underlying the latter is the argument that some understanding of religion(s) is needed to promote social cohesion and to enhance a range of aspects relevant to young people's development. For example, their social development might be enhanced through knowledge and understanding of culture, through engagement in democratic citizenship and through practices encouraging religious freedom and tolerance. At a personal level, engaging with religious diversity provides opportunities for young people's moral and spiritual development, and for clarifying their own ideas and values. The points on social and personal development accord with the voices of young people across Europe, which the REDCo project (e.g. Jackson 2012a),[3] sought to capture; the importance of listening to the voices of young people is also emphasised in the various projects concerning religion, education, and youth within the Religion and Society Programme.

The climate for the study of religions in publicly funded schools in England and Wales has undergone change, which can be related to two phases. The first, between the late 1960s and the late 1990s, was marked by secularising processes, the rise of Religious Studies in universities (bringing global awareness), and pluralisation through migration (with the creation of good community relations and of a laboratory for the study of diaspora religions). The second phase, from the late 1990s to the present, with special relevance of the post-9/11 period, is characterised by debates about the post-secular – the role of religion in the public sphere (for example, New Labour's stance on faith schools), increased awareness of global Islam, the Internet, New Labour's community cohesion agenda, and the current Coalition government's 'inadvertent' marginalisation of RE – a point to which we shall return below.

On the wider European level, a number of European institutions have – in the period following 9/11 – been concerned with the study of religions in schools: most notable are the Council of Europe (comprising 47 member states), the Organisation for Security and Co-operation in Europe (OSCE) (comprising 56 participant states), and the European Union (comprising 27 member states; the REDCo project was within the European Commission's Framework 6 research programme). The following sets out different aspects related to these European institutions.

Since 2002, the Council of Europe has given close attention to dealing with education about religions and non-religious convictions in public schools across Europe. In that year, the Council of Europe launched a major project on the study of religions as part of intercultural education entitled 'Intercultural Education and the Challenge of Religious Diversity and Dialogue in Europe' (Jackson 2007, 2010). The project had various outputs, but most importantly, the Committee of Ministers – the Foreign Ministers of all 47 member states – agreed (in December 2008) a policy recommendation on the dimension of religious and non-religious convictions within intercultural education. The Recommendation (Council of Europe 2008) was circulated to all member states.

In the light of the Council of Europe's tripartite aims – to protect human rights, pluralist democracy, and the rule of law; to promote awareness and development of Europe's cultural identity and diversity; and to seek solutions to social problems, such as discrimination against minorities, xenophobia, intolerance – its policy is set out in Intercultural Education and the Challenge of Religious Diversity and Dialogue (Council of Europe 2008) with dissemination by the European Wergeland Centre, Oslo, which – since its inauguration in May 2009 – supports intercultural, human rights, and citizenship education, including the dimension of religion.

The Council of Europe project on intercultural education and religious diversity and dialogue (2002–08) resulted in a book (published in various European languages) (Keast 2007) and a Ministerial Policy Recommendation (December 2008), with further follow-up projects (2011–13). The recommendation of the Committee of Ministers to member states on the dimension of religious and non-religious convictions within intercultural education include the following elements: principles, objectives, attitudes, educational preconditions, learning methods, initial and in-service teacher training, research/evaluation, with an emphasis on competences and values as well as on knowledge. To focus on two of the elements – objectives and educational preconditions – as most relevant here, the former include the following:

- developing a tolerant attitude and respect for the right to hold a particular belief
- nurturing a sensitivity to the diversity of religions and non-religious convictions
- promoting communication and dialogue
- providing opportunity to create spaces for dialogue
- addressing sensitive or controversial issues
- developing skills of critical evaluation and reflection
- combating prejudice and stereotypes

The educational preconditions comprise:

- sensitivity to the equal dignity of every individual
- capacity to put oneself in the place of others ... to establish ... mutual trust and understanding
- co-operative learning in which *peoples of all traditions* can be included and participate
- provision of a *safe learning space* to encourage expression without fear of being judged or held to ridicule

A joint project of the Council of Europe and the European Wergeland Centre is currently working on a 'road map' to assist member states in adapting and implementing the recommendation within their own particular contexts.

The Organisation for Security and Co-operation in Europe (OSCE) is the largest regional security organisation; formed in the 1970s, its approach to security includes the human dimension as well as the politico-military, the environmental and economic dimensions. In November 2007, the OSCE, through its Office for Democratic Institutions and Human Rights (ODIHR), launched the *Toledo Guiding Principles* (OSCE 2007), a standard-setting document issued by consensus of the OSCE's 56 Foreign Ministers, after having been drafted by an interdisciplinary and inclusive group of lawyers, academics, and educators. The twin aims of the *Principles* are: (a) to contribute to an improved understanding of the world's increasing religious diversity and the growing presence of religion in the public sphere; and (b) to assist OSCE participating states in promoting study of and knowledge about religions and beliefs in schools as a tool to enhance religious freedom and increase tolerance.

The current situation of RE in England and Wales, created by the impact of the current government's policy, has been marked by a trend towards marginalising the subject. This trend started in late 2010 with the White Paper on *The Importance of Teaching*, which ended the policy on community cohesion, and continued with: the omission of RE in the EBacc (English Baccalaureate) in July 2011, which means that many pupils will take only a 'recognized' humanities subject; the withdrawal of contributions to the continuing professional development costs for M-level courses for teachers; the closure of courses due to the number of PGCE (Post-Graduate Certificate in Education) RE places being halved; the erosion of national and local advice to support RE; and the Academies Act of 2010, which allows schools to leave the oversight of local authorities without any legal requirement to teach RE or maintain links with the local SACRE (Standard Advisory Council for Religious Education). At school level, the fallout of this trend is reflected in the findings of an online survey of RE teachers by the National Association of Teachers of Religious Education (NATRE), conducted over a ten-day period in May 2011, with the aim to examine the impact of the EBacc proposals on RE in English secondary schools (see also Chater 2011). Focusing its analysis on a sub-set of 1157 academies and community and grammar schools, NATRE (2011) found that

- the legal provision for RE at Key Stage 4 (upper secondary level) was not met in 24–31% schools (with the prediction that this rate would increase in 2011–12);
- 34–40% of the schools reported a drop in entries between 2010–11 and 2011–12 for GCSE exams at age 16;
- over 50% of the schools which had decreased entry levels gave the impact of the new EBacc as the reason;
- 25–30% of the schools reported reductions for 2011–12 in specialist RE staff; and
- in 10–14% of the schools, the statutory requirements for Key Stage 3 would not be met in 2011–12.

In contrast, research points to the importance of RE for young people. For example, at European level, the REDCo project found that: pupils see the RE classroom as a potentially 'safe space' for dialogue; pupils want peaceful co-existence based on knowledge about each other's religions and worldviews and sharing common interests or doing things together; and many pupils who have a firm religious commitment do not feel threatened by dialogue with others or by learning about others, although some feel vulnerable (Jackson 2012b).

Research also points to the importance of RE regarding policy and practice. Again, using REDCo findings, there was strong support from pupils for applying democratic principles in the school and the classroom, which accords with the Council of Europe documents cited above. The REDCo data also pointed to the need to contextualise these principles in each country. Hence also the need for more detailed research at national level; the Religion and Society Programme made an important preliminary contribution in this respect. Further, there is an urgent need for investment in RE, as other research (e.g. Jackson et al. 2010; Conroy, Lundie, and Baumfield 2012) and the report on RE by the government's Office for Standards in Education (Ofsted 2010) revealed: there are varying degrees of quality of RE teaching, which is in turn related to issues of resourcing and teacher training.

The contributions to this collection

As mentioned, this collection includes a selection of the papers presented at the conference and an additional contribution by Leslie J. Francis and colleagues. The essays mainly follow the organising principle of the conference, with the findings from the two large Programme projects forming the core. Thus, three contributions report on the Warwick project on 'Young People's Attitudes to Religious Diversity', with Julia Ipgrave focusing on the relationships between local patterns of religious practice and young people's attitudes to the religiosity of their peers, based on qualitative data from the project, and Leslie J. Francis and colleagues focusing on the quantitative data in two contributions, providing the theoretical approaches to the project in the first and presenting data analysis on religious diversity, empathy, and God in the second. Olga Schihalejev's response to Ipgrave thoughtfully draws out wider implications of this material for research on religion.

The next two contributions present findings and methodological approaches of the Glasgow-based project on 'Does Religious Education Work?' The first, by James Conroy, David Lundie, and Vivienne Baumfield exemplifies how failures of meaning occur in current RE teaching, drawing attention to the ways in which content, teaching, and examination-related issues interact. The second essay, by David Lundie and James Conroy, discusses the 'forum theatre approach' in eliciting ethnographic evidence in this study. Christina Osbeck's considered response to the first piece provides a critical reflection on 'failures of meaning' in the RE context, adducing other research to shed further light on the notion of meaning.

The following contributions draw on ethnographic or survey data which illuminate aspects of RE teaching, the role of RE teachers for young people or the formative influence of school or youth work in the formation of young people's religious identities. Judith Everington explores how beginning teachers use their personal life knowledge in the RE classroom and discusses the positive and negative aspects of doing this. Jenny Berglund extracts the standing of teachers in Muslim pupils' eyes from quantitative data, finding that young Muslims in Sweden entrust teachers with personal issues and problems, as they do parents and God. Jasjit Singh interrogates his interviews with older young British Sikhs to find how school and RE contributed to their sense of being nurtured in their religion, while Naomi Stanton focuses on Christian youth work, arguing that its different settings involve different sets of young people and thus fulfil different kinds of social needs. Taking a similar approach to Jasjit Singh, Sarah-Jane Page and Andrew Kam-Tuck Yip take the retrospective look of their interviewees – young adults – to explore how the prevailing religious and sexual cultures of their schools shaped their identities and attitudes.

Acknowledgements

We would like to express our gratitude to the Programme Director Professor Linda Woodhead who commissioned the conference on 'Religion in Education' and who unstintingly advised on and supported its design and organisation. The assistance of Peta Ainsworth, the Programme's Administrator, was invaluable for solving administrative challenges and Dr Rebecca Catto, the Programme Research Associate, ensured that the details related to the conference were posted on the AHRC's website. We would also like to thank our WRERU colleagues, especially Dr Ursula McKenna, and WRERU's Associate Fellows, for their assistance and support.

Notes

1. Further details about the conference, including the programme and a conference report, are available on the WRERU web site: http://www.warwick.ac.uk/go/WRERU
2. Further details about the range of projects and activities within the Programme can be found at its website: http://www.religionandsociety.org.uk/
3. The REDCo (Religion, Education, Dialogue, Conflict) Project was a three-year (2006–2009) European Commission Framework 6 project, involving a consortium of scholars from nine European universities and qualitative and quantitative studies both across and within participating countries. Further details can be found at: http://www.warwick.ac.uk/go/WRERU

References

Chater, M. 2011. Endpiece: The Gove who kicked the hornet's nest. *Resource: The Journal of the National Association of Teachers of Religious Education* 33, no. 3: 24–5.

Conroy, J.C., D. Lundie, and V. Baumfield. 2012. Failures of meaning in religious education. *Journal of Beliefs and Values* 33, no. 3: 307–21.

Council of Europe. 2008. Recommendation CM/Rec(2008)12 of the Committee of Ministers to member states on the dimension of religions and non-religious convictions within intercultural education. Available at: https://wcd.coe.int//ViewDoc.jsp?Ref=CM/Rec(2008)12&Language=lanEnglish&Ver=original&BackColorInternet=DBDCF2&BackColorIntranet=FDC864&BackColorLogged=FDC864.

Jackson, R. 2007. European institutions and the contribution of studies of religious diversity to education for democratic citizenship. *Religion and education in Europe: Developments, contexts and debates*, ed. R. Jackson, S. Miedema, W. Weisse, and J.-P. Willaime, 27–55. Münster: Waxmann.

Jackson, R. 2010a. Religious diversity and education for democratic citizenship: The contribution of the Council of Europe. *International handbook of inter-religious education. Religion, citizenship and human rights*, Vol. 4, ed. K. Engebretson, M. de Souza, G. Durka, and L. Gearon, 1121–51. Dordrecht: Springer Academic Publishers.

Jackson, R., ed. 2012a. *Religion, education, dialogue and conflict: Perspectives on religious education research*. London: Routledge.

Jackson, R. 2012b. Religion, education, dialogue and conflict: An introduction. *Religion, education, dialogue and conflict: Perspectives on religious education research*, ed. R. Jackson, 3–9. London: Routledge.

Jackson, R., J. Ipgrave, M. Hayward, P. Hopkins, N. Fancourt, M. Robbins, L. Francis, and U. McKenna. 2010. *Materials used to teach about world religions in schools in England*. University of Warwick: Department of Children, Schools and Families.

Keast, J., ed. 2007. *Religious diversity and intercultural education: A reference book for schools*. Strasbourg: Council of Europe Publishing.

NATRE (National Association of Teachers of Religious Education). 2011. An analysis of a survey of teachers on GCSE change and RE in light of the EBacc changes: A second survey – June 2011 (v2.2). Birmingham: NATRE. Available at: http://www.natre.org.uk/docstore/NATRE%20EBacc%20Survey2%20report_final.pdf.

Ofsted (Office for Standards in Education). 2010. *Transforming religious education: Religious education in schools 2006–9*. Manchester: Ofsted.

OSCE (Organisation for Security and Co-operation in Europe). 2007. *The Toledo guiding principles on teaching about religions and beliefs in public schools*. Warsaw: OSCE, Office for Democratic Institutions and Human Rights. Available at: http://www.osce.org/odihr/29154.

Elisabeth Arweck and Robert Jackson
WRERU, University of Warwick, UK

Relationships between local patterns of religious practice and young people's attitudes to the religiosity of their peers

Julia Ipgrave

Warwick Religions and Education Research Unit (WRERU), Institute of Education, University of Warwick, Coventry, UK

> This contribution reports research into young people's attitudes to religion and religious diversity in secondary schools across the UK. The data indicate that students' respect for the religiosity of their peers, or their lack of it, is due less to the influence of classroom RE (multi-faith or otherwise) than to the experience of religion in the neighbourhood and the degree to which being 'religious' is viewed as 'normal' there. The essay contrasts negativity experienced in schools by young people of strong practising religious faith in neighbourhoods where religious practice is not the norm with the greater tolerance and respect accorded to religious young people in schools serving neighbourhoods where religious practice is common and prominent. It considers the implications for religious education of this uneven experience.

Introduction

This essay reports data from two research projects carried out by the Warwick Religions and Education Research Unit (WRERU) into young people's attitudes to religious diversity. The first project was the English contribution to the European REDCo project (2006–2009)[1] and the second a UK-wide project funded by the AHRC/ESRC[2] Religion and Society Programme (2009–2012). The projects provide additional data for the growing body of research into young people's relationship with religion, notably the study by Hans-Georg Ziebertz and William Kay of religiosity among youth in Europe (2006). The projects have a distinctive contribution to make through their interest in young people's attitudes to the religion of others. Both combined quantitative and qualitative methods. My own involvement was with the qualitative strands, in particular with focus group discussions with 13- to 17-year-olds in a variety of school contexts. Young people's experience of Religious Education (RE) was one area given attention in both projects. In questionnaires completed for REDCo, student responses frequently echoed dominant national discourses about the benefits of multi-faith RE to the future harmony of society (Ipgrave and McKenna 2008, 138). They were generally in agreement with the 2010 Ofsted report on English RE, *Transforming Religious Education*, which remarked on the subject's positive contribution to the promotion of 'community cohesion' and 'understanding of the diverse nature of society' (2010, 5). However, focus group discussions that followed the REDCo surveys suggested greater complexities than were apparent in the questionnaires and highlighted the importance of contextual factors beyond the RE class.

The second WRERU project provided opportunities for a fuller exploration of students' experiences and perspectives. It expanded the investigation by covering all four nations of the UK, which involved discussion groups of teenagers in four schools in Northern Ireland, four in Scotland, three in Wales,[3] six in England, and three in London. Research contexts ranged from Sussex in the south of England to a Scottish island in the far northwest and included rural districts, towns, cities, and the metropolis, areas that were multi-religious or more religiously homogeneous, areas with an active religious culture and those without. There is some variation in RE across the nations, but they share many of the same principles. In Scottish Religious and Moral Education (RME) as in English RE, education for diversity and learning about a variety of religions is written into national guidance, although a larger proportion of curriculum time is given to Christianity. In 2007, world religions were given a place in the RE curriculum in Northern Ireland, but Christianity predominates to a greater degree than in other UK nations. In these diverse settings, the influence of context on young people's responses to religion was very evident. I shall illustrate this by focusing on the students' attitudes to religion when they encounter it in the lives of their 'religious' peers. A semi-grounded approach was taken in the collection and analysis of the data. Some common questions were shared across schools and groups, but the method also allowed new categories and themes to emerge within broad pre-defined areas of discussion (values, beliefs, social context). Citations used as illustrations in this essay have been selected to encapsulate some of these emerging themes in the young people's own language. Using material from a selection of schools participating in both projects, I shall describe settings where 'being religious' was viewed as 'abnormal' and others where it was viewed as 'normal.' There are positions in between these poles, but this essay aims to show through contrast the difference local patterns of religiosity can make. In each case (religiosity as 'abnormal' or 'normal') I will introduce the contexts, what the young people understood as 'religious', their attitudes towards 'religious' peers, and the impact these had upon those 'religious' young people. I shall end with a brief consideration of the challenges these findings pose for RE.

Where being 'religious' is abnormal

Contexts

In some schools, most students had limited encounter with religion outside RE, their communities having experienced a marked decline in religious practice over the generations. One such school (C)[4] was located in a country town in Cumbria in northwest England. The very low percentage of ethnic minorities in this county (0.7% in the 2001 Census) meant there were hardly any signs of non-Christian religions. School B was situated in a town in northeast England, which had similarly low levels of religious practice and a small minority of people of faiths other than Christianity, although there was a community of conservative Haredi Jews in the vicinity. In both schools, the young people distinguished between religious identity and religious practice, describing most inhabitants of their local area as Christians despite their lack of engagement in church life and worship:

> I think most people are Christened but don't really practise their religion as such. They just get christened and that's it – it's not the religious side of it. (B)[5]

> I think quite a lot of people are Christian, but I don't know if they actually go to church. They just think, 'Oh yeah, I'm Christian', but don't actually do anything. (C)

It was not a rebellion against religion; rather, people had 'lost interest in the whole religion thing' (B); 'everybody's not so fussed about religion anymore' (C); 'people round here aren't so bothered about it' (C). The decline of religion had not reached quite the same stage in the small town in northeast Scotland where School F was located, but students indicated this was the general trend. As one churchgoing Christian girl declared:

> We're more like a minority now, so the whole community has changed. (F)

Speaking of their generation in particular, one of her classmates described attitudes to religion as 'a bit wishy-washy; they don't really know what they think' (F).

There was a different flavour to the secularity of School A, an independent fee-paying school in the south of England. Although the school was a church foundation and had an energetic and much respected RE department, few of the students came from regularly practising church families. As most students were boarders, the influence of peers on attitudes and thinking could be quite intense. Students interviewed spoke of 'Dawkinsmania'[6] and an 'atheist cool' that had swept the school, so that, for example, when an RE class of 18 students were asked about their religion, all but three identified as atheist. The dominant view was that religion had been proved wrong by science.

What is 'religious'?

What does 'religious' mean in these contexts? One Christian student at School A reported that among his peers being 'religious' was associated with stupidity, with particular emphasis placed on the practices that go with religious commitment:

> It's 'Christianity's stupid' and 'are you religious?' rather than 'do you believe in God?' is the question and religious people do such and such and there are people and there are religious people – the stupid ones. (A)

Students at School B and C found the relationship between religious belief, religious identity, and being 'religious' complex, with 'religious-ness' proving most problematic. Several sought to 'de-religionise' local expressions of Christianity, so that 'Christening ... has got less religious, it's more of an occasion, it's just something you do when you're born' (B) and a grandmother who attended church was 'not massively religious and I don't think she believes in all that stuff – I think she goes 'cos it's a bit of a social link really' (C). Some had difficulty discerning what being 'religious' actually meant, but most of those who used the word wished to distance themselves from it:

> You can be kind of religious without being religious as such – using all the technical words. You can believe in God but not be a Christian. You can still be kind of religious, without being religious, if you know what I mean. (C)

In the context of Christianity the word 'religious' had negative connotations; it was coupled with the word 'Bible-bashers' at School C and F and used as the opposite of open-mindedness: '[if you're religious] you're not open-minded, you're stubborn' (C); religious Christians might want 'to stop people having their own views' and 'extreme Christians' 'don't like homosexuals and all that'. There was a 'killjoy' element, as the 'religious' were characterised as very strict, not drinking or swearing or going out at the weekend (C). Being 'religious' was a stigma that even religiously committed Christians in these contexts might wish to dissociate themselves from, as with a churchgoing Anglican at School A who decided not to join the school chapel choir because people would say 'so-and-so's religious and I'm not'.

In some localities, religious practice was so little in evidence that being 'religious' was immediately associated with 'foreigners' and minorities such as the distinctive Haredi Jewish community who were easily recognizable to students at School B by their dress. In Cumbria, when asked whether there were many religious people in the neighbourhood, one boy automatically thought of Muslims:

> I don't know. I don't know many people that wear big dresses and stuff like Muslims ... you don't really get them round here. (C)

For some, to show one's religion in dress or practice was abnormal, even, occasionally, a subject for ridicule. At School B students reported peers making 'funny jokes' about the Haredi community and teasing a local Sikh shopkeeper about his turban. At School C they remembered how students had peered through the door and laughed at a Muslim teacher performing his prayers.

Relating to 'religious' peers

The negative associations of 'religious-ness' influenced students' attitudes towards their religious peers. At School B there was a very small number of Muslim and Sikh students. They reported that religion was little talked about at school, but when it was, it became a focus for criticism or ridicule. There was a direct correlation between teasing and lack of experience of religion:

> I think it's basically because most English people are not Christians or they don't have a religion, so they think because they're non-religious, they can say what they want about other people's religions or judge it any kind of way that they possibly can. (B)

Learning about different religions did not necessarily improve the situation. These students felt uncomfortable studying their own religions in RE classes. They recalled peers making fun of the name of Muhammad or Sikh turbans and claimed that the subject provided ammunition for others being unkind. A Muslim student described how classmates once held a ham sandwich under his nose at lunch time; if it had not been for RE, 'they wouldn't know about it – because they don't know many things' (B). These comments and similar instances reported in another school challenge the common-sense view that learning about diversity necessarily generates positive attitudes to difference. Students contrasted the purposes of RE with its actual outcomes:

> I think they just make [RE] compulsory to try and break down the ethnic barriers between Christians and Muslims and Hindus and trying to stop racism, which as far as I've seen just doesn't seem to work – the more they seem to learn about it, the more jokes they can make. (B)

There is some evidence that 'non-religious' young people were made uneasy by their peers showing signs of religious commitment, while 'religious' students recorded a lack of comprehension:

> People find it strange. Like some people think it's weird like what you're doing and ... 'why do you do all that?'. (B)

Some students found it hard to imagine that others of their age group accepted the obligations and restrictions that religion imposes, as one Muslim girl reported:

> My friends don't understand anything ... It's when they're doing something and you can't and they're like, 'why can't you?' and then you have to explain everything ... I go over it again and again and they still don't understand. (B)

However, at these schools, there was little evidence of a separation of religious and non-religious into antagonistic camps. Generally, if religion was left out of the equation, relationships between the majority and small 'religious' minority were fairly harmonious. 'Religious' students sought to fit into the teenage culture of their 'non-religious' peers, although there were limits to this conformity. A Turkish girl in School B reported negative ('really judgemental') reactions from her friends when they discovered that as a Muslim she did not believe in sex outside marriage. Religious *identity* was not perceived to be problematic, but religious *practice* was viewed as socially awkward, cutting across 'normal' teenage activity.

> You probably get on better with people who aren't really tied down with their religion, like where the Muslims pray five times a day, it's just easier to hang around with someone who doesn't have to do that all the time. (B)

Not 'being tied down' with one's religion was important to good relations; it was fine to belong to a religion as long as you were not conscientious in your practice or, as one boy described it, not 'uptight':

> I've got a Sikh friend, but it doesn't make a difference, they don't really practise Sikhism ... I think that my Sikh friends, they have a really relaxed attitude ... they're relaxed and we're relaxed and it makes it easier – we're not uptight about it and they're not uptight about it and it doesn't create an awkward atmosphere like how it does with the Jews.[7] (B)

Impact on the 'religious' students

Some 'religious' young people risk social exclusion if their religious commitment and practices are generally known at school. In a discussion students recalled the problems one of them had faced when it was discovered that she was a regular churchgoer:

> Sometimes people can bully you and stuff for your beliefs/[8] you're judged/ yeah, like labelled – like you don't want to be friends with so and so because they go to church. (B)

In such contexts, it required real courage to speak about or practise one's religion publicly, as 'non-religious' students in School F recognized:

> It depends how religious you are, because if you're really religious, you won't mind, because it's what you believe in, but sometimes peer pressure can make people pull your leg and call you 'Bible-bashers' and that/And you're afraid of being criticised for your belief. (F)

Christian students at School A spoke about the bravery and strength of commitment required to receive a blessing or communion in the chapel Eucharist, knowing that their peers would sneer at them: 'it takes a real step of courage to go up and get a blessing'; it is 'a great sign of respect to stand up before 500 people to get up and affirm your faith in Christ'.

For others the art was to avoid being seen as 'religious', as one boy explained:

> Many people think it's not cool to be religious – but you don't have to express your views; you can just keep them very quiet and not tell anybody about it. (A)

Students in other schools also recognized the imperative to keep quiet:

> I think you'd keep it quiet; if you are [religious], you wouldn't talk about it. (C)

> We don't generally speak about it much ... because we're very outnumbered ... When I speak about it, I'm afraid that people will look at me a lot differently. (F)

The students were not excluded from school life on account of their religion, but their religion was excluded; for some this meant that a significant part of their lives was unacknowledged. A student in School F, for example, spoke about her excitement at first taking communion in her Church of Scotland church, her role as a Sunday schoolteacher, her duties of reading lessons and ringing the bells (F), yet these were things she felt she could not talk about with her school friends.

Where being 'religious' is normal
Contexts

Nigel Biggar and Linda Hogan have observed that in the UK there is 'no simple trajectory towards either secularism or religiosity' (2009, 1); the reality is hugely complex, incorporating stories of decline, persistence, and revitalisation. I have reported from schools where the majority viewed religious practice as 'abnormal'. I also visited schools where religion was viewed as 'normal', woven into the fabric of the local community. In Northern Ireland and the Scottish islands, for example, there are areas that may be seen as the last strongholds of conservative Protestantism of the Scottish Reformed tradition and there are also large city contexts where there has been an increase in religious practice, partly (although not exclusively) due to immigration patterns.

Among the Northern Irish schools, there were two 'Protestant schools',[9] one a girls' school (E) in a town in the west, the other a mixed rural comprehensive (G) in Co. Tyrone. Both served religiously practising communities, the majority of pupils regularly attending church with their families and participating in Christian camps, church youth groups, and traditional church-based uniformed organisations such as the Girls' and the Boys' Brigades. The Scottish island community served by School H was characterised by similar regular churchgoing which was supported by strong family structures. Here Sabbath-Day observance was very important; the idea of no work and no sports on Sunday was part of the island's culture, although under threat from secularising influences, the migration of families, and visits of tourists from the mainland. The students' descriptions of their community were not very different from those of the Northern Irish contexts:

> Most people go to church or to Sunday School or either their parents or grandparents go, if they don't go personally. Everyone has a church link – everyone knows what it means to be Christian. (H)

Students in predominantly Muslim areas of English cities were also very familiar with religion. Interviews for the REDCo project took place in a Bradford school (I) which served a large religiously observant Pakistani population. As one student said:

> Bradford is religious, like there are loads of churches and mosques ... and people actually go to them. (I)

There was a similar dynamic in a school in southeast Birmingham (J). Here students described their neighbourhood as 'a solid society', 'a close knit community ... majority Muslim and we have loads of mosques'.

Two South London schools (K, L) were involved in the research, both Church of England schools with large West African populations, predominantly Christian with a minority of Muslim students and several from mixed-faith families. In School K there was also a significant number of white (English and Irish heritage) students. The degree of religious practice among black students in these schools was high, for the Christians often involving church attendance several times a week and frequent Bible study. Several attended youth churches and youth groups in addition to their family churches. One student described her neighbourhood as follows:

> The part of [name of South London area] I live in is like a black community and it's like most people go to my church anyway, so we're all just – it's like a really together community; it's actually quite religious. The two main religions are Muslim and Christianity, so I think it's actually quite religious; like every Sunday we find it hard to find [people] at home until like the mid-afternoon when everyone's come back from church, so it's actually quite a religious area. (K)

What is 'religious'?

As in the other schools, students associated 'religious-ness' with practice and commitment, but the degree and type of practice and commitment required for being 'religious' were different. In School E, I interviewed a group of girls who all believed in the fundamental tenets of the Christian faith and attended church every Sunday, with some also attending the church youth group on Wednesdays, yet they categorised themselves as 'non-religious'. They distinguished themselves from their 'religious' peers, the *'strong believers'*, who regularly spoke about their faith in public, made frequent reference to the Bible, did not swear, drink or attend discos.

Interestingly those to whom others in these schools referred as 'religious' did not accept the category, because 'religion' meant rites and rituals and did not describe their sense of relationship with Jesus. An African Christian in School L made the same point. In the Northern Irish and island schools, another distinction was made: between 'Christian' and 'un-Christian' (or 'not Christian'), the latter being the churchgoing 'non-religious' mentioned above. The distinction was explained in evangelical terms of 'being saved'. In Schools E and G, 'Christian' students could identify life-transforming moments when they had been called and made a choice to be a 'Christian'.

Among the Muslim and African Christian students, 'religious' was also understood as practice and commitment beyond the minimum of formal worship. It was closely bound up with morality:

> It depends on what you count as a religious person – in this school there's loads of Christians; loads of people who say, 'yeah, I go to church on a Sunday, I believe in God', but … it's one thing to practise what you believe, so I think there's only a limited amount of people that actually practise and show what they're like. (K)

> People who are brought up religious … they behave in a certain way and we kind of pick that up straight away … like there's something about the way they behave. (J)

In the London schools, against a backdrop of street crime and gang culture, religious life was often couched in terms of a moral battle, of resisting temptation and directing one's passions aright:

> So even if they're going to church every day with their Mum, it doesn't mean that the day after they're gonna not go and commit a crime, so I don't really think going to church really helps you. I think it's more like your beliefs, like what you think your passion is. (K)

> When you're reading the Qur'an, your heart just forgets about all the street – like hanging around with your friends and doing bad things – and you're concentrating on the one thing that you're reciting, like the Arabic in the Qur'an. (L)

In these schools, for both Muslims and Christians, being 'religious' was associated with seriousness, maturity, and taking on responsibilities. It was something they aspired to and hoped they would acquire and exercise to a greater degree as they got older:

> As you get older, your religion also brings more responsibilities, so as you get older, you're going to take those responsibilities into your home; so if you do, it'll make you more religious. (I)

> When you grow up – like I want to christen my children and be a good teacher to them – so you're going to feel stronger [in your religion], so you're going to pass it on, what your beliefs [are]. (K)

Relating to 'religious' peers

Despite general familiarity with religion in their communities, there was some differentiation in the 'religious-ness' of the student population by state ('Christian' or 'un-Christian'; 'religious' or 'non-religious') or by position along a spectrum towards religious maturity. The question here is how young people relate to those *more* religious than themselves. In School E both those who categorised themselves as 'non-religious' and those whom they categorised as 'religious' voiced more respect towards each other than was evident in the schools described earlier. The 'religious' girls could recall very few occasions when their religious perspective affected the way people treated them. This accords with comments from their 'non-religious' peers:

> There's definitely a group within the school who are religious and you know if you ever wanted to go with them, you're more than welcome; they're really nice girls, but you know that they are religious people ... they are very open about it. (E)

> Everyone just respects that that's their choice, just like they respect that it's other girls' choice not to do what they do. (E)

In School H, students related a similar easy relationship to the pervading religious culture of the island:

> There's never really a problem with the religious and non-religious people, nothing like 'Oh, I don't like him because he's religious' or whatever, I've never known that. ... We ['non-religious'] people are from a sort of religious background, so there's always someone like your Gran or your Granddad who's religious, so it's always been kind of there. (H)

In schools I, J, K, and L, students did not talk directly about fellow students they viewed as particularly religious, although they evidently had respect for those who acted according to the moral principles of their religion and disapproval for those who did not. Students in School K linked religion to moral integrity when they argued that it would be beneficial if more people in school were 'religious':

> Everyone would live their life by a doctrine kind of thing ... the school would be better, like life would be better in the school, like there wouldn't be bullying, there wouldn't be verbal abuse. (K)

Impact on the 'religious' students

In this more sympathetic environment students felt able to be more explicit about their faith and include it in everyday conversation. As one girl in the island school noted:

> [Here] you have religious friends and they're just speaking about it – even out of lessons and on ... Saturdays it's pretty much 'I've got to get everything done today because I know I can't do it tomorrow because it's Sunday'. (H)

For some, it would be more of an issue if people did not know that they were religious – if you were a Christian, 'it has to show' (H).

The confidence of these young people meant that they could contribute as 'religious' people to the life of the school. There was a significant difference between the students who kept quiet about their religion for fear of being teased and the confident organisers of the Scripture Union at School E, for example. This student-run organisation met once or twice a week, held classroom prayer meetings and occasional weekend or special events, including formal dinners. There was also a strong student-run Scripture Union in the island school, which met each Wednesday with invited Christian speakers (e.g. a speaker from the Corrymeela Community[10]) attracting numbers beyond the core members; a recent event had been attended by 110 students. 'Religious' students were not just welcomed within the school, but acted as hosts. As one of the organisers said:

> One of the things that we really don't want is it just to be a little group of Christians that just stay in their own little corner and don't come out of it ... we want it to be open for Christians and non-Christians, people who believe and who don't believe. (E)

As well as the personal benefits of faith, the religious commitment of these students afforded them social capital when understood in terms of building social networks and relationships of trust and, to use Robert Putnam's distinction (2000, 1), not just *bonding* with like, which could be a sign of defensiveness, but *bridging* by relating to others in confidence.

From a position of confidence in their own religious expression, several students were feeling their way towards relations with other religions. In the London schools there was familiarity with religious difference and relationships existed across religious divides:

> I talk with my Muslim friends about religion ... it's just sort of things that's interesting to talk about because it's like finding out about their religion and our religion and how it kind of links. (L)

Some expressed the view that security in one's own religion was not an obstacle but rather a spur to dialogue with other faiths:

> You could be strong in your religion, but you could be open-minded as well and you could maybe link someone else's religion to your own like and see how different religions come together as well. (L)

Among those unaccustomed to meeting people of other religions (Muslims in School I and Christians in School E and G), there was a degree of apprehension and acute consciousness of cultural difference (e.g. in food and dress). Nevertheless, there was also recognition of the affinity between people with strong faith, who have God as the key reference in their lives. Protestant girls in Northern Ireland recognized that 'there are some Catholic people who do love God, like LOVE God', who, like them, 'have a relationship with Him' (E). 'Christians' could identify commonalties of belief (in God, in God's creation, in prayer) with Islam, compared Muslims' 'strictness with their religion' to their own attempts to live in accordance with biblical teaching, and appreciated Muslims' preparedness to 'stand up for your religion' (G). At the same time, there was some hesitancy about how to handle conflicting truth claims and reconcile a desire that others should benefit from knowledge of the truth (as perceived by them) with respect for their religious commitment:

> I don't really like to say to them 'you're wrong', because then they can say, 'well, you're wrong'. I don't know what to say to them really. (G)

Some sensed that answers to these questions might be found within their own faith traditions; for example, a Muslim student looked to the Qur'an for guidance:

> If you read the Qur'an properly, if you take it in properly and read yourself and study yourself and get the right advice from the right people, you'd actually be able to associate with people from other religions. (J)

The search for answers could be theologically informed. Whether or not people of non-Christian faiths would be saved was a question for debate among the 'Christians', but knowledge that religion and faith are the result of God's activity, not just personal choice, ultimately left the judgement to Him:

> A lot of Muslims are searching for God in their religion and God has revealed himself to a lot of Muslims as well, so really someone who's seeking to find God they will – and God will reveal Himself. (E)

> It's not for us to judge, 'oh, you're going to heaven and you're not'. God in his perfection and justice will like be able to say. (E)

Implications for RE

There is a sharp contrast between contexts where religious expression is stigmatised and excluded from teenage interaction and those where it is valued and permitted to contribute to the life of the school. The issue is not just the personal well-being of individuals who might be marginalised or discriminated against (although that is of concern), but also the general well-being of school communities that seek to include and benefit from the full participation of all members. It is a particular issue for RE because of the role it has recently been afforded in promoting 'community cohesion' and education for diversity. Cohesion and diversity require inclusion and integration, but not assimilation; as different members of society come together, they should retain the distinctions that constitute diversity. These distinctions run deeper than mere identity-signifiers (Sikh, Christian, Muslim), they entail strongly felt reasons and motivations. Therefore, 'religious' students should not have to put aside their religious perspectives to engage with their peers and those peers have an obligation (in the interests of inclusion) to be responsive to them and their contributions.

These observations relate the research findings with wider questions about religion in the public arena. In recent years, the idea that, in liberal democracies, religious voices should be relegated to the private sphere has come under increasing criticism from prominent thinkers. Jürgen Habermas writes that religious citizens should feel able to express and justify their convictions in religious language, so that they are freed from the undue '*mental* and *psychological* burden' of having continually to translate their reasons into secular language for public discourse (2006, 9–10) and so that society as a whole does not risk cutting itself off from 'key sources for the creation of meaning' (10). Both consequences of the suppression of religious voices were observable in some schools. In *Democracy and Tradition*, Jeffrey Stout argues that 'civility requires recognition of each person's deepest commitment; members of a democratic society owe reasons to each other when taking stands on important issues, including reasons that are only fully justifiable within our own tradition' (2005, 184–5). Where the young people could express their religious reasons freely, Stout's conditions of civility were met.

RE has aspirations to play a significant role in the promotion of a diverse and cohesive society. The nature of the subject means that it has particular responsibility within this wider vision for encouraging the harmonious inclusion of religious perspectives within that diversity. The schools that have been the focus of this study have offered several examples where this has evidently not happened and others where the successful inclusion may have more to do with the patterns of religious practice in the local community than with the teaching of religion in school. These findings have implications for the subject. Firstly, they indicate that multi-faith RE cannot be relied upon to ensure the development of positive attitudes, unless other conditions are in place. Whatever students learn about religious diversity and respect for difference has little value, unless they are prepared to listen to and reflect upon their meanings when they encounter 'religious' people (including from their own religious heritage). A school community can only be diverse and cohesive if young people with strong religious commitments are able to share their experiences with their fellow students, see their religion valued, and contribute their faith perspectives to public discourse.

Secondly, while our sympathies may lie primarily with 'religious' students in contexts where their perspectives are marginalised, their peers are victims of the ignorance and religious illiteracy that characterises some sectors of British society. The young people who viewed religious practice and commitment as 'weird' or ridiculous were generally of Christian heritage, often identifying as Christian but having become disconnected from their cultural roots. The issue in the educational context is not so much loss of faith as loss of ability to comprehend and empathise. Engaging in depth with the tradition that is part of their family and community history could help to overcome that sense of the strangeness of religion (whatever religion) and of those who practise it. The same Ofsted report that spoke of RE's positive role in educating for diversity also noted concerning weaknesses in teaching about Christianity; evidently significant improvements are needed, if detailed study of this religion is to be part of the solution.

Finally, the difference that context makes to students' experiences and responses is marked, their starting points for the study of religions contrasting sharply between those who can say, 'We have RE in the way we live, in our personal lives and our society' (I), and those who admit that 'In a school like ours, [students] don't know what religion is at all, so they need to be taught' (C). This means that the learning needs of students in Cumbria are not the same as the needs of students in South London, that students in School B would benefit from detailed exploration of what it means to be religiously committed (the baseline of religious literacy), while those in School E are ready to tackle the challenges of interreligious dialogue. Rather than seek consistency, RE needs to acknowledge inequalities of experience and respond with differentiated content and approach according to the particularities of local circumstances and their impact on young people's lives.

Notes

1. The full title of REDCo is 'Religion in Education: A contribution to Dialogue or a factor of Conflict in transforming societies of European Countries.' The research was funded through EC Framework 6.
2. The Arts and Humanities Research Council and the Economic and Social Research Council.

3. Research in Welsh schools (as well as in some English and London schools) was carried out by another WRERU colleague, Elisabeth Arweck. All the schools used here as examples are schools where I undertook the fieldwork.
4. The contexts of schools referred to in this article can be characterised as:

   A—independent fee-paying school with a Christian foundation in rural south of England; many pupils are boarders; fairly low levels of religious practice in community.

   B—maintained school in town in northeast England; low levels of religious practice in community; small minority of people from faiths other than Christianity; local community of Haredi Jews.

   C—maintained school in country town in northwest England; low levels of religious practice.

   E—maintained girls' school in town in western Northern Ireland; community where practising Christianity is common.

   F—maintained school in small town in northeast Scotland, with general trend away from churchgoing in the community.

   G—maintained rural school in Co. Tyrone, Northern Ireland; serving largely Protestant practising community.

   H—maintained school; Scottish island community; largely Protestant practising community.

   I—maintained school in Bradford, northern England; serving religiously practising Muslim community.

   J—southeast Birmingham; serving observant Muslim community.

   K—Church of England school, south London, large West African school population from religiously practising community; significant numbers of white English and Irish heritage.

   L—Church of England school, serving predominantly West African community; population largely Christian; minority of Muslim and other faith students; religiously practising community.

5. Letters indicate schools rather than individual students.
6. Reference to prominent atheist Richard Dawkins.
7. This refers to the local Haredi community.
8. The use of / indicates change of speaker.
9. There are no official Protestant schools in the NI education system, but many are Protestant by default, because Roman Catholic students tend to be educated in the Roman Catholic sector.
10. This a peace-building organisation in Northern Ireland.

References

Biggar, N., and L. Hogan, eds. 2009. *Religious voices in public places*. Oxford: Oxford University Press.

Habermas, J. 2006. Religion in the public sphere. *European Journal of Philosophy* 14, no. 1: 1–25.

Ipgrave, J., and U. McKenna. 2008. Diverse experiences and common vision: English students' perspectives on religion and religious education. *Encountering religious pluralism in school and society: A qualitative study of teenage perspectives in Europe*, ed. T. Knauth, D.-P. Jozsa, G. Bertram-Troost, and J. Ipgrave, 113–47. Münster: Waxmann.

Ofsted. 2010. *Transforming religious education*. London: HMI.

Putnam, R.D. 2000. *Bowling alone: The collapse and revival of American community*. New York: Simon and Schuster.

Stout, J. 2005. *Democracy and tradition*. Princeton, NJ: Princeton University Press.

Ziebertz, H.-G., and W. Kay, eds. 2006. *Youth in Europe II: An international empirical study about religiosity*. Berlin: LIT-Verlag.

Contextuality of young people's attitudes and its implications for research on religion: a response to Julia Ipgrave

Olga Schihalejev

Faculty of Theology, University of Tartu, Tartu, Estonia

> This is a response to Julia Ipgrave's contribution on the contextuality of young people's views on religion and religious diversity in this collection of essays on 'Religion in Education'. First I will highlight and reflect on methodological issues raised by Ipgrave's observations in the light of my own research. The first problem highlighted is the use of the same words while they have different emotional connotations in different regional settings and for different groups. Then I will reflect on the ambivalent results concerning learning about religions from the point of view of implementing the research findings in relation to everyday school practices.

Since 1994, the Warwick Religions and Education Research Unit (WRERU) has been successful in winning substantial research grants, including the recent EC Framework 6 project on religion, education, dialogue, and conflict (REDCo) (e.g. Jackson 2012) and a major project for the UK Government's Department for Children, Schools and Families on materials used to teach about world religions in schools in England (Jackson et al. 2010). All of WRERU's projects were very complex, using different sets and combinations of methods and involving researchers who work with integrity and creativity and who co-operate closely. Between 2009 and 2012, WRERU staff were engaged in a major AHRC/ESRC[1] research project in the Religion and Society Programme, exploring young people's attitudes in the UK to religious diversity.

The investigation of a variety of contexts provides an opportunity to consider the impact and appropriateness of generalising assumptions about the nature of religious diversity and appropriate pedagogies to deal with diversity. The part of the project reported by Julia Ipgrave (2012, in this collection) investigated pupils in different local settings, their experiences of and perspectives on religion and religious diversity and attempted to identify factors that influenced their attitudes. The data from this part of the study are extremely interesting and rich, exploring different contextual settings in different parts of the UK. The findings not only raise urgent questions for policy makers and teachers in the different parts of the UK, but also offer a methodological challenge to any (but especially to quantitative) research on religion. In this response to Ipgrave's essay I shall point out some methodological challenges and look more closely at one of the (in my view) most interesting questions posed by the findings.

Methodological challenges

The use of a mixed method approach has been a growing trend in large research studies, whether concerning research as part of a doctoral thesis (e.g. Hussein 2009; Phipps 2009), national studies (e.g. Smith et al. 2011; Madge 2013) or international projects (e.g. Ziebertz and Kay 2006; Weisse 2012). The qualitative work reported in Ipgrave (2012, in this collection) makes a contribution to such mixed method studies. This type of research helps to clarify complex issues but also points to important methodological problems.

Along with members of the WRERU team and other European research groups, I worked on the REDCo project and one (of many) challenges in this research was how to translate the questionnaire of the quantitative survey into eight different languages so that the meaning of the questions remained consistent. It seemed to be an easy task at the beginning, but we soon realised that it was almost impossible to find the exact equivalents in the different national and linguistic contexts.

Ipgrave's essay points to the next level of this problem: the study investigated *inter alia* how young people speak about being religious in different local settings and within different groups. The findings show clearly that the same words may have very diverse connotations, even across the same country. Religion and the way it is understood have not only semantic but also emotional connotations, including attitudes; thus the word 'religious', for example, can mean different things in different local settings, as illustrated in Ipgrave's text. It shows that, in one context, 'religious' means 'being born again' and, in another context, it means 'following dead practices', with young people using the word 'faith' instead of 'having a relation with Jesus'. Therefore, if the word 'religious' is used in a questionnaire, it will mean different things for different respondents, which will invalidate the results, especially when combined with other dispositional or comparable scales (often–rarely, important–unimportant). For example, if the question is 'how often do you pray?', the answer 'often' may mean for one respondent 'once a month' and 'rarely' may mean for another respondent '(only) every other day'. Also, the response 'not very important' to the question 'how important is religion to you?' may indicate very different things, as my study in Estonia showed (Schihalejev 2008). There is no easy answer to the question of how to implement this finding in quantitative research. Maybe one day, every questionnaire will be carefully translated not only into different languages but also into 'local contexts', using the dialects of local youth culture.

Multi-faith religious education: a reason to tease

A part of the REDCO study in Estonia involved a quantitative study in 21 schools (Schihalejev 2010). Although it was found that pupils who studied religious education (RE) were more tolerant than those who had not done such studies, the results were more blurred when looked at more closely, school by school. I wrote a report for every participating school and found that there were some schools which offered RE, where students held intolerant views, but there was also a school which offered no RE, where students held the most tolerant views. Similar 'school-related' results were found in other countries where REDCo researchers had prepared individual 'school reports', for example, in Russia (Kozyrev and Valk 2009). The REDCo team could not explain this and felt that there was a need to study school culture more deeply in order to shed light on this finding.

The research carried out by the WRERU team at Warwick University may suggest some reasons for such differences, namely that RE may not be the only or the most important influence on young people's attitudes. Ipgrave reports the rather uncomfortable finding – especially for proponents of RE – that multi-faith religious education, in contexts with low levels of religious literacy and with a small minority of pupils from religions other than Christianity, gives pupils tools to tease peers from other religions instead of promoting mutual understanding. As one pupil put it, 'the more they seem to learn about it, the more jokes they can make.' One can only agree with the views of these young people – that 'knowing about' religion is not a sufficient aim of any form of RE. Scholars of education, among them Robert Jackson, have made the point that genuine knowledge and understanding might be a necessary, but not sufficient condition for encouraging positive attitudes or increase of tolerance (Jackson 2005). If religion is squeezed into only the private and hidden sphere of life, it may threaten democratic principles. As Ipgrave formulates it:

> A school community can only be diverse and cohesive if young people with strong religious commitments are able to share their experiences with their fellow students, see their religion valued, and contribute their faith perspectives to public discourse.

The school is a potentially 'safe place' where respectful and intelligent dialogue about religious and worldview issues can be learned and experienced. The qualitative data Ipgrave reports show that context strongly influences the attitudes of young people. Thus we should be cautious about putting all the responsibility for creating a safe space on the RE subject and its teachers. Although I agree with the proposal that RE should 'respond with differentiated content and approach according to the particularities of local circumstances and their impact on young people's lives', I think that this should not only be the task for RE, but for the whole school. The whole school culture needs to be modified through the co-operation of staff, pupils, and parents in order to define and justify ideals of mutual understanding and respect and to plan ways of approaching them. The attitudes held in the area in which the school is situated might remain beyond the reach of such change, but the changes in the school culture may help to improve the situation, as studies in youth aggression (Reis, Trockel, and Mulhall 2007) and multicultural education have shown (Nieto and Bode 2012).

Ipgrave's findings thus contributes to both further discussions about the productive ways of promoting active tolerance in a school setting and the question about more valid and reliable ways to investigate religion in different contextual settings.

Acknowledgements

This research was supported by the European Union through the European Regional Development Fund (Center of Excellence in Cultural Theory) and ETF grant 9108 "Contextual factors of young people's attitudes and convictions in relation to religion and religious diversity".

Note

1. The AHRC (Arts and Humanities Research Council) and ESRC (Economic and Social Research Council) are two major public funding bodies in the UK.

References

Hussein, R. 2009. *Teaching about religion: A mixed methods study of teachers' attitudes, knowledge, and preparation, with a focus on Islam and Muslims.* University of North Florida. Theses and Dissertations. Paper 206. Available at: http://digitalcommons.unf.edu/etd/206.

Ipgrave, J. 2012. Relationships between local patterns of religious practice and young people's attitudes to the religiosity of their peers. *Journal of Beliefs and Values* 33, no. 3: 261–74.

Jackson, R. 2005. Intercultural education, religious plurality and teaching for tolerance. Interpretive and dialogical approaches. *Intercultural education and religious plurality: Oslo occasional papers* 1, ed. R. Jackson and U. McKenna, 5–13. Oslo: The Oslo Coalition on Freedom of Religion or Belief.

Jackson, R., ed. 2012. *Religion, education, dialogue and conflict: Perspectives on religious education research.* London: Routledge.

Jackson, R., J. Ipgrave, M. Hayward, P. Hopkins, N. Fancourt, M. Robbins, L.J. Francis, and U. McKenna. 2010. *Materials used to teach about world religions in schools in England.* London: Department for Children, Schools and Families. Available at: http://www2.warwick.ac.uk/fac/soc/wie/research/wreru/research/completed/dcsf.

Kozyrev, F., and P. Valk. 2009. Saint-Petersburg students' views about religion in education. *Teenagers' perspectives on the role of religion in their lives, schools and societies: A European study*, ed. P. Valk, G. Bertram-Troost, M. Friederici, and C. Beraud, 311–49. Münster: Waxmann.

Madge, N. 2013. *Youth on religion: The development, negotiation and impact of faith and non-faith identity.* Abingdon: Routledge.

Nieto, S., and P. Bode. 2012. *Affirming diversity: The sociopolitical context of multicultural education.* 6th ed. Boston, MA: Pearson.

Reis, J., M. Trockel, and P. Mulhall. 2007. Individual and school predictors of middle school aggression. *Youth and Society* 38, no. 3: 322–47.

Phipps, K. A. 2009. *Same direction—different paths: A mixed methods examination of leaders' openness to religious difference using the Intercultural Development Inventory.* Electronic Theses and Dissertations collection for University of Nebraska–Lincoln. Paper AAI3379730. Available at: http://digitalcommons.unl.edu/dissertations/AAI3379730.

Schihalejev, O. 2008. Meeting diversity: Students' perspectives in Estonia. In *Encountering religious pluralism in school and society: A qualitative study of teenage perspectives in Europe*, ed. T. Knauth, D.-P. Jozsa, G. Bertram-Troost, and J. Ipgrave, 247–78. Münster: Waxmann.

Schihalejev, O. 2010. *From indifference to dialogue? Estonian young people, the school and religious diversity.* Münster: Waxmann.

Smith, C., K. Christoffersen, H. Davidson, and P.H. Snell. 2011. *Lost in transition: The dark side of emerging adulthood.* New York: Oxford University Press.

Weisse, W. 2012. Reflections on REDCo project. *Religion, education, dialogue and conflict*, ed. R. Jackson, 10–24. London: Routledge.

Ziebertz, H.-G., and W. Kay, eds. 2006. *Youth in Europe II: An international empirical study and religiosity.* Berlin: LIT-Verlag.

Young people's attitudes to religious diversity: quantitative approaches from social psychology and empirical theology

Leslie J. Francis[a], Jennifer S. Croft[a], Alice Pyke[a] and Mandy Robbins[b]

[a]*Warwick Religions and Education Research Unit (WRERU), University of Warwick, Coventry, UK;* [b]*Glyndŵr University, Wrexham, Wales, UK*

> This essay discusses the design of the quantitative component of the 'Young People's Attitudes to Religious Diversity' project, conceived by Professor Robert Jackson within the Warwick Religions and Education Research Unit, and presents some preliminary findings from the data. The quantitative component followed and built on the qualitative component within a mixed method design. The argument is advanced in seven steps: introducing the major sources of theory on which the quantitative approach builds from the psychology of religion and from empirical theology; locating the empirical traditions of research among young people that have shaped the study; clarifying the notions and levels of measurement employed in the study anticipating the potential for various forms of data analysis; discussing some of the established measures incorporated in the survey; defining the ways in which the sample was structured to reflect the four nations of the UK, and London; illustrating the potential within largely descriptive cross-tabulation forms of analysis; and illustrating the potential within more sophisticated multivariate analytic models.

Introduction

The 'Young People's Attitudes to Religious Diversity' project, conceived and directed by Professor Robert Jackson within the Warwick Religions and Education Research Unit (WRERU), was designed to maximise the research insights of both qualitative and quantitative methods. Within the time constraints of a three-year project, it was decided to begin with the qualitative research and to allow the findings of the qualitative approach to inform aspects of the quantitative approach. At the current stage of the project, the quantitative data are still being prepared for analysis.

Therefore, the aims of the present contributions are to discuss the design of the quantitative study and to display some of the ways in which the data can be analysed, drawing on the data of the first 3020 completed questionnaires. The argument will be advanced in seven steps: introducing the major sources of theory on which the quantitative approach builds; locating the empirical traditions of research among young people that have shaped the study; clarifying the notions and levels of measurement employed in the study; discussing some of the established measures incorporated in the survey; defining the ways in which the sample was structured; illustrating the potential within largely descriptive cross-tabulation forms of analysis; and illustrating the potential within more sophisticated multivariate analytic models.

Sources of theory

The rich and thick data generated by the qualitative study raised a number of key issues both about how young people expressed their attitudes towards religious diversity and about the factors that helped to shape those attitudes. Such influences included sociological factors (like family), personal factors (like sex), psychological factors (like personality), and theological factors (like ideas about God). These key issues resonated with work already well established within various quantitative research traditions. Two particularly relevant quantitative research traditions are provided by the psychology of religion and by empirical theology.

Quantitative research in the psychology of religion has its roots in the late nineteenth and early twentieth century, but it was not until the mid-1950s that sufficient independent studies were conducted to provide the basis for beginning to co-ordinate evidence and to draw useful conclusions. Argyle's (1958) pioneering book *Religious behaviour* clearly demonstrated that a body of empirically based knowledge was beginning to emerge in the psychology of religion. Argyle significantly updated his original review of the literature in the mid-1970s and the mid-1990s (Argyle and Beit-Hallahmi 1975; Beit-Hallahmi and Argyle 1997).

Essentially, Argyle's work stands within the individual differences tradition of psychology. In the 1950s, he concluded that the major individual difference associated with religion was that of sex. Routinely, empirical studies showed women to be more religious than men, at least when religion is defined in terms of Christian beliefs, practices, and values. By the 1990s Argyle concluded that the connection between religion and personality was a second secure finding, drawing on the explosion of studies that had concentrated on testing this association from the early 1980s (see Francis et al. 1981a, 1981b; Francis, Pearson, and Kay, 1982). The trends charted by Argyle have been brought further up-to-date (from an American perspective) by Hood, Hill, and Spilka (2009).

The quantitative phase of the 'Young People's Attitudes to Religious Diversity' project draws on theories developed within the individual differences approach to the psychology of religion, including theories concerned with the influence of sex and the influence of personality. By taking such theories into account in designing the quantitative phase of the project, the findings from the study are likely to inform current debates rehearsed in journals like *Archive for the Psychology of Religion*, *International Journal for the Psychology of Religion, Mental Health, Religion and Culture,* and *Psychology of Religion and Spirituality.*

Quantitative research in empirical theology has its roots in the 1970s and was shaped by theologians working with methods and theories informed by the social sciences. Empirical theology was conceived in the Netherlands by Hans van der Ven as an interdisciplinary activity whereby the tools of the social sciences were taken into theology and tested by the theological academy. Empirical theology was conceived in England and Wales by Francis as an interdisciplinary activity whereby the practitioners of empirical theology sought to have their work tested both by the theological academy and by social scientists. The debate between these two perspectives was well captured by Cartledge (1999) in *Journal of Beliefs and Values*.

As a relatively new and emerging discipline, it is still too early for major reviews to have drawn together key findings, although clear patterns are emerging with *Journal of Empirical Theology*, through the conferences of the International Society for Empirical Research in Theology and through the series of essays published by Brill, including *Religion Inside and Outside Traditional Institutions* (Streib 2007), *Empirical Theology in Texts and Tables: Qualitative, Quantitative and Comparative Perspectives* (Francis, Robbins, and Astley 2009), and *The Public Significance of Religion* (Francis and Ziebertz 2011).

At heart empirical theology is concerned with conceptualising and operationalising constructs informed by theological rather than sociological or psychological debate. One good example of such constructs is provided by the notion of God images as displayed by Ziebertz (2001) in the collection of essays *Imaging God* and by Hegy (2007) in the collection of essays *What do we Imagine God to be?*. God images may be concerned with key theological concepts like the debate between the God of mercy and the God of justice. A second good example of such constructs is provided by the notion of the theology of individual differences as displayed by Francis (2005) and by Francis and Village (2008). Drawing on a strong doctrine of creation shaped by Genesis 1:27, the theology of individual differences posits fundamental human differences (like sex, ethnicity, and psychological type) as reflecting the image of the divine creator.

The quantitative phase of the 'Young People's Attitudes to Religious Diversity' project draws on theories developed within the individual differences approach to empirical theology, including theories concerned with the influence of God images. By taking such theories into account in designing the quantitative phase of the project, the findings from the study are likely to inform the current debates rehearsed in journals like *International Journal of Practical Theology, Journal of Empirical Theology, Review of Religious Research*, and *Journal of Psychology and Theology*.

Empirical traditions

The quantitative phase of the 'Young People's Attitudes to Religious Diversity' project was not developed within a vacuum, but built on three traditions of empirical research already well established within the capacity of the WRERU, namely the Teenage Religion and Values Project, the Attitudes toward Religion Project, and the Outgroup Prejudice Project.

The Teenage Religions and Values Project had its roots in a series of studies published during the 1980s and 1990s, including *Youth in Transit* (Francis 1982), *Teenagers and the Church* (Francis 1984), and *Teenage Religion and Values* (Francis and Kay 1995), all concerned with modelling the association between various aspects of religion and spirituality and various areas of values and attitudes. During the 1990s, the Teenage Religions and Values Project set out to compile a database of 34,000 Year 9 and Year 10 pupils drawn from across England and Wales and reflecting the distribution of young people within state maintained and independent schools, including schools with a religious character. Findings from this project were published in two major books, *The Values Debate* (Francis 2001) and *Urban Hope and Spiritual Health* (Francis and Robbins 2005) and in a wide range of focused journal papers.

The Teenage Religion and Values Project brought to the quantitative phase of the 'Young People's Attitudes to Religious Diversity' project a number of strengths, including experience in the design and administration of questionnaires among a large number of young people, sets of well-tested items, and a secure platform of empirical evidence against which findings from the new survey could be located. In particular, this project offered a helpful recognition of the multi-dimensional nature of religion operationalised in empirical research, distinguishing between five dimensions. These five dimensions are now included in the quantitative component of the 'Young People's Attitudes to Religious Diversity' project.

The first dimension is self-assigned religious affiliation. This is the dimension of religiosity routinely gathered in many countries within the context of the national census and included for the first time in 2001 in the census for England and Wales and for Scotland. In England and Wales the census distinguished between the six main faith traditions (Buddhism, Christianity, Hinduism, Islam, Judaism, and Sikhism). In Scotland the census also distinguished between denominational strands within Christianity. Recognizing the importance of the denominational differences within Christianity, the Teenage Religion and Values Survey made fine distinctions between different groups.

The second dimension is self-reported attendance at public centres of worship (including churches, synagogues, and mosques). Public religious practice taps the extrinsic aspects of religiosity.

The third dimension is self-reported personal prayer and self-reported reading of scripture. Personal religious practice taps the intrinsic aspects of religiosity.

The fourth dimension is religious belief. Belief in God may operate independently of self-assigned religious affiliation and self-reported public and personal religious practice.

The fifth dimension is God images. Alongside a well-established research tradition concerned with assessing the social significance of belief in God, a second research tradition has examined the importance of the *kind* of God in whom people believe (that is to say their image of God). The Teenage Religion and Values Survey included items concerned both with belief in God and with the *kind* of God in whom individuals believe.

Alongside theses indicators of conventional religiosity, the Teenage Religion and Values Survey also included a range of markers tapping aspects of alternative spiritualities. One key aspect of this area focused on the paranormal and on paranormal beliefs.

The Attitudes toward Religion Project had its roots in a study published in the late 1970s (Francis 1978) that argued for the primacy of the attitudinal dimension of religion in building a co-ordinated approach to the psychology of religion. Initially this body of research was shaped entirely within the Christian tradition, drawing on the Francis Scale of Attitude toward Christianity, and by the mid-1990s Kay and Francis (1996) were able to integrate the findings from the first 100 studies to use that instrument.

The scope of the Attitude toward Religion Project was subsequently extended to other faith traditions through the Katz–Francis Scale of Attitude toward Judaism (Francis and Katz 2007), the Sahin–Francis Scale of Attitude toward Islam (Sahin and Francis 2002; Francis, Sahin, and Al-Failakawi 2008), and the Santosh–Francis Scale toward Hinduism (Francis et al. 2008). More recently, the Astley–Francis Scale Attitude toward Theistic Faith has allowed comparable studies to employ the same instrument within Christian, Islamic, and Jewish as well as secular contexts (Astley, Francis, and Robbins 2012). In order to locate its findings alongside the growing body of empirical evidence organised by the Attitudes toward Religion Project, the quantitative component of the 'Young People's Attitudes to Religious Diversity' project now includes the Astley–Francis Scale of Attitude toward Theistic Faith.

The Outgroup Prejudice Project has its roots in collaborative work with Brockett and Village at York St John University. The first database developed by this project was employed by Brockett, Village, and Francis (2009) to develop the Attitude toward Muslim Proximity Index by analysing attitudes of 1777 non-Muslim secondary school children in northern England. The scale was based on physical and social distance, using items related to the idea of having Muslims living at various distances from the respondent, to having Muslims marry into the family, and to mixing with Muslims wearing cultural dress (the *hijab*). The study showed that the notion of proximity could be used to measure prejudice towards Muslims among non-Muslim secondary school pupils. The advantage of the scale was that it was based on a range of notions surrounding 'proximity' of the outgroup, including different levels of proximity. One limitation of the scale was that it was applicable to non-Muslim attitudes towards Muslims and not *vice versa*.

The second database developed by the Outgroup Prejudice Project was designed to develop a scale using concepts related to the Attitude toward Muslim Proximity Index, but one that could be generalised across ethnic or religious groups. This second database, comprising 930 pupils from Blackburn, 1376 pupils from Kirklees, and 2116 pupils from York, was employed by Brockett, Village, and Francis (2010) and Village (2011) to develop and test the Outgroup Prejudice Index as a reliable and valid scale that was comparable in measuring attitudes towards outgroup among Christians, among Muslims, and among those of no religious affiliation.

Drawing on the Outgroup Prejudice Project, the quantitative component of the 'Young People's Attitudes to Religious Diversity' project now includes a wide range of proximity measures.

Levels of measurement

At the design stage, a quantitative survey needs to be clear about the levels of measurement to be achieved by the data, since this in turn shapes the statistical techniques that can be employed to interrogate the data at a later stage. The quantitative component of the 'Young People's Attitudes to Religious Diversity' project was designed to be amenable to all kinds of statistical analysis up to multi-level linear models. Different parts of the survey included nominal, ordinal, interval, and scaled levels of measurement.

Nominal levels of measurement include the question concerning religious affiliation. Such questions allow individuals to be placed within categories, but there is no natural progression within and between these categories. The question concerning sex is also a nominal variable, but since there are only two categories, this is a nominal variable that can be conventionally employed in linear models.

Ordinal levels of measurement allow individuals to be placed in rank order without making assumptions about the equality of distances between the points within the ranking. The question concerning frequency of praying may fall into this category when individuals are invited to check one of the five options: nearly every day, at least once a week, at least once a month, occasionally, and never. Although the intervals between the points are clearly not equal, such variables may be employed in linear models.

Interval levels of measurement allow assumptions about the equality of distances between the points. Within the social sciences this assumption is conventionally made with Likert (1932) scaling. The form of Likert scaling employed in the quantitative component of the 'Young People's Attitudes to Religious Diversity' project invited pupils to assess clear well-focused statements on the conventional five point scale: agree strongly, agree, not certain, disagree, and disagree strongly.

Scaled levels of measurement go one stage further and combine a set of items to assess a broader underlying construct. There are three main benefits from this process of scaling. The first is that it is possible to build a more complex theoretical understanding of what is being measured. For example, the notion of *extraversion* is more complex than something that can be captured by a single item, but may be more adequately captured by a set of items. The second benefit is that, while the individual's responses to a single item may fluctuate from day to day, the overall pattern of responses to a set of items remains much more stable. Scales access a deeper level of personal stability. The third benefit is that when a set of items are brought together, the range of scores is expanded. For example, on the Likert scale, each item has a range of just five points (1 to 5), but when 10 Likert items are combined, the range expands (10 to 50). This provides greater differentiation between individuals. To be effective, scales require careful development and testing.

Instruments of measurement

As well as providing the opportunity for the development of new scales, the quantitative component of the 'Young People's Attitudes to Religious Diversity' project included a range of recognized and established instruments in order to link the findings from this new study with established and developing fields of enquiry. Such established scales include measures of attitude towards religion, God images, self-esteem, empathy, and personality. This aspect of measurement will be illustrated by reference to the Eysenckian dimensional model of personality and to the family of instruments designed to access and assess these dimensions.

Eysenck's dimensional model of personality was selected for inclusion in the quantitative component of the 'Young People's Attitudes to Religious Diversity' project for three reasons. First, the model proposes an economical and robust account of individual differences in terms of three higher order factors that have been shown to be stable across cultures and across the age range. Moreover, the model proposes a continuum from normal to abnormal personality that in turn may function as an index of individual differences in psychological health. Second, as Beit-Hallahmi and Argyle (1997) demonstrated, since the 1980s, there has been a concerted research interest in establishing both the theoretical and the empirical connection between the model of personality and individual differences in religiosity. Third, the model has played a key role in the three earlier projects on which this project builds, namely the Teenage Religion and Values Project, the Attitudes toward Religion Project, and the Outgroup Prejudice Project.

Eysenck's three higher order dimensions of personality are all named by the high scoring pole of the continuum: extraversion, neuroticism, and psychoticism. Eysenck's choice of terms like 'neuroticism' and 'psychoticism' to describe aspects of normal personality is both illuminating and unhelpful. It is illuminating in the sense of underscoring the Eysenckian view that neurotic and psychotic disorders are not discrete categories discontinuous from normal personality. It is unhelpful in the sense of describing perfectly healthy aspects of normal personality with terms redolent of poor psychological health. These three dimensions have been measured among adults by the Eysenck Personality Questionnaire (Eysenck and Eysenck 1975) and the Eysenck Personality Questionnaire Revised (Eysenck, Eysenck, and Barrett 1985). They have been measured among young people by the Junior Eysenck Personality Questionnaire (Eysenck and Eysenck 1975) and the Junior Eysenck Personality Questionnaire Revised (Corulla 1990). These instruments also routinely include a lie scale. Alongside the full versions of these measures, abbreviated forms have been produced for use among adults (Francis, Brown, and Philipchalk 1992) and for use among young people (Francis 1996). It is the abbreviated form of the Junior Eysenck Personality Questionnaire Revised that was included in the quantitative component of the 'Young People's Attitudes to Religious Diversity' project.

The first dimension assesses introversion, through ambiversion to extraversion. Eysenck's extraversion scales measure sociability and impulsivity. The opposite of extraversion is introversion. The middle range between extraversion and introversion is often referred to as 'ambiversion'. The high scorer on the extraversion scale is characterised by the test manual (Eysenck and Eysenck 1975) as a sociable individual, who likes parties, has many friends, needs to have people to talk to, and prefers meeting people to reading or studying alone. The typical extravert craves excitement, takes chances, acts on the spur of the moment, is carefree, easy-going, optimistic, and likes to 'laugh and be merry'. In the survey, extraversion is accessed by items like, 'Do you like going out a lot?' and 'Would you rather be alone instead of being with other people?'.

The second dimension assesses emotional stability, through emotional lability to neurotic disorder. Eysenck's neuroticism scales identify the underlying personality traits which at one extreme define neurotic mental disorder, including emotional lability and over-reactivity. The opposite of neuroticism is emotional stability. The high scorer on the neuroticism scale is characterised by the test manual as an anxious, worrying individual, who is moody and frequently depressed, likely to sleep badly and to suffer from various psychosomatic disorders. Eysenck and Eysenck (1975) suggest that if the high scorer on the neuroticism scale has to be described in one word, one might say that he was a *worrier*; his main characteristic is a constant preoccupation with things that might go wrong, and with a strong emotional reaction of anxiety to these thoughts. In the survey, neuroticism is accessed by items like 'Are your feelings easily hurt?' and 'Do you often feel "fed up"?'.

The third dimension assesses tender-mindedness, through tough-mindedness to psychotic disorder. Eysenck's psychoticism scales identify the underlying personality traits which at one extreme define psychotic mental disorders. The opposite of psychoticism is normal personality. The high scorer on the psychoticism scale is characterised by Eysenck and Eysenck (1976), in their study of psychoticism as a dimension of personality, as being cold, impersonal, hostile, lacking in sympathy, unfriendly, untrustful, odd, unemotional, unhelpful, lacking in insight, strange, with paranoid ideas that people were against him. In the survey, psychoticism is accessed by items like 'Do you enjoy hurting people you like?' and 'Would you enjoy practical jokes that could sometimes hurt people?'.

The lie scale was originally introduced to personality tests to identify individuals who were trying to create a good impression, but subsequently scores recorded on the lie scale have been interpreted more broadly to reflect a form of social conformity or social acquiescence. In the survey, this construct is accessed by items like 'Have you ever said anything bad or nasty about anyone?' and 'Have you ever taken anything (even a sweet) that belonged to someone else?'.

Designing the survey

As in all good quantitative studies, the first step was to design a pilot survey. At this stage a long questionnaire was devised containing options from which choices could be made. This long questionnaire was administered throughout one school that was particularly interested in working on the project. This pilot study involved both cognitive testing and quantitative testing in order to check how the sections worked and to select the better performing components.

The main project was designed to collect data from at least 2000 Year 9 and Year 10 pupils from each of the 'five nations' of the UK, defined as England, Northern Ireland, Scotland, Wales, and London. Within each nation half of the pupils were recruited from schools with a religious character. For England, Northern Ireland, Scotland, and Wales, half of the pupils were recruited from urban areas and half from rural areas. Within London, half of the pupils were recruited from inner London and half from outer London.

The interim analyses reported in the following sections were conducted at the end of June 2011 when 3020 completed questionnaires were available for interrogation. This sample comprised 1587 males and 1433 females; 1892 pupils from schools with a religious character and 1128 from secular schools.

Cross-tabulation

One of the simpler forms of analysis through which a database of this nature can be interrogated is that of cross-tabulation. The potential within this method will be illustrated by identifying an appropriate research question. The question concerns the connection between the pupils' religious identity and their personal well-being, their views on religion and equality, and their attitudes towards Islam.

First, however, the notion of 'religious identity' requires clarification and clear operationalistion within the contextual constraints of the survey. Religious identity is often regarded as synonymous with self-assigned religious affiliation. It is this level of information that is collected by the national census and it was also available within the survey. Religious affiliation by itself, however, is a fairly crude measure of religious identity. A somewhat more refined construct is generated by taking religious practice into account as well. The 'Young People's Attitudes to Religious Diversity' project asked both about religious affiliation and about religious practice in terms of attendance at religious worship services (e.g. in a church, mosque or synagogue). After the 2001 census in England and Wales had reported that 72% of the population self-identified as 'Christian', academic debate focused on the extent to which religious affiliation without practice becomes a meaningless category. In his analysis of British Social Attitudes Survey data, Francis (2003) demonstrated that non-practising, self-identified Christians display a distinctive profile of values compared with those who self-identify as having 'no religion'. Building on this basis, the following analyses distinguish between three religious identities: no religious affiliation and no religious attendance, Christian affiliation and no religious attendance, and Christian affiliation with weekly attendance. To avoid contamination by sex differences, the following analyses were conducted among female pupils only.

Table 1 takes the three categories of religious identity and cross-tabulates them against 13 items from the questionnaire (three concerned with personal well-being; five concerned with religion and equality; five concerned with attitudes towards Islam). In the questionnaire, each of the 13 items was rated on a five-point Likert scale. In order to generate cross-tabulated data, the five points of the Likert scale were reduced to two categories: yes (agree strongly and agree) and no (disagree strongly, disagree, and uncertain). The significance of the differences between the responses of the three religious identity categories to each of the attitude items was tested by the chi-square contingency statistic and expressed in Table 1 in terms of the probability level. Table 1 shows that on 11 of the 13 items the differences between the three religious identity groups reached the highest level of statistical significance ($p < .001$).

In terms of personal well-being, the non-attending Christians recorded higher levels of purpose in life and lower levels of depression and suicidal ideation in

Table 1. Religious identity and personal and social attitudes.[1]

affiliation attendance	none none[2] %	Christian none[3] %	Christian weekly[4] %	$p <$ [5]
Personal well-being				
I feel my life has a sense of purpose.	39	55	73	.001
I often feel depressed.	36	31	24	.01
I have sometimes considered taking my own life.	22	16	14	.05
Religion and equality				
Promoting equality in society is important to me.	53	52	74	.001
We must respect all religions.	73	78	93	.001
Learning about different religions in school is interesting.	47	55	73	.001
Religion is mainly a force for bad in the world.	25	19	8	.001
Religious people are often intolerant of others.	31	24	21	.01
Attitudes towards Islam				
A lot of good is done in the world by Muslims.	23	21	35	.001
I am interested in finding out about Muslims.	27	40	55	.001
Studying religion is school has shaped my view about Muslims.	38	47	60	.001
Muslims should be allowed to wear the headscarf in schools.	60	59	79	.001
Muslims should be allowed to wear the Burka in schools.	51	52	63	.001

Notes:
1. based on responses of 1,433 female pupils
2. no religious affiliation and no attendance
3. Christian affiliation and no attendance
4. Christian affiliation and weekly attendance
5. probability level based on χ^2

comparison with the non-attending non-affiliates. The highest level of personal well-being was experienced by the attending Christians.

In terms of religion and equality, generally, the non-attending Christians took a more positive view in comparison with the non-attending non-affiliates, but a less positive view than the attending Christians.

In terms of attitudes towards Islam, the most positive and accepting view was taken by the churchgoing Christians. These findings suggest that a negative view of Muslims is more prevalent among secular young people than among young people who are practising members of Christian churches. In this sense Christianity is seen to promote acceptance, not rejection, of adherents of Islam.

Correlational and multivariate models

A more powerful and more complex way of handling the data generated by the 'Young People's Attitudes to Religious Diversity' project is offered by correlational and multivariate statistical models. The potential within this method will be illustrated by identifying an appropriate research question. The question concerns identifying the relative power of personal, psychological, theological, and contextual factors in shaping young people's attitudes towards religious diversity.

First, however, the notion of 'attitudes towards religious diversity' requires clarification and clear operationalisation within the context and constraints of the survey. The questionnaire contained a wide range of items relevant to this broad underlying construct. Table 2 presents the 11 items identified by exploratory factor and correlational analyses (five negatively phrased items and six positively phrased items) as cohering most satisfactorily into a unidimensional scale. Table 2 presents the correlations between each individual item and the sum of the other items (ranging between .47 and .74) and the alpha coefficient (Cronbach 1951). The alpha coefficient is well in excess of DeVellis's (2003) minimum threshold of .65.

Second, the notion of personal, psychological, theological, and contextual factors also requires clarification and clear operationalisation. Within the survey, personal factors are represented by sex and age; psychological factors are represented by the

Table 2. Attitude toward Religious Diversity Index (ARDI).[1]

	r
I would not like to live next door to a Buddhist.[2]	.71
I would not like to live next door to a Hindu.[2]	.74
I would not like to live next door to a Jew.[2]	.70
I would not like to live next door to a Muslim.[2]	.72
I would not like to live next door to a Sikh.[2]	.73
We must respect all religions.	.58
Learning about different religions in school is interesting.	.47
I would be happy about a close relative marrying someone from a different faith.	.54
I would be happy to go out with someone from a different faith.	.56
Having people from different religious backgrounds makes my school an interesting place.	.53
People from different religious backgrounds make where I live an interesting place.	.50
alpha	.89

Notes:
1. based on responses of 2,578 male and female pupils
2. These items were reverse coded to generate the scale.

four measures proposed by the abbreviated form of the Junior Eysenck Personality Questionnaire Revised (extraversion, neuroticism, psychoticism, the lie scale); theological factors are represented by the Astley–Francis Scale of Attitude toward Theistic Faith and the God images index; and contextual factors are represented by school type (schools with a religious character and secular schools).

Table 3 explores the predictive power of these personal, psychological, theological, and contextual factors on attitude towards religious diversity in three steps (reflected in the three columns). Step one (in the first column) presents the bivariate Pearson correlation coefficients between sex and age and attitude towards religious diversity. Considered separately, both correlations are significant. A more positive attitude towards religious diversity is held by females than males and this applies to Year 9 pupils rather than Year 10 pupils.

Step two (in the second column) presents the bivariate partial correlations between attitude towards religious diversity and the psychological, theological, and contextual variables after controlling for sex and age. Considered separately, three of the four Eysenckian measures and both of the theological measures have statistically significant associations with attitudes towards religious diversity.

Step three (in the third column) employs multiple regression to assess the simultaneous influence on attitudes towards religious diversity of the personal, psychological, theological, and contextual factors. The beta weights now clarify the picture and demonstrate that the apparent influence of the lie scale and of attitudes towards theistic belief (indicated by the partial correlation coefficient) was an artifact of other correlations within the overall system. Table 3 shows that personal factors (sex and age), psychological factors (neuroticism and psychoticism), and theological factors (God images) are all implicated in predicting attitudes towards religious diversity. The most positive attitude towards religious diversity is held by younger females who are tender-minded (low on psychoticism) and more emotionally engaged (high on neuroticism) and who believe in a loving God of mercy (God image). Schools with a religious character, however, are not implicated in predicting attitudes towards religious diversity when all these other factors are taken into account.

Table 3. Predictors of attitude towards religious diversity.[1]

	r^2	partial r^3	beta[4]
sex	.24***		.12***
age	−.06***		−.04*
extraversion		−.04	.00
neuroticism		.08***	.07***
psychoticism		−.32***	−.27***
lie scale		.12***	.03
theism		.22***	−.01
God image		.27***	.20***
school type		.01	.01

Notes:
1. based on responses of 2578 male and female pupils
2. Pearson correlation coefficients
3. partial correlation coefficients controlling for age and sex
4. beta weights (standardised regression coefficients)

Conclusion

This essay set out to offer an overview of the design and scope of the quantitative component of the 'Young People's Attitudes to Religious Diversity' project, conceived by Professor Robert Jackson within the Warwick Religions and Education Research Unit as a project within the Religion and Society Programme which was jointly sponsored by the AHRC and ESRC. The essay has illustrated ways in which the data generated by the quantitative component of the project may be explored to provide insights into the nature of young people's attitudes towards religious diversity, individual differences in these attitudes, and the correlates of these attitudes. Such analyses may be used to test a wide range of theories regarding the correlates, antecedents, and consequences of the variety of approaches that young people take to make sense of the lives within religiously diverse and religiously complex societies. The rich source of data now assembled is ready for such analyses to proceed.

Note

'Young People's Attitudes to Religious Diversity' (AHRC Reference AH/G014035/1) was a large-scale mixed methods research project investigating the attitudes of 13- to 16-year-old pupils across the UK. Young people from a variety of socio-economic, cultural, ethnic, and religious backgrounds from different parts of England, Wales, Northern Ireland, and Scotland, and including London as a special case, took part in the study. Professor Robert Jackson was principal investigator and Professor Leslie J. Francis co-investigator. Together they led a team of qualitative and quantitative researchers based in WRERU, within the Institute of Education at the University of Warwick. The project was part of the AHRC/ESRC Religion and Society Programme and ran from 2009–2012.

References

Argyle, M. 1958. *Religious behaviour*. London: Routledge and Kegan Paul.
Argyle, M., and B. Beit-Hallahmi. 1975. *The social psychology of religion*. London: Routledge and Kegan Paul.
Astley, J., L.J. Francis, and M. Robbins. 2012. Assessing attitude toward religion: The Astley-Francis Scale of Attitude toward Theistic Belief. *British Journal of Religious Education* 34, no. 2: 183–93.
Beit-Hallahmi, B., and M. Argyle. 1997. *The psychology of religious behaviour, belief and experience*. London: Routledge.
Brockett, A., A. Village, and L.J. Francis. 2009. Internal consistency reliability and construct validity of the Attitude toward Muslim Proximity Index (AMPI): A measure of social distance. *British Journal of Religious Education* 31, no. 3: 241–9.
Brockett, A., A. Village, and L.J. Francis. 2010. Assessing outgroup prejudice among secondary pupils in Northern England: Introducing the Outgroup Prejudice Index (OPI). *Research in Education* 86, no. 1: 67–77.
Cartledge, M.J. 1999. Empirical theology: Inter- or intra-disciplinary? *Journal of Beliefs and Values* 20, no. 1: 98–104.
Cronbach, L.J. 1951. Coefficient alpha and the internal structure of tests. *Psychometrika* 16, no. 3: 297–334.
Corulla, W.J. 1990. A revised version of the psychoticism scale for children. *Personality and Individual Differences* 11, no. 1: 65–76.
DeVellis, R.F. 2003. *Scale development: Theory and applications*. London: Sage.
Eysenck, H.J., and S.B.G. Eysenck. 1975. *Manual of the Eysenck Personality Questionnaire (adult and junior)*. London: Hodder and Stoughton.

Eysenck, H.J., and S.B.G. Eysenck. 1976. *Psychoticism as a dimension of personality.* London: Hodder and Stoughton.

Eysenck, S.B.G., H.J. Eysenck, and P. Barrett. 1985. A revised version of the psychoticism scale. *Personality and Individual Differences* 6, no. 1: 21–9.

Francis, L.J. 1978. Measurement reapplied: Research into the child's attitude towards religion. *British Journal of Religious Education* 1, no. 2: 45–51.

Francis, L.J. 1982. *Youth in transit: A profile of 16–25 year olds.* Aldershot: Gower.

Francis, L.J. 1984. *Teenagers and the Church: A profile of church-going youth in the 1980s.* London: Collins Liturgical Publications.

Francis, L.J. 1996. The development of an abbreviated form of the Revised Eysenck Personality Questionnaire (JEPQR-A) among 13–15-year-olds. *Personality and Individual Differences* 21, no. 6: 835–44.

Francis, L.J. 2001. *The values debate: A voice from the pupils.* London: Woburn Press.

Francis, L.J. 2003. Religion and social capital: The flaw in the 2001 census in England and Wales. In *Public faith: The state of religious belief and practice in Britain*, ed. P. Avis, 45–64. London: SPCK.

Francis, L.J. 2005. *Faith and psychology: Personality, religion and the individual.* London: Darton, Longman and Todd.

Francis, L.J., L.B. Brown, and R. Philipchalk. 1992. The development of an abbreviated form of the Revised Eysenck Personality Questionnaire (EPQR-A): Its use among students in England, Canada, the USA and Australia. *Personality and Individual Differences* 13, no. 4: 443–9.

Francis, L.J., and Y.J. Katz. 2007. Measuring attitude toward Judaism: The internal consistency reliability of the Katz–Francis Scale of Attitude toward Judaism. *Mental Health, Religion and Culture* 10, no. 4: 309–24.

Francis, L.J., and W.K. Kay. 1995. *Teenage religion and values.* Leominster: Gracewing.

Francis, L.J., P.R. Pearson, M. Carter, and W.K. Kay. 1981a. Are introverts more religious? *British Journal of Social Psychology* 20, no. 2: 101–4.

Francis, L.J., P.R. Pearson, M. Carter, and W.K. Kay. 1981b. The relationship between neuroticism and religiosity among English 15 and 16-year-olds. *Journal of Social Psychology* 114, no. 1: 99–102.

Francis, L.J., P.R. Pearson, and W.K. Kay. 1982. Eysenck's personality quadrants and religiosity. *British Journal of Social Psychology* 21, no. 3: 262–4.

Francis, L.J., and M. Robbins. 2005. *Urban hope and spiritual health: The adolescent voice.* Peterborough: Epworth.

Francis, L.J., M. Robbins, and J. Astley, eds. 2009. *Empirical theology in texts and tables: Qualitative, quantitative and comparative perspectives.* Leiden: Brill.

Francis, L.J., A. Sahin, and F. Al-Failakawi. 2008. Psychometric properties of two Islamic measures among young adults in Kuwait: The Sahin–Francis Scale of Attitude toward Islam and the Sahin Index of Islamic Moral Values. *Journal of Muslim Mental Health* 3, no. 1: 9–34.

Francis, L.J., Y.R. Santosh, M. Robbins, and S. Vij. 2008. Assessing attitude toward Hinduism: The Santosh–Francis Scale. *Mental Health, Religion and Culture* 11, no. 6: 609–21.

Francis, L.J., and A. Village. 2008. *Preaching with all our souls.* London: Continuum.

Francis, L.J., and H.-G. Ziebertz, eds. 2011. *The public significance of religion.* Leiden: Brill.

Hegy, P., ed. 2007. *What do we imagine God to be? The function of 'God images' in our lives.* Lewiston, NY: Edwin Mellen Press.

Hood, R.W., Jr., P.C. Hill, and B. Spilka. 2009. *The psychology of religion: An empirical approach.* 4th ed. New York: The Guilford Press.

Kay, W.K., and L.J. Francis. 1996. *Drift from the churches: Attitude toward Christianity during childhood and adolescence.* Cardiff: University of Wales Press.

Likert, R. 1932. A technique for the measurement of attitudes. *Archives of Psychology* 140, no. 22: 1–55.

Sahin, A., and L.J. Francis. 2002. Assessing attitude toward Islam among Muslim adolescents: The psychometric properties of the Sahin–Francis scale. *Muslim Education Quarterly* 19, no. 4: 35–47.

Streib, H., ed. 2007. *Religion inside or outside traditional institutions*. Leiden: Brill.
Village, A. 2011. Outgroup prejudice, personality and religiosity: Disentangling a complex web of relationships among adolescents in the UK. *Psychology of Religion and Spirituality* 3, no. 4: 269–84.
Ziebertz, H.-G., ed. 2001. *Imagining God: Empirical explanations from an international perspective*. Münster: LIT-Verlag.

Religious diversity, empathy, and God images: perspectives from the psychology of religion shaping a study among adolescents in the UK

Leslie J. Francis, Jennifer S. Croft and Alice Pyke

Warwick Religions and Education Research Unit (WRERU), University of Warwick, Coventry, UK

> Major religious traditions agree in advocating and promoting love of neighbour as well as love of God. Love of neighbour is reflected in altruistic behaviour and empathy stands as a key motivational factor underpinning altruism. This study employs the empathy scale from the Junior Eysenck Impulsiveness Questionnaire to assess the association between empathy and God images among a sample of 5993 religiously diverse adolescents (13–15 years old) attending state maintained schools in England, Northern Ireland, Scotland, Wales, and London. The key psychological theory being tested by these data concerns the linkage between God images and individual differences in empathy. The data demonstrate that religious identity (e.g. Christian, Muslim) and religious attendance are less important than the God images which young people hold. The image of God as a God of mercy is associated with higher empathy scores, while the image of God as a God of justice is associated with lower empathy scores.

Introduction

The 'Young People's Attitudes to Religious Diversity' project was established within the Warwick Religions and Education Research Unit (WRERU) by Professor Robert Jackson to explore how young people between the ages of 13 and 16 years respond to living in the context of increasing religious diversity within the UK. The project was conceived as employing mixed methods and drawing on a broad range of theoretical backgrounds. The present study is situated within the quantitative component of the mixed methods project and perspectives shaped by the psychology of individual differences and the psychology of religion.

The quantitative component of the project was designed to collect the responses of at least 10,000 Year 9 and Year 10 pupils (13–15 years old) educated within the state maintained system of schools within the four 'nations' of the UK – England, Northern Ireland, Scotland, Wales – and London. The distinctiveness of London justifies special treatment within the context of religious diversity. The present analysis was conducted with an interim dataset of nearly 6000 pupils.

The research problem addressed by the present study arises from an earlier analysis of the interim data that identified empathy as a key psychological construct capable of exploring significant variance in the attitude of young people towards accepting others from diverse religious backgrounds. Given the key role of empathy in equipping young people for life in a religiously diverse context, the present study examines the connection between empathy and religiosity (broadly conceived) from theoretical and empirical perspectives, drawing on insights from the psychology of religion and from empirical theology. Major religious traditions agree in advocating and promoting love of neighbour as well as love of God. Love of neighbour is reflected in altruistic behaviour and empathy stands as a key motivational factor underpinning altruism.

Empathy and religion

Within the psychology of religion, empirical research concerned with the connection between empathy and religion can be traced back to Batson's early 'Good Samaritan' experiments (Batson, Schoenrade, and Pych 1985). Batson et al. argued that the theological account of the relationship between empathy and religion derives from the theory that religion promotes helping behaviour, as exemplified by the Parable of the Good Samaritan, while empathy is understood as fundamental to helping behaviour (Rushton 1980). On this account, one would hypothesise a positive correlation between belonging to a religious group and empathy. The problem with this theological view is that it appeared to be contradicted by the bulk of the empirical evidence emerging from Batson's early studies within the psychology of religion. The experiments reported by Darley and Batson (1973), Batson (1976), and Batson and Gray (1981) found no support for the notion that religion promotes pro-social or helping behaviour. At the same time, Batson's early work was the subject of a number of methodological criticisms that began to undermine the confidence that could be placed in the conclusions drawn from this strand of experimental research in the psychology of religion.

A second strand of empirical research within the psychology of religion has involved examining the direct relationship between psychometric measures of empathy and measures of religion. Examples of this strand of research are provided by Watson et al. (1984), Watson, Hood, and Morris (1985), Francis and Pearson (1987), Duriez (2004a, 2004b), Furrow, King, and White (2004), Khan, Watson, and Habib (2005), Paek (2006), and Markstrom et al. (2010). The main conclusion of these studies is that the relationship between empathy and religion varies according to the conceptualisation and operationalisation of religiosity employed.

Watson et al. (1984) administered the scales of intrinsic and extrinsic religiosity developed by Allport and Ross (1967) together with the Questionnaire Measure of Emotional Empathy (Mehrabian and Epstein 1972) and the Hogan Empathy Scale (Hogan 1969) to a sample of 180 undergraduate students. They found a positive correlation between empathy and intrinsic religiosity, but a negative correlation between empathy and extrinsic religiosity. A second study reported by Watson et al. (1985) conducted among 215 undergraduate volunteers from an introductory psychology class, employing the intrinsic and extrinsic scales developed by Allport and Ross (1967) and the Interpersonal Reactivity Index developed by Davis (1983), confirmed a positive correlation between intrinsic religiosity and empathic concern and a negative correlation between extrinsic religiosity and empathic concern. Clearly religious orientation is a matter of importance in this debate.

Somewhat different findings concerning the connection between religious orientation and empathy were reported in the studies by Khan, Watson, and Habib

(2005) and Paek (2006). The first (Khan, Watson, and Habib 2005) found a positive association between empathy and intrinsic religiosity among 168 Muslim students in Pakistan who completed the extrinsic and intrinsic measures proposed by Gorsuch and Venable (1983) and a three-item measure of empathic concern extracted from the seven-item measure proposed by Davis (1983). The second study (Paek 2006) provided further support for the association between Davis's measure of empathic concern and intrinsic religiosity but not extrinsic religiosity among 148 Christian churchgoers.

Francis and Pearson (1987) administered the Junior Eysenck Impulsiveness Inventory (Eysenck, Easting, and Pearson 1984) together with the Francis Scale of Attitude toward Christianity (Francis and Stubbs 1987) to a sample of 569 11- to 17-year-old pupils. They found a positive correlation between empathy and religiosity, after controlling for age and sex. In the light of the study by Watson et al. (1984), this finding is consistent with the view that the Francis Scale of Attitude toward Christianity assesses a form of intrinsic religiosity (Francis and Orchard 1999; Hills and Francis 2003).

Duriez (2004a) administered to a sample of 375 first-year psychology students a Dutch translation of the Interpersonal Reactivity Index (Davis 1983) together with the Post-Critical Belief Scale (Duriez, Fontaine, and Hutsebaut 2000). The strength of this measure is that it distinguishes between two aspects of religiosity: being religious or not (exclusion versus inclusion of transcendence) and the way in which religious contents are processed (literal versus symbolic). Duriez (2004a) found no relationship between empathy and the index of being religious or not, and a positive relationship between empathy and higher scores in the direction of processing religious content in a symbolic way. This finding was subsequently replicated by Duriez (2004b), using the same instruments for two further samples: 1133 university students following an introductory course in psychology and 397 adults. In the third sample, comprising 338 secondary school pupils (mean age = 16 years, SD = 0.93), reported in the same article, a positive correlation was found between empathy and being religious (a tendency to include transcendence) as well as between empathy and processing religious content in a symbolic way.

Furrow, King, and White (2004) investigated the connection between religious identity and pro-social concerns among a sample of 801 urban public high-school pupils ranging in age from 13 to 21 years, employing the 56-item Prosocial Personality Battery (Penner et al. 1995). They reported positive correlations between three components of religious identity (active in church life, committed to religiously informed ethical standards, and holding traditional beliefs) and three aspects of empathy (affective empathy, cognitive empathy, and self-oriented empathy).

Markstrom et al. (2010) investigated the connection between two measures of religiosity (frequency of religious attendance and importance of spiritual or religious beliefs), two measures of empathy (empathic concern and perspective taking accessed by Davis 1983), among 428 pupils in grades 10 and 11. They reported a positive connection between both measures of empathy and importance of belief, but no connection between these measures of empathy and frequency of religious attendance.

Within empirical theology, empirical research concerned with the connection between empathy and religion can be traced back to the more recent work by Francis (2007). Francis argued that the ways in which individuals feel about themselves and other people is connected with the way in which they imagine that God feels about them. In other words, Francis posits a correlation between God images and images of self and images of others. According to this theory, images of God as the God of mercy may be reflected in a more positive self-concept and in higher levels of empathy with and for others, while images of God as the God of justice may be reflected in a less positive self-concept and in lower levels of empathy with and for others.

This theologically driven theory which links images of God with individual differences in self-concept connects with and helps to interpret findings from early research reported by Benson and Spilka (1973) and by Spilka, Addison, and Rosensohn (1975). Both studies assessed self-esteem by means of a modified form of the Coopersmith Self-Esteem Inventory (Coopersmith 1967). The first study (Benson and Spilka 1973), involving 128 male pupils attending a Catholic high school who regarded religion as personally important, found that self-esteem scores were positively correlated with loving God images, but negatively correlated with rejecting, impersonal, vindictive, and controlling God images. The second study (Spilka, Addison, and Rosensohn 1975), involving 116 male and 82 female 16-year-olds attending three Catholic high schools, found that, for male pupils, self-esteem was negatively related to a wrathful God image. For female pupils, self-esteem was negatively related to a deistic God image and positively related to a loving God image, a traditional God image, and a kind God image.

Benson and Spilka's (1973) findings are consistent with the findings of several other studies working within different traditions. For example, Chartier and Goehner (1976) employed form B of the Coopersmith Self-Esteem Inventory (Coopersmith 1967) alongside the loving God semantic differential measure developed by Benson and Spilka (1973) among 84 male and female 10th and 11th grade pupils enrolled at Western Christian High School in Glendova, California. This study found that self-esteem scores were positively correlated with loving God images. Buri and Mueller (1993) employed the Tennessee Self Concept Scale (Fitts 1965) alongside eight bi-polar adjectives from Gorsuch's (1968) primary factors of the wrathfulness and kindliness of God among 213 Catholic college students from the University of St Thomas. They found a strong positive correlation between self-esteem and more loving, comforting, and nurturing God images. Other studies, however, provide only partial confirmation of these findings, with varying outcomes according to the populations studied and the instruments employed (Chartier and Goehner 1976; Potvin 1977; Jolley and Taulbee 1986; Greenway, Milne, and Clarke 2003).

The relationship between God images and other aspects of personal well-being and psychological adjustment have been explored by Schwab and Petersen (1990), Schaefer and Gorsuch (1991), Brokaw and Edwards (1994), Tisdale et al. (1997), Francis, Gibson, and Robbins (2001), Francis (2001), and Schaap-Jonker et al. (2002). For example, Francis, Gibson, and Robbins (2001) explored the relationship between God images and self-worth among a sample of 866 12- to 15-year-olds in Scotland. Self-worth was assessed by an eight-item index which included items like 'I feel my life has a sense of purpose,' 'I feel I am in control of my life', 'I often feel depressed,' and 'I have sometimes considered taking my own life'. The data demonstrated a positive relationship between self-worth and images of God as loving and forgiving and a negative relationship between self-worth and images of God as cruel and punishing. Francis (2001) explored the relationship between God images and personal well-being among a sample of 26,733 13- to 15-year-olds in England and Wales. In this study personal well-being was assessed by a nine-item index which included items like 'I find life really worth living', 'I feel I am not worth much as a person', 'I am worried about how I get on with other people', and 'Sometimes I have considered taking my own life'. The data demonstrated a negative correlation between a punishing image of God and good personal well-being.

Extending this earlier research from exploring the connection between God images and self-related concepts, Francis (2007) examined the relationship between empathy, as assessed by the empathy scale of the Junior Eysenck Impulsiveness Questionnaire (Eysenck, Easting, and Pearson 1984), and God images, as assessed in terms of uni-dimensional semantic space ranging from negative affect to positive affect (Francis, Robbins, and Gibson 2006), among a sample of 1826 secondary school pupils in England. After controlling for sex, school year, and individual differences in personality, as assessed by the short-form Revised Junior Eysenck Personality Questionnaire (Corulla 1990), the data demonstrated a significant link between high levels of empathy and positive God images and a significant link between low levels of empathy and negative God images.

Research question

Against this background, the aim of the present study is to test the connection between empathy and God images after allowing for the effect of other personal, psychological, and religious factors to be taken into account. First, however, it is important to clarify the research background to the key constructs being employed.

The understanding and measurement of *empathy* employed by the present study was pioneered by Mehrabian and Epstein (1972) in their Questionnaire Measure of Emotional Empathy. Their understanding of empathy focuses on the ability to experience vicariously the feelings of another and emphasises the empathic emotional response, in contrast to the Hogan Empathy Scale (Hogan 1969) which focuses on a cognitive view of empathy as the ability to take another's viewpoint (see Chlopan et al. 1985). The empirical components of empathy within Mehrabian and Epstein's measure are defined as: susceptibility to emotional contagion, appreciation of the feelings of unfamiliar and distant others, extreme emotional responsiveness, tendency to be moved by others' positive emotional experiences, tendency to be moved by others' negative emotional experiences, sympathetic tendency, and willingness to be in contact with others who have problems.

The Mehrabian and Epstein scale was adopted by Eysenck and Eysenck (1978) and adapted by Eysenck and Eysenck (1980) to form a junior measure of empathy. Further refinement by Eysenck (1981), Saklofske and Eysenck (1983), and Eysenck, Easting, and Pearson (1984) led to the development of a 23-item measure of emotional empathy for use among adolescents. It is reasonable to assume that the junior version of the scale measures the same psychological dimension as the adult version. It is this instrument that is employed in the present study. Two example items from the Eysenckian junior measure of empathy are: 'Would you feel sorry for a lonely stranger in a crowd?' and 'Do you often get very interested in your friends' problems?'.

The understanding and measurement of *God images* employed by the present study was pioneered by Benson and Spilka (1973) who employed a 10-item semantic differential grid which they claimed to generate two indices assessing a loving God image and a controlling God image. This instrument, known as the 'Loving and Controlling God Scales', has been employed effectively in a number of subsequent studies, including Spilka, Addison, and Rosensohn (1975), Chartier and Goehner (1976), Jolley and Taulbee (1986), Gabbard, Howard, and Tageson (1986),

Bowman et al. (1987), Kirkpatrick and Shaver (1990, 1992), Park and Cohen (1993), Brokaw and Edwards (1994), Pritt (1998), Kirkpatrick (1998), and Rowatt and Kirkpatrick (2002).

Francis, Robbins, and Gibson (2006) proposed a revised form of Benson and Spilka's (1973) instrument because they found that the factor structure of the original instrument was not recoverable among pupils who were less theologically educated than the group among whom the scales were originally constructed, namely a homogeneous religious sample of Catholic pupils who had been members of a Catholic parish for at least 10 years. Among their less theologically educated group of pupils Francis, Robbins, and Gibson (2006) found that the deletion of two items resulted in an improved eight-item uni-dimensional index, defining semantic space related to God images ranging from negative affect to positive affect.

A further refinement of the semantic differential grid assessment of God images proposed by Benson and Spilka (1973) and modified by Francis, Robbins, and Gibson (2006) was advanced by Francis (under review). The core constructs employed in the semantic differential grid were re-presented for scoring on a conventional five-point Likert scale (agree strongly, agree, not certain, disagree, and disagree strongly) in order to allow the God image items to be absorbed unobtrusively among a range of other items. It is this instrument that is employed in the present study. Two example items from Francis's New Index of God Images are 'I think of God as loving' and 'I think of God as strict'.

The understanding of *personal factors* employed in the present study concern sex and age (measured in terms of school year). These two personal factors are taken into account because of their key role in predicting individual differences in religiosity (Kay and Francis 1996) and in empathy (Francis and Pearson 1987).

The understanding of *psychological factors* employed in the present study is rooted in Eysenck's dimensional model of personality (Eysenck and Eysenck 1991). This model of personality is taken into account since two different strands of research have demonstrated the power of this model to predict individual differences in both religiosity and empathy. On the one hand, a number of studies have drawn attention to the consistent relationship between psychoticism scores and religious attitudes in general (Francis 1992; Fearn, Lewis, and Francis 2003) and to God images in particular (Francis 2005). On the other hand, a number of studies have drawn attention to the consistent relationship between both psychoticism and neuroticism scores and empathy (Eysenck and Eysenck 1980; Eysenck and McGurk 1980; Eysenck 1981). According to Eysenck's dimensional model of personality, individual differences can be most adequately and economically summarised in terms of the three higher order factors of extraversion, neuroticism, and psychoticism.

Eysenck's three-dimensional model of personality has been operationalised for use among adults by the Eysenck Personality Questionnaire (Eysenck and Eysenck 1975) and by the Eysenck Personality Questionnaire Revised (Eysenck, Eysenck, and Barrett 1985) and for use among young people by the Junior Eysenck Personality Questionnaire (Eysenck and Eysenck 1975) and by the Junior Eysenck Personality Questionnaire Revised (Corulla 1990). Both the junior and the adult forms of the revised instruments are available in the full and short form of 48 items. It is the short form of the Junior Eysenck Personality Questionnaire Revised that is employed in the present study. In respect of this instrument, two example items from the extraversion scale are 'Can you get a party going?' and 'Do you like going out a lot?'. Two example items from the neuroticism scale are 'Do you find it hard to get to sleep at night because you are worrying about things?' and 'Are your feelings rather easily hurt?'. Two example items from the psychoticism scale are 'Would you enjoy practical jokes that could sometimes harm people?' and 'Do you sometimes like teasing animals?'. Two example items from the lie scale are 'Have you ever said anything bad or nasty about anyone?' and 'Did you ever take anything (even a sweet) that belonged to someone else?'.

The understanding of additional *religious factors* employed in the present study sets alongside God images two well established sociological measures of religiosity, self-assigned religious affiliation, and self-reported religious attendance. Both measures have also been routinely employed within the psychology of religion. The inclusion of these measures in the study enables the predictive power of God images to be tested against the power of more conventionally employed measures of religiosity.

Method

Procedure

The 'Young People's Attitude to Religious Diversity' project set out to obtain responses from at least 2000 Year 9 and Year 10 pupils attending state maintained schools in each of the four nations of the UK – England, Northern Ireland, Scotland, Wales – and London. In each area, half the pupils were recruited from schools with a religious character (Anglican, Catholic or joint Anglican/Catholic) and half from schools without a religious character. Within the participating schools, questionnaires were administered by the religious education teachers within examination-like conditions. Pupils were assured of anonymity and confidentiality and given the option not to participate in the project.

Measures

Empathy was assessed by the empathy scale of the Junior Eysenck Impulsiveness Questionnaire (JIVE: Eysenck, Easting, and Pearson 1984). This instrument contains 23 empathy-related items developed from the adult measure of emotional empathy proposed by Mehrabian and Epstein (1972). Each item is assessed on a dichotomous scale: *yes* and *no*.

God images was assessed by the New Index of God Images (NIGI) proposed by Francis (under review). This instrument contains three positive images (reflecting the God of mercy) and three negative images (reflecting the God of justice) derived from the original conceptualisation proposed by Benson and Spilka (1973). These items are posed so that they can be addressed both by those who believe in God and by those who do not believe in God. Each item is assessed on a five-point scale: *agree strongly, agree, not certain, disagree*, and *disagree strongly*.

Personality was measured by the short Revised Junior Eysenck Personality Questionnaire (JEPQR-S: Corulla 1990). This instrument proposes three 12-item measures of extraversion, neuroticism, and psychoticism, together with a 12-item lie scale. Each item is assessed on a dichotomous scale: *yes* and *no*.

Religious attendance was assessed by the question 'Apart from special occasions (like weddings) how often do you attend a religious worship service (e.g. in a church, mosque or synagogue)?'. Responses were recorded on a seven-point scale: never, sometimes, at least once a year, at least six times a year, at least once a month, nearly every week, and several times a week.

Religious affiliation was recorded by a check list of world faiths and Christian denominations in response to the question 'What is your religion?'. For the analyses, two dummy variables were constructed from the responses to the question: one identifying the students who self-assigned as Christian and the other identifying the students who self-assigned as Muslim. In order to allow these two dummy variables to be compared with students of no religious affiliation, those affiliated with other world faiths were omitted from the analyses.

Sex and school year were both recorded as dichotomous variables: male = 1, female = 2; Year 9 = 1, Year 10 = 2.

Sample

The analyses were conducted on the interim dataset, including the responses of the first 5993 pupils. This sample included 3564 pupils who described themselves as Christians, 107 who described themselves as Muslims, and 2122 who described themselves as religiously unaffiliated. The remaining 200 pupils who identified with other faith traditions were omitted from the analyses. Of the total sample, 54% claimed never to attend religious services; 48% were male and 52% female; 45% were in Year 9 and 55% in Year 10.

Results

Table 1 presents the scale properties of the six measures employed in the study: God image, empathy, extraversion, neuroticism, psychoticism, and the lie scale. The alpha coefficients demonstrate that four of the indices (God image, empathy, extraversion, neuroticism) reached the threshold of .65 proposed by DeVellis (2003) for acceptable internal consistency reliability. The lower alpha coefficient recorded by the psychoticism scale is consistent with the difficulties associated with measuring this dimension of personality (Francis, Brown, and Philipchalk 1992). The poor performance of the lie scale deserves closer investigation.

In view of the centrality and novelty of the measure of God image employed in the present study, Table 2 examines the properties of the measure in greater detail. For this analysis, the negative items were reverse coded so that a high scale score indicates a positive God image and a low scale score indicates a negative God image. The item rest-of-test correlations confirm the uni-dimensionality and homogeneity of the construct being assessed.

Table 3 presents the bi-variate Pearson correlations between empathy, God image, sex, school year (age), extraversion, neuroticism, psychoticism, lie scale,

Table 1. Scale properties.

Scale	N items	alpha	mean	sd	range low	range high
Extraversion	6	.68	4.6	1.6	0	6
Neuroticism	6	.70	3.0	1.8	0	6
Psychoticism	6	.59	1.2	1.4	0	6
Lie scale	6	.50	2.4	1.4	0	6
God image	6	.89	18.7	5.9	6	30
Empathy	23	.78	13.8	4.2	0	23

Table 2. Scale of God images: item rest-of-test correlations.

	r
I think of God as loving	.77
I think of God as forgiving	.79
I think of God as accepting	.76
I think of God as strict*	.69
I think of God as disapproving*	.60
I think of God as demanding*	.58

Note: * these items are reverse coded
r indicates that the correlation between the individual item and the sum of the other five items

Table 3. Correlation matrix.

	Emp.	Mu	Ch	At	GI	L	P	N	E	Y
Sex	.24***	.02	.04**	.03*	.08***	.05***	−.25***	.26***	.10***	.04**
School year (Y)	.06***	−.01	.04***	.06***	.02	−.09***	.00	.02	.04**	
Extraversion (E)	.20***	−.06***	.02	−.01	−.02	−.20***	.07***	−.06***		
Neuroticism (N)	.49***	−.02	.01	.03*	.10***	−.14***	.03*			
Psychoticism (P)	−.06***	−.02	−.11***	−.13***	−.14***	−.33***				
Lie scale (L)	−.10***	.02	.01	.01	.08***					
God image (GI)	.20***	.08***	.38***	.35***						
Attendance (At)	.09***	.03	.39***							
Christian (Ch)	.06***									
Muslim (Mu)	−.01									

Note: * $p < .05$; ** $p < .01$; *** $p < .001$

religious attendance, self-assigned religious affiliation as Christian, and self-assigned religious affiliation as Muslim. Three main features of these data are of particular relevance to the present study.

First, God image scores are significantly correlated with some personal factors (sex), some psychological factors (neuroticism and psychoticism), and some religious factors (religious attendance and self-assigned religious affiliation), but with neither school year nor extraversion. A more positive God image (as operationalised by the New index of God Images) is associated with being female, with tender-mindedness (lower psychoticism scores), with greater emotionality (higher neuroticism scores), with higher levels of religious attendance, and with self-assigned religious affiliation as Christian or Muslim.

Second, empathy scores are significantly correlated with personal factors (sex and school year), with personality factors (extraversion, neuroticism, and psychoticism), and religious factors (religious attendance and self-assigned religious affiliated as Christian). Greater empathic capacity (as operationalised by the Eysenckian empathy measure) is associated with being female, being older, with greater emotionality (higher neuroticism scores), with tender-mindedness (lower psychoticism scores), with extraversion (higher extraversion scores), with higher levels of religious attendance, and with self-assigned affiliation as Christian (although not as Muslim).

Third, in terms of the key research question posed by the present study, there is significant correlation between God image and empathy scores. Greater empathic capacity is associated with a more positive God image.

Table 4. Regression model.

	r^2	increase r^2	F	p <	beta	t	p
Sex	.05	.05	234.6	.001	.08	5.7	.001
School year	.05	.00	0.7	NS	.01	0.7	NS
Extraversion	.05	.00	18.8	.001	.14	10.7	.001
Neuroticism	.22	.16	998.2	.001	.42	31.2	.001
Psychoticism	.22	.01	35.6	.001	−.05	−3.8	.001
Lie scale	.22	.00	1.9	NS	.01	0.9	NS
God image	.24	.02	132.7	.001	.14	9.9	.001
Attendance	.24	.00	4.4	.05	.03	2.2	.05
Christian	.24	.00	0.2	NS	−.01	−0.8	NS
Muslim	.24	.00	1.5	NS	−.02	−1.2	NS

In view of the complex pattern of significant correlation between sex, age, personality, religious attendance, religious affiliation, empathy, and God images, Table 4 employs multiple regression analysis to take into account the possible contaminating effects of personal factors (sex and school year) and psychological factors (extraversion, neuroticism, psychoticism, and the lie scale) before examining the relationship between God image and empathy. Religious factors (religious attendance and religious affiliation) are entered last to examine whether these factors account for additional variance after taking God images into account. In this model, empathy stands as the dependent variable and the predictor variables were entered in the fixed order of sex, school year (the two personal factors), extraversion, neuroticism, psychoticism, the lie scale (the four psychological factors) and God image, followed by religious attendance, Christian affiliation, and Muslim affiliation (the three religious factors).

Two main features of these data are of particular relevance to the present study. First, and most importantly, the increase in r^2 demonstrates that a positive God image is a statistically significant predictor of greater empathic capacity, even after controlling for individual differences in sex, school year, and personality. Given the significant variance in empathy accounted for by sex and by personality, it is particularly impressive that God images are able to provide significant additional predictive power. After taking God images into account, the additional variance explained by other religious factors (religious attendance and self-assigned religious affiliation) is trivial. Second, the beta weights demonstrate that the three most powerful factors in the model associated with individual differences in empathy are neuroticism (.42), extraversion (.14), and God images (.14).

Conclusion

The present study was designed to build on the findings from the earlier exploration of the data that empathy functioned as a key psychological construct capable of explaining significant variance in the attitude of young people towards accepting others from diverse religious backgrounds. Against this background the present study drew on theoretical perspectives and empirical evidence advanced by both the psychology of religion and empirical theology concerning the contribution of religion to the development of empathic capacity. Three main conclusions emerge.

The first is that research concerned with the association between religion and empathy needs to be nested within the broader framework of the individual differences tradition of research. The correlation matrix demonstrated that sex differences are important in shaping empathy, religious attendance, and God images; that neuroticism scores are important in shaping empathy, religious attendance, and God images; and that psychoticism scores are important in shaping empathy, religious attendance, and God images. Such findings are consistent with previous research and serve to underscore the importance of taking such potential contaminants into account before examining the association between religion and empathy.

The second conclusion is that the correlation between empathy and either religious attendance or religious affiliation is quite small compared with the correlations between empathy and sex, neuroticism and extraversion. Such findings are consistent with previous research and suggest that measures of external religiosity like religious attendance and religious affiliation (that may often be the only measures available) may not always be the most effective means of capturing the empirical importance of religion within individual lives.

The third conclusion is that God images serve as a more powerful predictor of individual differences in empathy than religious attendance and religious affiliation. This finding is consistent with one previous study that has explored the association between God images and empathy reported by Francis (2007). The notion of God images provides a key interface between the psychology of religion and empirical theology. The present findings underscore the value of taking perspectives from empirical theology into account when shaping empirical research exploring the connection between religion and empathy.

The key finding from the present study and from the earlier study by Francis (2007) is that there is a positive association between God images and empathic capacity. Different interpretations of this finding can be given from the perspective of the psychology of religion and from the perspective of empirical theology. Both perspectives will embrace a third construct: self image.

Within the psychology of religion, the three psychological constructs of a positive or loving God image, a positive self-concept or good level of self-esteem, and a well-developed capacity for empathy can be linked in two different ways. On the one hand, one strand of psychological theory conceives the direction of causality to emanate from God images: how we see ourselves is influenced by how we believe God sees us. Believing that God sees us as lovable and as loved encourages us to see ourselves as lovable. In turn, people who accept themselves may have the greater confidence and capacity to show empathy with others. On the other hand, another strand of psychological theory conceives the direction of causality to begin with self-concept. According to this account, based on consistency theory, individuals who have a low regard for themselves cannot reconcile with that low self-evaluation the view that they are acceptable to a loving God. Low self-regard generates a view of God as hostile and unloving. In turn, people who perceive God as basically unloving towards them are influenced by this role model to respond to others in an equally unloving and unempathic manner.

Within empirical theology, the two psychological constructs (a positive self-concept or good level of self-esteem and a well-developed capacity for empathy) and the theological construct of a God of mercy can be linked by the theological concept of love. One Christian line of argument based on the theological concept of love takes the following form. The first point is that the New Testament in general and the Johannine literature in particular argues that God is love (1 John 4:8). The second point is that the human response to encounter with the love of God is love for God: we love God because God first loved us (1 John 4:19). The third point is that the second commandment defines love for others as involving also love for self: thou shalt love thy neighbour as thy self (Mark 12:31). In this sense, love of self implies positive self-concept or good level of self-esteem. The fourth point is that love for God also entails love for others: if God so loved us, we ought also love one another (1 John 4:11). In this sense, love for one another implies showing empathy. While this theological explanation holds good only within the Christian contexts, similar theological models may be constructed within the context of other faith traditions.

Note

Young People's Attitudes to Religious Diversity (AHRC Reference: AH/G014035/1) was a large-scale mixed methods research project investigating the attitudes of 13- to16-year-old students across the UK. Young people from a variety of socio-economic, cultural, ethnic, and religious backgrounds from different parts of England, Wales, Northern Ireland, and Scotland, and including London as a special case, took part in the study. Professor Robert Jackson was principal investigator and Professor Leslie J. Francis co-investigator. Together they led a team of qualitative and quantitative researchers based in the Warwick Religions and Education Research Unit, within the Institute of Education at the University of Warwick. The project was part of the AHRC/ESRC Religion and Society Programme and ran from 2009 to 2012.

References

Allport, G.W., and J.M. Ross. 1967. Personal religious orientation and prejudice. *Journal of Personality and Social Psychology* 5, no. 4: 432–43.

Batson, C.D. 1976. Religion as prosocial: Agent or double agent? *Journal for the Scientific Study of Religion* 15, no. 1: 29–45.

Batson, C.D., and P.A. Gray. 1981. Religious orientation and helping behaviour: Responding to one's own or to the victim's needs? *Journal of Personality and Social Psychology* 40, no. 3: 511–20.

Batson, C.D., P.A. Schoenrade, and V. Pych. 1985. Brotherly love or self-concern? Behavioural consequences of religion In *Advances in the psychology of religion*, ed. L.B. Brown, 185–208. Oxford: Pergamon Press.

Benson, P.L., and B.P. Spilka. 1973. God-image as a function of self-esteem and locus of control. *Journal for the Scientific Study of Religion* 12, no. 3: 297–310.

Bowman, E.S., P. M. Coons, R. S. Jones, and M. Oldstrom. 1987. Religious psychodynamics in multiple personalities: Suggestions for treatment. *American Journal of Psychotherapy* 41, no. 4: 542–54.

Brokaw, B.F., and K.J. Edwards. 1994. The relationship of God image to level of object relations development. *Journal of Psychology and Theology* 22, no. 4: 352–71.

Buri, J.R., and R.A. Mueller. 1993. Psychoanalytic theory and loving God concepts: Parent referencing versus self-referencing. *Journal of Psychology* 127, no. 1: 17–27.

Chartier, M.R., and L.A. Goehner. 1976. A study of the relationship of parental-adolescent communication, self-esteem, and God image. *Journal of Psychology and Theology* 4: 227–32.

Chlopan, B.E., M.L. McCain, J.L. Carbonell, and R.L. Hagen. 1985. Empathy: Review of available measures. *Journal of Personality and Social Psychology* 48, no. 3: 635–53.

Coopersmith, S. 1967. *The antecedents of self-esteem*. San Francisco, CA: Freeman.

Corulla, W.J. 1990. A revised version of the psychoticism scale for children. *Personality and Individual Differences* 11, no. 1: 65–76.

Darley, J., and C.D. Batson. 1973. From Jerusalem to Jericho: A study of situational and dispositional variables in helping behaviour. *Journal of Personality and Social Psychology* 27, no. 1: 100–8.

Davis, M.H. 1983. Measuring individual differences in empathy: Evidence for a multidimensional approach. *Journal of Personality and Social Psychology* 44, no. 1: 113–26.

DeVellis, R.F. 2003. *Scale development: Theory and applications*. London: Sage.

Duriez, B. 2004a. Are religious people nicer people? Taking a closer look at the religion–empathy relationship. *Mental Health, Religion and Culture* 7, no. 3: 249–54.

Duriez, B. 2004b. A research note on the relation between religiosity and racism: The importance of the way in which religious contents are being processed. *International Journal for the Psychology of Religion* 14, no. 3: 177–91.

Duriez, B., J.R.J. Fontaine, and D. Hutsebaut. 2000. A further elaboration of the Post-Critical Belief scale: Evidence for the existence of four different approaches to religion in Flanders-Belgium. *Psychologica Belgica* 40: 153–81.

Eysenck, H.J., and S.B.G. Eysenck. 1975. *Manual of the Eysenck Personality Questionnaire (adult and junior)*. London: Hodder and Stoughton.

Eysenck, H.J., and S.B.G. Eysenck. 1991. *Manual of the Eysenck personality scales*. London: Hodder and Stoughton.

Eysenck, S.B.G. 1981. Impulsiveness and antisocial behaviour in children. *Current Psychological Research* 1, no. 1: 31–7.

Eysenck, S.B.G., G. Easting, and P.R. Pearson. 1984. Age norms for impulsiveness in children. *Personality and Individual Differences* 5, no. 3: 315–21.

Eysenck, S.B.G., and H.J. Eysenck. 1978. Impulsiveness and venturesomeness: Their position in a dimensional system of personality. *Psychological Reports* 43, no. 3: 1247–55.

Eysenck, S.B.G., and H.J. Eysenck. 1980. Impulsiveness and venturesomeness in children. *Personality and Individual Differences* 1, no. 1: 73–8.

Eysenck, S.B.G., H.J. Eysenck, and P. Barrett. 1985. A revised version of the psychoticism scale. *Personality and Individual Differences* 6, no. 1: 21–9.

Eysenck, S.B.G., and B.J. McGurk. 1980. Impulsiveness and venturesomeness in a detention centre population. *Psychological Reports* 47, no. 3: 1299–306.

Fearn, M., C.A. Lewis, and L.J. Francis. 2003. Religion and personality among religious studies students: A replication. *Psychological Reports* 93, no. 3: 819–22.

Fitts, W.H. 1965. *Tennessee Self-Concept Scale: Manual*. Los Angeles, CA: Western Psychological Services.

Francis, L.J. 1992. Is psychoticism really a dimension of personality fundamental to religiosity? *Personality and Individual Differences* 13, no. 6: 645–52.

Francis, L.J. 2001. God images, personal wellbeing and moral values: A survey among 13–15 year olds in England and Wales. In *Imagining God: Empirical explorations from an international perspective*, ed. H.-G. Ziebertz, 125–44. Münster: LIT–Verlag.

Francis, L.J. 2005. God images and self-esteem: A study among 11 to 18-year-olds. *Research in the Social Scientific Study of Religion* 16: 105–21.

Francis, L.J. 2007. God images and empathy: A study among secondary school pupils in England. In *What do we imagine God to be? The function of 'God images' in our lives*, ed. P. Heggy, 67–88. Lampeter: Edwin Mellen Press.

Francis, L.J. under review. Distinguishing between negative and positive God images: Introducing the New Index of God Images (NIGI).

Francis, L.J., L.B. Brown, and R. Philipchalk. 1992. The development of an abbreviated form of the Revised Eysenck Personality Questionnaire (EPQR-A): Its use among students in England, Canada, the USA and Australia. *Personality and Individual Differences* 13, no. 4: 443–9.

Francis, L.J., H.M. Gibson, and M. Robbins. 2001. God images and self-worth during adolescence. *Mental Health, Religion and Culture* 4, no. 2: 103–8.

Francis, L.J., and A. Orchard. 1999. The relationship between the Francis Scale of Attitude toward Christianity and measures of intrinsic, extrinsic and quest religiosity. *Pastoral Psychology* 47, no. 5: 365–71.

Francis, L.J., and P.R. Pearson. 1987. Empathic development during adolescence. Religiosity the missing link? *Personality and Individual Differences* 8, no. 1: 145–8.

Francis, L.J., M. Robbins, and H.M. Gibson. 2006. A revised semantic differential scale distinguishing between negative and positive God images. *Journal of Beliefs and Values* 27, no. 2: 237–40.

Francis, L.J., and M.T. Stubbs. 1987. Measuring attitudes towards Christianity: From childhood into adulthood. *Personality and Individual Differences* 8, no. 5: 741–3.

Furrow, L.J., P.E. King, and K. White. 2004. Religion and positive youth development: Identity, meaning, and prosocial concerns. *Applied Developmental Sciences* 8, no. 1: 17–26.

Gabbard, C.E., G.S. Howard, and C.W. Tageson. 1986. Assessing locus of control with religious populations. *Journal of Research in Personality* 20, no. 3: 292–308.

Gorsuch, R.L. 1968. The conceptualisation of God as seen in adjective ratings. *Journal for the Scientific Study of Religion* 7, no. 1: 56–64.

Gorsuch, R.L., and G.D. Venable. 1983. Development of an 'age-universal' I-E scale. *Journal for the Scientific Study of Religion* 28, no. 2: 348–54.

Greenway, A.P., L.C. Milne, and V. Clarke. 2003. Personality variables, self-esteem and depression and an individual's perception of God. *Mental Health, Religion and Culture* 6, no. 1: 45–58.

Hills, P., and L.J. Francis. 2003. Discriminant validity of the Francis Scale of Attitude toward Christianity with respect to religious orientation. *Mental Health, Religion and Culture* 6, no. 3: 277–82.

Hogan, R. 1969. Development of an empathy scale. *Journal of Consulting and Clinical Psychology* 33, no. 3: 307–16.

Jolley, J.C., and S.J. Taulbee. 1986. Assessing perceptions of self and God's comparison of prisoners and normals. *Psychological Reports* 59, no. 3: 1139–46.

Kay, W.K., and L.J. Francis. 1996. *Drift from the Churches: Attitude toward Christianity during childhood and adolescence*. Cardiff: University of Wales Press.

Khan, Z.H., P.J. Watson, and F. Habib. 2005. Muslim attitudes toward religion, religious orientation and empathy among Pakistanis. *Mental Health, Religion and Culture* 8, no. 1: 49–61.

Kirkpatrick, L.A. 1998. God as a substitute attachment figure: A longitudinal study of attachment style and religious change in college students. *Personality and Social Psychology Bulletin* 24, no. 9: 961–73.

Kirkpatrick, L.A., and P.R. Shaver. 1990. Attachment theory and religion: Childhood attachments, religious beliefs, and conversion. *Journal for the Scientific Study of Religion* 29, no. 3: 315–34.

Kirkpatrick, L.A., and P.R. Shaver. 1992. An attachment–theoretical approach to romantic love and religious belief. *Personality and Social Psychology Bulletin* 18, no. 3: 226–75.

Markstrom, C.A., E. Huey, B.M. Stiles, and A.L. Krause. 2010. Framework of caring and helping in adolescence. Are empathy, religiosity, and spirituality related constructs? *Youth and Society* 42, no. 1: 59–80.

Mehrabian, A., and N. Epstein. 1972. A measure of emotional empathy. *Journal of Personality* 40, no. 4: 525–43.

Paek, E. 2006. Religiosity and perceived emotional intelligence among Christians. *Personality and Individual Differences* 41, no. 3: 479–90.

Park, C.L., and L.H. Cohen. 1993. Religious and nonreligious coping with the death of a friend. *Cognitive Therapy and Research* 17, no. 6: 561–77.

Penner, L.A., B.A. Fritzsche, J.P. Craiger, and T.S. Freifield. 1995. Measuring the prosocial personality. In *Advances in personality assessment*, ed. J.N. Butcher and C.D. Spielberger, 147–63. Hillside, NJ: Lawrence Erlbaum.

Potvin, R.H. 1977. Adolescent God images. *Review of Religious Research* 19, no. 1: 43–53.

Pritt, A.F. 1998. Spiritual correlates of reported sexual abuse among Mormon women. *Journal for the Scientific Study of Religion* 37, no. 2: 273–85.

Rowatt, W.C., and L.A. Kirkpatrick. 2002. Two dimensions of attachment to God and their relation to affect, religiosity, and personality constructs. *Journal for the Scientific Study of Religion* 41, no. 4: 637–51.

Rushton, J.P. 1980. *Altruism, socialisation and society*. Englewood Cliffs, NJ: Prentice Hall.

Saklofske, D.H., and S.B.G. Eysenck. 1983. Impulsiveness and venturesomeness in Canadian children. *Psychological Reports* 52, no. 1: 147–52.

Schaap-Jonker, H., E. Eurelings-Bontekoe, P.J. Verhagen, and H. Zock. 2002. Image of God and personality pathology: An exploratory study among psychiatric patients. *Mental Health, Religion and Culture* 5, no. 1: 55–71.

Schaefer, C.A., and R.L. Gorsuch. 1991. Psychological adjustment and religiousness: The multivariate belief–motivation theory of religiousness. *Journal for the Scientific Study of Religion* 30, no. 4: 448–61.

Schwab, R., and K.U. Petersen. 1990. Religiousness: Its relation to loneliness, neuroticism and subjective well-being. *Journal for the Scientific Study of Religion* 29, no. 3: 335–45.

Spilka, B., J. Addison, and M. Rosensohn. 1975. Parents, self and God: A test of competing theories of individual-religion relationships. *Review of Religious Research* 16, no. 3: 154–65.

Tisdale, T.C., T.L. Key, K.J. Edwards, B.F. Brokaw, and S.R. Kemperman. 1997. Impact of treatment on God image and personal adjustment, and correlations of God image to personal adjustment and object relations development. *Journal of Psychology and Theology* 25, no. 2: 227–39.

Watson, P.J., R.W. Hood, and R.J. Morris. 1985. Dimensions of religiosity and empathy. *Journal of Psychology and Christianity* 4, no. 3: 73–85.

Watson, P.J., R.W. Hood, R.J. Morris, and J.R. Hall. 1984. Empathy, religious orientation and social desirability. *Journal of Psychology* 117, no. 2: 211–6.

Failures of meaning in religious education

James C. Conroy[a], David Lundie[b] and Vivienne Baumfield[a]

[a]School of Education, University of Glasgow, Glasgow, UK; [b]Faculty of Education, Liverpool Hope University, Liverpool, UK

> The educational aims of religious education (RE) in the UK as evinced, for example, by Ofsted have been couched in the language of meaning making. Based on an ESRC funded three-year ethnographic study of 24 schools across the UK, this essay represents one attempt to interrogate how such meanings are shaped, or indeed fail to be shaped, in the day-to-day transactions of the school. We do this by locating RE in current discussions of efficacy, as manifest in inspectoral reports and allied scholarship, illustrate how complex the entailments and purposes of RE are, explore some of the ethnographic and related data to understand how meaning is shaped inside and outside the classroom, and, finally, attempt to locate that material in more general observations about the nature of meaning in RE – observations that are informed by contemporary readings of meaning making in the work of, among others, Baudrillard. We observe that RE, so dependent upon meaning for educational justification, is too frequently a site which witnesses failures of meaning.

Introduction

Arguably anxiety is one, if not the, defining characteristic of late industrial societies; it insinuates itself into the interstitial spaces of common and personal life and is manifest in a scepticism that a range of social practices and institutions can provide epistemologically, ethically, and ontologically adequate resources for our day-to-day living. Philosophers and social theorists have increasingly replaced the 'search for truth' with the 'search for meaning' – a quest that has come to shape our discourse about the purposes of religious education (RE) in not only common schools but also in religiously denominated schools. If pupils are no longer required to attend to the truth claims of religion, they should certainly attend to the meaning these claims have for their adherents. Moreover, they should draw on the insights of religious belief systems to inform their own 'meaning making' (learning from religion). The displacement of a more traditional, epistemologically loaded study of religion by such personal 'meaning making' was intended to enhance the relevance of the subject and its efficacy as a resource for living with oneself and with the other. It is, we suggest, not unreasonable to ask whether the pre-eminent place afforded meaning in RE has conduced to the realisation of such enhanced efficacy.

This essay offers one attempt to investigate how such questions of meaning are treated in the day-to-day transactions between religious educators and pupils in and beyond the classroom.

In 2007, the UK's Arts and Humanities Research Council (AHRC) and Economic and Social Research Council (ESRC) launched their joint programme on 'Religion and Society', which funded the study that informs this essay. The project had the simple title, 'Does Religious Education Work?', with its centrepiece an ethnographic study in 24 schools (common and religiously denominated) across the UK of the practices that surround and inhere in RE. In addition to our multi-modal ethnography (Walford 2008), we conducted professional seminars using the Delphi method (Baumfield et al. 2011), textbook and policy analyses, participant research, and an online questionnaire made available to pupils in all the participating schools. As far as possible, we allowed the ethnographic data to speak for themselves and used an 'emergent themes' process to foreground our interrogations. One emergent theme was 'meaning making'. We did not begin with the question, 'what does x mean?', but with the data. Hence we do not, at the beginning, offer a substantive account of meaning in RE but defer that discussion to the end. In that way we hope to free the material from being overly determined. How pupils experience RE as depicted in the case studies offers some uncomfortable insights into their perceptions of the nature of the subject, particularly in the preparation for public examinations. We have selected particular instances[1] where the pupils themselves highlighted discrepancies between the aims and the enactment of RE in the classroom. We make no claim to uniformity or universality of experience but suggest that these discrepancies point to important tropes in the experiences and practices of the subject in secondary schools. The extent to which our concerns represent a fundamental fracture in the fabric of RE in UK schools can be tested cumulatively through the replication of the methods we have used in the project, which is why our data sets will be available online.

The following attempts to contextualise RE in current discussions of efficacy, as manifest in inspectoral reports and allied scholarship, to illustrate how complex the entailments and purposes of RE are, to explore some of the ethnographic and related data, to understand how meaning is transacted in the lived experience of the classroom and, finally, to locate that material in more general observations about the nature of meaning in RE.

The context and the purposes of religious education

With its explicit mention, some 11 times, the most recent Ofsted subject report *Transforming RE* (2010) foregrounds 'meaning' as a central, perhaps *the* central, feature of religious education. Such a concern is not evident in cognate subject reports, such as the one on history, which mentions it not once (Ofsted 2011).[2] Even the recent Ofsted (2012) report on the teaching of English, *Moving English Forward*, features only seven mentions of meaning – only one of which is actually concerned with the meaning of language, with the majority focused on activities that are 'meaningful' for pupils. Hence meaning here becomes a synonym for 'relevance' and may not be considered primarily as concerned with the meaning of the object of study in and for itself.

Given the centrality that meaning appears to play in the espoused purposes of RE, it is important to understand the nature and extent of its instantiation in the practices of religious education in the schools that formed the locations for this study. Somewhat ironically, in *Transforming RE*, success at Key Stage 4 was considered not with respect to its efficacy in unfolding meaning but in the 'increase in the number of students leaving with an accredited qualification' (Ofsted 2010, 32). In the light of many observations about weaknesses in teaching, the increase in uptake does not self-evidently appear to be the consequence of improved quality, nor indeed to have led to a concomitant increase in resources (material or time allocation). The concerns raised in the Ofsted report (2010) are echoed in the analysis by Jackson et al. (2010) of materials used in RE teaching, which points out that there was a widespread perception (among academic consultants) that 'many of the resources fell short in conveying a real sense of the deeper significance and power of religions in the lives of the believer' (6). The concern with the deeper significance and power of religion is of course another way of pointing to the centrality of meaning in RE.

A series of additional comments in the Ofsted report, with 24 discussions of specific weaknesses, suggests that the provision of high-quality RE is in a parlous state across a substantial range of entailments, including specifically religious content, intellectual challenge, assessment, limited access to subject specialists, and time-tabling difficulties. It might be suggested that these weaknesses are contingent, reflecting little more than the fact that RE is often taught by inadequately prepared, and often non-specialist, teachers and under-led and resourced by senior managers in schools. Indeed, our own research exposes such contingent weaknesses in many of the schools we studied (Conroy et al. 2011). However, this cannot be the sole explanation for systemic weakness, given that we found, during our ethnographic work, varied and complex failures of meaning, despite the schools stating that they had confidence in their RE provision. Rather, we suggest, everyday RE is striated with failures of meaning that emanate from foundational or constitutive confusions in the conduct of the subject that are deep-seated. These constitutive failures, we propose, emerge from epistemic and values confusions about the very purposes and meaning of RE in a late industrial society.

While the purposes of RE are multiple and complex, at its core two competing impulses rub awkwardly against each other: the epistemological impulse to understand the nature of the thing in itself and the ethical impulse to appropriate the study of religion as a means to cultivate certain moral dispositions and attitudes (Grimmitt 1987). This conflation potentially gives rise to a crisis of meaning in so far as the first impulse must perforce rest on a position of substantive epistemic neutrality, while the second must abjure such neutrality, to a greater or lesser extent. This epistemic and ethical conflict in turn gives rise to a conflict regarding the meanings of the activities. Hence the anxieties (expressed by Ofsted and others) about the efficacy of RE may equally be anxieties about meaning.

To expand on this: *from our analysis of the claims and practices of RE and arguably as a consequence of maintaining many of the structural features of RE, which were created in the nineteenth century*, both policymakers and professionals are unclear about the specifically educational purposes of RE (Baumfield et al. 2011). They do not wish to 'give up' religious education for significant political and cultural reasons, but have burdened it with many competing imperatives. These include substantial contributions to the following educational entailments,[3] many of which have overlapping elements, but some are, at least *prima facie*, in conflict with one another:

(a) religious literacy (knowledge and understanding of religious ideas and language and their social and cultural impact)
(b) dealing with truth claims and pluralism
(c) philosophical understanding
(d) understanding heritage
(e) citizenship education
(f) multi-cultural sensitivity and awareness
(g) spiritual and social cohesion – contributing to school ethos
(h) nurturing pupils in particular communities (including catechesis)
(i) moral development
(j) spiritual life and religious observance
(k) enhancing local demographic considerations
(l) very particular 'Socratic dispositions'.
(m) sex and relationships education

We must overlay this complex concatenation with further entailments, such as examination success, personal development, the cultivation of creativity, the promotion of community cohesion, etc. While we do not wish, at this stage, to further disaggregate these entailments, we would point out that they provide a formidable account of what RE is intended to offer pupils. Although we might not expect every pupil in every circumstance to attend consciously to the myriad features of RE, we are nevertheless likely to desire that they are able to make sense of (understand and interpret) as well as ascribe meaning to those entailments that comprise religion as a whole. Consequently, if they understand only fragments, can they be said to be religiously educated? Moreover, can we ever say that we have a legitimate expectation that pupils acquire such a synoptic view if we are unclear as to whether or not the teacher has the same view? The answer to these questions must surely reside in the actual cases of pupils and teachers. In the next section we shall therefore look at some such cases in order to understand more how meaning is or is not transacted in the everyday experience of the classroom. We shall then use them to uncover and reflect on more general issues of meaning in the social practices of teaching RE.

Fieldwork

Example 1: interview with a pupil in the lower sixth form in a London comprehensive

Interviewer (I): ... you were saying that the philosophy is quite different?

Pupil (P): Yes, I think it's very different actually. Because in RS [Religious Studies] it's more about 'this is what this religion thinks and this is what that religion thinks, compare this view' at best! Compare this and that, whereas with philosophy it's more of a coming to those ideas. Before you even get to these theological issues...

I: You're saying that a lot of them don't really know why they're Muslim. Do you think RS helps with that at all?

P: No.

I: No?

P: No. Because RS...RS isn't philosophy. RS is just saying 'this is the way things are'. It can help in some ways to say 'this is what this faith believes, so when you find Islam, this is what Islam says'.... I think it's ... the way RS is taught is, 'these are the rules. This is what people do', but Islamicly, the way I see it, the way Islam should be taught really is not about, 'these are the rules', it's 'these are the principles and this is how you come to the rules'. So it's .... I think that's kind of the problem. People will say, 'ok I have to fast and pray five times a day and this that and the other', but for me that's not where it should start. It should start before that. So .... Because whoever's teaching would have to be able to fully appreciate the, not the idea, but the style of thinking and stuff.

The pupil's observations in this interview point to our first concern with meaning. Operating from within a particular religious tradition (Islam), the pupil considers the teaching of RE to be flawed in so far as it is concerned with comparative descriptions of social phenomena and practices rather than with religion as a way of not only construing, but being in, the world. Moreover, this resonates with other pupil comments and ethnographic observations of pupils in schools with relatively large numbers of religiously affiliated pupils. Inadvertently, the pupil touches on the well-trodden Wittgensteinian path of the incommensurability of religious outlooks, suggesting that there are questions around the full appreciation of 'the style of thinking'. We are not persuaded that incommensurability *simpliciter* is at issue here – after all people from different religious traditions can communicate their ideas reasonably well in a wide range of contexts. And, as Ricoeur points out, while:

... an event belonging to one stream of consciousness cannot be transferred as such into another stream of consciousness. Yet, nevertheless, something passes from me to you.... This something is not the experience as experienced, but its meaning. Here is the miracle. The experience as experienced, as lived, remains private, but its sense, its meaning becomes public. (1976, 16)

But even if the communication failures are not straightforward, it is possible to see them embedded in the clash not between a set of religious claims, but between pedagogical purposes – a theme that emerges repeatedly in our ethnographic and policy studies. Following Ricoeur we can see that it is not that pupils misunderstand or misrepresent to themselves what is communicated, rather it is that they deem the morphological discussion of religion within the classroom as having little salience in their religious lives. As the pupil cited above goes on,

Because they are second-, third-generation Bengalis ... school is a completely different experience all together and the way they're taught.... RS would probably have been the first time they would have seen it in that kind of context in that way. So it's almost like you get two opposite ends of the spectrum. Like you get the cultural stuff and then you get the ... what they learn in school.... I wouldn't say it's exactly what Islam is. It's different.... I dunno ... it's strange.

What may be at stake here is the way in which the purposes of RE are enacted in the conversational space. The gap between pupil and teacher emanates from the different meanings ascribed not to the religious *cogitationes* but to the purpose of RE. The pupil considers that the purposes of teaching religion in his classroom appeared to be dominated by somewhat basic comparisons, which misrepresent the 'being-in-the-world' nature of religious attachment. In this case the pupil considers RE to have been shaped by somewhat prosaic morphological considerations to which she ascribes little meaning and which fail to connect with the meaning she invests in religious being. There is a gap between the classroom or school attribution of meaning to the activity of studying religion and that of the pupil – a gap summarised in a group discussion in another school where a pupil observed that 'I think the stuff the school teaches us.... I think we have to kind of accept it when we're in school because that's what comes up in exams' (Girls' Comprehensive School, London). Here we can clearly see an important distinction between purpose and meaning – passing examinations is purposeful but not meaningful.

Let us now turn to the second example; a set of field notes from one of the ethnographers on the project.

Example 2: field notes from a church school in the north-east

The consequences for the meaning of RE and religion itself of the, possibly excessive, priority afforded examinations was to be seen in quite a number of the schools in our study. As one of the ethnographers observed while waiting in the departmental office, 'the notice boards had a lot of information about targets and performance graphs for RE, broken down into small units of analysis'. In the revision class of a Year 10 top set:

> ... there was persistent low level disruption.... The ... point at which the [students] did become engaged was when the teacher went through the results of the mock exam and the predicted ... grades. Interestingly, even the apparently most disaffected pupils evidently cared about the grades and were quite competitive.

> The Department has a VLE [Virtual Learning Environment] where past papers can be found with marks schemes for the questions – there are also tally counts of how often keywords/terms come up and pupils are encouraged to check this and make sure they have the definitions clear and learn them. The [particular] lesson [observed] focused on one question and mark scheme.

> Question: How might the presence of religion in the world demonstrate the existence of God?

> Marks Scheme: 2 marks per bullet point
> - Many different people believe in God.
> - Religions have a common focus and share some key ideas.
> - Prayers sometimes seem to be answered.
> - Believing in God helps people in their life.

> I found that the class were not really engaged in the lesson and overheard the following: 'I've written it so that I won't seem very clever.' – 'I don't believe in any of them – why do I have to pretend?'

Once again, albeit from a different perspective, the purpose of RE is subject to scrutiny from its students. The activity of breaking down the information into examination-sized gobbets within the lesson appears to echo a significant functional purpose of the activity – the passing of examinations. With substantial corroboration by other parts of the field notes, it appears that, for this group of pupils, religious education is both facile and futile.

Perhaps more importantly, the examination question itself indicates a further difficulty with meaning. Prima facie, it provides a meaningful task, but closer inspection reveals it as conceptually confused. The relationship between the verb 'to demonstrate' and the possible putative answers suggest a significant gap in the communication of the concept of demonstrable belief – indeed what belief might mean for adherents. How, we might ask, can the existence of adherents demonstrate the existence of God any more than the existence of children who believe in Santa Claus can lead us to believe in the actual existence of Santa Claus? The issue at stake here is whether the question is itself meaningful. We suggest that it is both logically and existentially meaningless and leads to more confusion than clarity about what constitutes an appropriate question in the domain of religion. The third – overlapping – example is a focus group discussion with GCSE pupils.

Example 3: focus group in a London community school

Interviewer (I): What are your impressions of RE lessons in your school?

Pupil 1 (P1): I am not sure of the structure of the lessons; it just seems to be random work on people's feelings.

Pupil 2 (P2): [It] would be useful to have an overview at the start…

Pupil 3 (P3): … like what is in the exam…

P2: What happened in the lessons wasn't in the mock exam.

Pupil 4 (P4): The book [revision guide] was useful and the crammer sessions were OK because only the people serious about learning came to them. In school time the lessons are just people messing around.

P1: Don't want to always just work to the test though; I like things like the Truth Tube stuff. Could be a little less vague if we did a section at a time, there's lots of bits.

P2: Need to make the aims clear right at the start of the lesson.

Pupil 5 (P5): It's helpful if we know what we are doing.

P1: But there's no specific answer; it's your own opinions, so you can't be wrong.

P5: The arguments and clashes are good, good for discussion.

I: How do RE lessons compare with other lessons in school?

P1: … more relaxed … you feel that you can express your opinions.

P3: RE's down to what people believe, so it's relaxed.

P1: But some people use the subject and its advantages against the teacher; it's annoying because they take advantage…

Pupil 6 (P6): It's about different beliefs, but some people ... won't learn because they think there is nothing to learn because it is just what I believe.

P2: ... it's not a good 'cool' subject and this affects how much you want to join in.

P1: RE is not taken seriously, even in mock exam we were messing about. Students were running a competition about how many times a phrase...

P3: ... like 'Gordon Brown's tie'...

P1: ... could be used in an answer.

The sense of boredom and scepticism underlying this conversation points to one of RE's central challenges: coherence as to purpose and meaning. Pupils appeared to have absorbed the view that the purposes of RE are vague and possibly meaningless and that RE primarily serves as a forum for expressing personal opinions. The meaning of religion as an object of study inheres in its being a site for opinion forming; the meaning of RE is the provision of a site for agonistic self-expression. Superficially this appears to be the cultivation of a kind of Socratic engagement. Such a move can be seductive, but, in the dialogues, Plato is not much given to the view that 'it's your own opinion so you can't be wrong'. Nevertheless, we repeatedly witnessed, by teachers and pupils, the articulation of strongly relativist accounts of religious and ethical value and the reification and consequent valorisation of personal opinion as the core purpose of religious education. Ironically, the meaning of religion is apt to be lost in the perceived purpose of RE as the site for personal positioning and (although this is less evident in practice than might be assumed) personal meaning making.

In the interstices of these commentaries and recordings what emerges is a clash of purpose with purpose and purpose with meaning, summarised in the following extract from our Delphi expert discussion:

A: I'm troubled by this; still religious education by and large does entail some moral commitment.... This of course gets us on to some very tricky territory because religions enshrine different conceptions of justice and fairness...

B: Going back to the non-statutory national framework, the description of Religious Education at Key Stage 3 was in another context a 'beliefs and issues' agenda...

C: You're talking about ideas, but I'm talking about people...

While the discussion here may be somewhat more sophisticated than in the case of pupils, similar conflicts of purpose emerge – the clash between those purposes concerned with ideas as locked into the performative categories of curricular and examination frameworks and those purposes concerned with nurturing certain perceived forms of human (personal) development and flourishing. It might be argued that similar conflicts of purpose can be found in other curriculum subjects, but that merely reinforces the more general educational challenge. More importantly, religious education is a different kind of social practice to, say, maths education. The two may share similarities to the extent that they are both concerned with disclosing features of the world to pupils. However, in the case of maths any ethical or indeed existential import is of a second-order kind – for example, having a sophisticated grasp of numbers might offer a resource for understanding better how national income might be effectively re-distributed to reduce certain social inequalities. In the case of religious education as a social practice, the ethical and existential are internal to the practice itself. Further, the purpose of maths is understanding; to understand the formal operations of trigonometry does not require that we freight the exercise of learning how to do trigonometry with an expectation that it will change us ethically.[4] Alternatively, the purpose of RE *is*, as the participants cited above have variously intimated, the creation of meaning; neither understanding nor evaluation will do.

So many 'meanings' – so little meaning

However, what do we intend to convey when we talk about meaning in such a context? It is clear from the model agreed syllabuses in England (SCAA 1994a, 1994b) (despite subsequent developments), from the work of a large number of scholars, from the teacher comments and practices – and indeed from the pupil reactions and conversations – that meaning in RE is dominated by recourse to the personal. Even where colleagues disagree about how to bring about the 'learning *from* religion', there seems little doubt that they wish to communicate that the meanings internal to religion should also, in various ways, be internal to the pupil. Of course, few teachers in our study regarded the cultivation of such internal meanings as entirely individualistic. Rather, teachers considered that they should be nurturing meaning in some of the following ways:

- personal
- inter-personal – inter subjective
- transpersonal–transcendent other: openness to the claims of transcendent religious experience and claim ('I' and 'Thou')
- institutional meanings: RE as an institutional social practice deemed to draw pupils together within a school community
- meanings within socio-religious communities (which differ from the educational institution's ascription of meaning)
- meaning as intention: 'this is what I mean by x'

Despite recourse to so many refractions of 'meaning', it appears that much religious education continues to fail to secure, for pupils (and for many teachers), either epistemic or ethical meaning. There is in fact no strong sense in our ethnographic records that RE offers: (1) an insight into the meaning theological claims have for their adherents; (2) a coherent ground upon which the individual creates his/her own meanings rooted in something more substantial than oddly conceived personal preferences; (3) a transcendent ground for ethical attachment and moral behaviour. If meaning is constitutive of RE properly conceived, as we suggested at the outset, it appears that the kinds of failures and confusions of meaning discussed above radically compromise religious education as an intentional social practice.

What might we possibly mean by the term 'failures of meaning'? To come to some understanding of what such a failure of meaning might denote we need to consider 'meaning' itself. This is no straightforward task since there is more than one answer to the question 'what does X mean?'. In delineating but some senses of meaning we see that it can refer to the import ascribed to particular linguistic utterances, as in 'what does Mary mean when she says she can't complete the task?', or to the ethico-religious import of particular actions, such as the meaning of *zakat* for an observant Muslim. It can indicate the significance that someone attaches to his/her life. Or, as in the case of one school in our study (a religiously denominated school), an icon attached to the wall (see Figure 1) might signify a Catholic school. Simultaneously, it may signify (to the believer) that the incarnation is God's redemptive act. Looked at another way, and juxtaposed as it was with a collection of examination-focused targets and descriptions, it may merely reinforce certain regulatory and examination norms. Or it might suggest an interesting causal connection between veneration of the nativity and examination success.

The point is that meaning is a notoriously and simultaneously allusive and elusive term and that it loses none of its characteristic slipperiness when used with respect to particular educational entailments. Hence, when we ask what education means, some will argue that the question is 'meaningless' (as some of our participants in the Delphi seminar indeed did), by which they point out that there is no singular account of education that will satisfy all those who wish to employ the term. For example, the liberal educational tradition, represented by Peters (1967) and his successors (e.g. White 2003), has considered the meaning of education to be located in the claim that it points to certain liberal intellectual values; for Maritain (1960), its meaning is in the preparation for the assumption of particular kinds of 'spiritual ' freedom; for Robert Owen, among many others, its meaning is secured in the twin aims of emancipation and material success aiming to meld the imperatives of character formation and securing the interests of capital 'around the

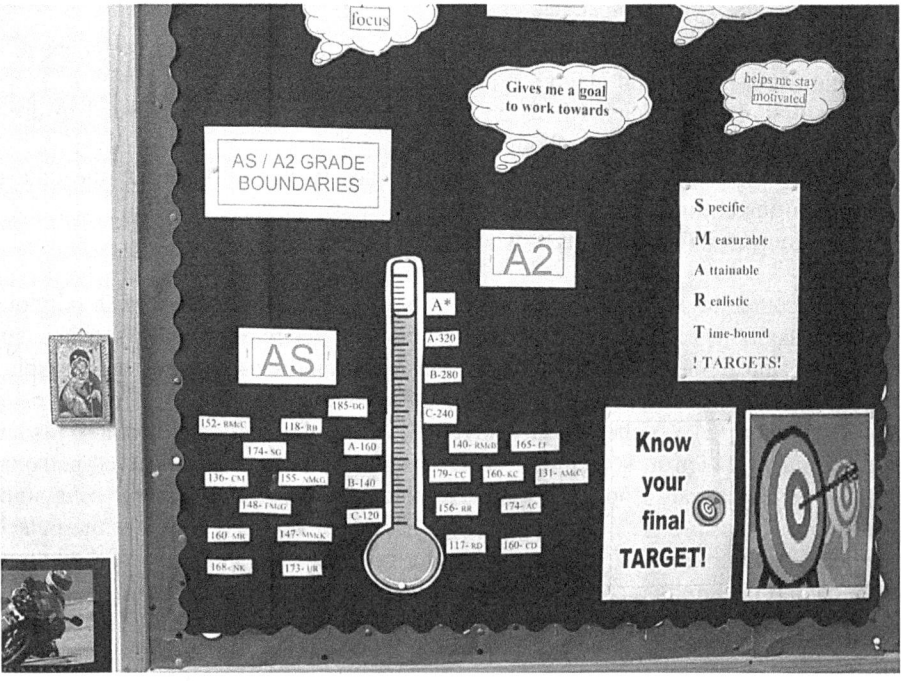

Figure 1. Examination encouragement.

collaborative pursuit of material prosperity' (Davis and O'Hagan 2010, 83). These meanings but scratch the surface.

As our ethnographic excursuses have demonstrated, modern education often conflates 'meaning' and 'purpose'. In some of the examples cited above, it can be a challenge to disaggregate the inscription of a meaning from the purposes of a particular activity. Hence meaning is intrinsic to the very activity of RE. In the case of religious studies (the study of religion), the purpose may be to enhance understanding of the phenomena. One is not required to have a meaningful encounter with the beliefs under scrutiny; in RE, one is so required (at least theoretically). Nowhere is this more evident than in the textbooks and syllabuses for public examinations, where any claim to meaning is displaced by the drive to fulfil one of the purposes we outlined above – passing an examination. Working at Key Stage 4, teachers often found themselves caught between the competing imperatives of education and examination. Their desire to help pupils understand the complex and subtle nature of religious systems, beliefs, and practices was often in conflict with their fear that a lack of success in securing high pass rates would undermine an already fragile professional identity. Hence meaning surrenders to purpose with amazing facility. Indeed, we argue, an important consequence of the rise of performativity has been the displacement of meaning by purpose, although – arguably – meaning itself, as suggested earlier, displaced 'truth'. The difficulty for RE lies precisely in this displacement. When it is encumbered by myriad entailments, in the belief that this will somehow make religious education stronger and therefore more resistant to the predations of performativity, there are two significant consequences. The first is that we turn RE into its own antithesis and the second is the dilution of the character of meaning. And, as shown above, the classroom becomes a site of non-meaning or at least of the elision of meaning. Thus RE finds itself caught between two silences where it can make no substantive claims in the face of a performative and sceptical culture on the one hand and the mythical silence of the incommunicable and irreducible self on the other.

The inability to speak meaningfully about religion in the classroom leads to the cultivation of language without exchange value, where words fail to signify anything that resonates in the life of the pupil, where confusions, contradictions, and conflations abound. Following Baudrillard, we recognize that it is precisely the illusion of neo-individualism (1994, 106) with its atomistic approach to meaning (where pupils suggest that RE is the site *par excellence* for rendering public their unanchored opinions) which flattens the power of language and meaning, rendering void the space wherein imaginary networks and self-representations may be exchanged for meaning. This flattening leads to expunging controversy by eliding what is disturbing and discordant (Conroy 2004, 180). But it is also 'entirely profane ... above all, sad, like everything that exhausts meaning. Lastly, it's utterly boring' (Baudrillard and Noailles 2007, 10). This exasperated sigh, evoking the 'boring', echoes in many pupil responses in our study.

Baudrillard's model of language, interpreted in the light of Conroy's (2009) work on liminality and 'enstrangement',[5] suggests the need for managed discomfort if religious education is to be emotionally transformative and to restore its primary role as a site for meaning making. Religious language must escape the mundane, that 'circuit of "liberated" words, gratuitously useable, circulating as exchange value' (Baudrillard 1993, 203), resisting simplifications or totally alienated significations.

The constraints of the examination context, coupled with an inattention to meaning are manifest in not only the spoken attitudes of teachers, but also the tasks and questions posed to pupils at this level and in the pupils' work. Two examples from different schools serve to illustrate this point. In the first (Figure 2), a set of GCSE examination questions, the theological meanings of forgiveness are displaced by its being aligned to the political considerations of war. Lest one be in any doubt as to the relative importance of forgiveness, the mark scheme gives the game away! How, we might ask, is a pupil to grasp the enormous theological complexity of a concept like forgiveness when: (a) all that is required is a simplistic definition; and (b) it is merely there to serve a subordinate function in the socio-moral discussion of war? The examinations process thus evacuates the endeavour of religious meaning. Further, the triumph of purpose over meaning is witnessed in the instruction that pupils should use the 'correct GCSE technique'. In the second example (Figure 3), the *reductio ad absurdum* is witnessed in the facile summation of a distinction between Catholicism and Anglicanism, although it is not clear whether such a distinction is theological, social or philosophical. And it will not do to dismiss this as just the work of a poor pupil, given that these serve only as examples of a much wider pattern of 'meaning void' questions and answers.

The questionnaire distributed to pupils in the schools, the structure of which emanated from emergent themes of the ethnography, offered further insights, especially into pupils' perceptions of how RE compared to other curriculum subjects. An emerging consensus suggests that RE was indeed different from 'normal classes'. In some respects, this difference can be construed as positive, in so far as pupils felt that RE lessons provided opportunities for greater engagement with social issues and they enjoyed a more open and approachable style of teaching. However, they also rated RE as less important than other subjects. The quantitative data position RE as a subject concerned with sharing opinions rather than reaching any significant conclusions, which coheres with findings from the case studies. That most pupils did not ascribe any utilitarian worth to RE is a double-edged sword, as they enjoyed not feeling any pressure, but did not see any need to 'press for meaning'. This also suggests that attempts to enhance the status of RE by making it an examination subject is, as seen in the case studies, unlikely to be successful.

TEST FOR YEAR 10 LONG COURSE RS GCSE

Answer using the correct GCSE technique for answering the different kinds of questions: a), b), c) and d). See coloured information sheet.

a). What is forgiveness? (2 marks)

b) Choose ONE religious person, community or organisation working for world peace. Outline its work. (6 marks)

c) Explain why nuclear weapons cause problems for religious believers (8 marks)

d). 'All religious people should support their country's armed forces.'

Do you agree? Give reasons for your opinion, showing you have considered another point of view. In your answer, you should refer to at least one religion. (4 marks)

Figure 2. GCSE Examination Questions.

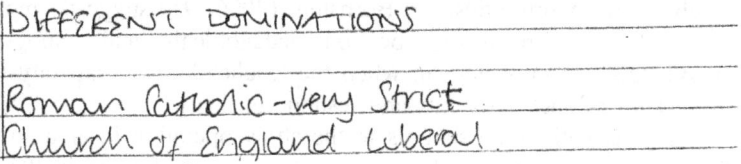

Figure 3. A student response.

In the cases cited in this essay we see the inattention to meaning and the service of purpose without meaning. If RE is to distinguish itself from other educational entailments, it does so surely on the grounds that it brings something different – religious experience – to bear in the educational space. Of course, religious experience makes steep demands; it invites the enquirer to enter a space which is the property of neither the atomised individual nor the community as a structurally closed static phenomenon, a space which belongs to the Ultimate. In this context, the individual – pupil and teacher – ought to be brought face to face with the incompleteness of their condition, their 'enstranged' self. In this way, religious language, to remain meaningful to its users, opens up the borderlands of individuals' imaginings and is 'neither restrictive nor penurious in this context: it is the fundamental rule of the symbolic' (Baudrillard 1993, 204).

When we asked the question 'Does religious education work?', we were immediately faced with a retreat from the complexity of meaning by recourse to Pinker's (2008, 374) 'plausible deniability'. During the Delphi seminar, several colleagues attempted to declare the question unanswerable, because – in sublime circularity – there were too many potential purposes and we would not know what 'working' meant in each case. Rather than succumb to plausible deniability, is it not better to turn our attention from all those purposes and ask, 'Does it work in cultivating and communicating meaning?' Repeatedly, questions of meaning were deferred and potentially interesting discussions were cut short so as to deliver on the purposes of RE – to get through the syllabus. Too often we observed that by succumbing to the demands of the examination, the clock was run down with fatuous exercises and the question of meaning could not rear its *unconsoling* head. Often this was the result of succumbing to the weight of the examination system.

Conclusion

In this essay we have illustrated the ways in which RE teachers in a variety of contexts have been unable to foreground meaning so that it might reflect its constitutive position within the subject. It is no part of our argument that attention to meaning invariably has to affirm the claims of religious communities. Nor do our findings suggest that there is some singular account of meaning to be valorised. Indeed, as Engelke and Tomlinson (2006, 2) argue, failures of meaning making allow for approaches to meaning as a contested and uncertain process, rather than an entity waiting to be uncovered. The contested conception of meaning allows for the consideration of cultural artifacts, images, and events that follow, not as the bars of a rigid cultural cage within which pupils and teachers are caught, but as the strands from which pupils and teachers weave a tapestry or tapestries of meaning. The hollowing out of religion and religious education in late industrial societies offers precisely such opportunities. As Bornstein (2006, 91) suggests, moments of meaninglessness for participants may be both pedagogically and ethnographically meaningful. But this can only happen when the teacher has the capacity to recognize the significance of such moments and respond to them.

On occasion – as with some schools in the study operating in areas of secularism, indifference, and hostility to religion – the tapestry can be almost blank, offering no points of reference from which to begin an exploration of the processes of meaning making within a given religious culture. In the end the enterprise of cultivating meaning is likely to fail as long as religious education, both theoretically and as a practice, continues to foreground purposes that perforce offer too many contradictions: e.g. between the intellectual and the affective, the public and the private, the metaphorical and the literal, self-determination and civic cohesion. The displacement of meaning by purpose leaves RE bereft of its single distinguishing feature: that meaning inheres in its very definition.

Central to the project design and our deliberations on the findings has been the interdisciplinary nature of the research team. In our reflections on the data and consequent analysis we had to face the possibility that our analysis might be considered no more than a lament for the loss of, or failure to realise, some putative golden age of RE. In our defence, two observations can be made. First, the move from aspiration to enactment is one of the key areas for analysis in the original project design and, secondly, the 'lament' – if it is indeed one – can be seen in the disappointment expressed by the pupils as much as in the researchers' interpretation.

Notes

1. We could have substituted many other examples for those highlighted here. The examples were chosen because they exemplified very particular kinds of failures of meaning.
2. The report *History for All* uses 'meaningful' twice, but – like the English report – this is in connection with making the activities meaningful for pupils as an educational exercise.
3. The following list derives from the findings of: (1) a two-day Delphi seminar for professionals from a range of interest groups in the field; (2) reports from teachers involved in the project; and (3) published policy and pedagogical materials. It is intended not to be exhaustive but to be representative.
4. Even in areas where evaluation appears intrinsic to the pedagogic intentions it is, with notable exceptions such as citizenship, which shares crucial features with religious education that make it vulnerable to similar challenges.
5. When commentators and scholars consider notions of alienation, they tend to draw on the concept of estrangement, rooted in the nineteenth century (largely Marxist and post-Marxist) idea that the material conditions of the world are the proximate cause of such alienation. Conroy however, restores and refurbishes the more ancient notion of 'enstrangement' to suggest that human beings are made strange from within rather than from without.

References

Baudrillard, J. 1993. *Symbolic exchange and death*. London: Sage.
Baudrillard, J. 1994. *The illusion of the end*. Cambridge: Polity Press.
Baudrillard, J., and E.V. Noailles. 2007. *Exiles from dialogue* (Trans. C. Turner). Cambridge: Polity Press.
Baumfield, V., J. Conroy, R. Davis, and D. Lundie. 2011. The Delphi method: Gathering expert perspectives in religious education. *British Journal of Religious Education* 34, no. 1: 5–19.

Bornstein, E. 2006. Rituals without final acts: Prayer and success in World Vision Zimbabwe's humanitarian work. In *The limits of meaning: Case studies in the anthropology of Christianity*, ed. M. Engelke and M. Tomlinson, 85–104. New York: Berghahn.
Conroy, J. 2004. *Betwixt and between: The liminal imagination, education and democracy.* New York: Peter Lang.
Conroy, J. 2009. The enstranged self: Recovering some grounds for pluralism in education. *Journal of Moral Education* 38, no. 2: 145–64.
Conroy, J. et al. 2011. *Does religious education work? A three-year investigation into the practices and outcomes of religious education: A briefing paper.* Glasgow: University of Glasgow. http://www.gla.ac.uk/schools/education/research/currentresearchprojects/doesreligiouseducationwork/#d.en.153511.
Davis, R., and F. O'Hagan. 2010. *Robert Owen.* London: Continuum.
Engelke, M., and M. Tomlinson, eds. 2006. *The Limits of meaning: Case studies in the anthropology of Christianity.* New York: Berghahn.
Grimmitt, M. 1987. *Religious education and human development: The relationship between studying religions and personal, social and moral education.* Great Wakering: McCrimmons.
Jackson, R., J. Ipgrave, M. Hayward, P. Hopkins, N. Fancourt, M. Robbins, L. Francis, and U. McKenna. 2010. *Materials used to teach about world religions in schools in England.* Warwick, RI: Department of Children, Schools and Families.
Maritain, J. 1960. *Education at the crossroads.* New Haven: Yale University Press.
Ofsted (Office for Standards in Education). 2010. *Transforming religious education: Religious education in schools 2006–09.* Manchester: Ofsted.
Ofsted (Office for Standards in Education). 2011. *History for all: History in English schools 2007–10.* London: Ofsted. http://www.ofsted.gov.uk/resources/history-for-all (accessed April 4, 2012).
Ofsted (Office for Standards in Education). 2012. *Moving English Forward: Action to raise standards in English.* London: Ofsted.
Peters, R. 1967. *Ethics and education.* London: Allen and Unwin.
Pinker, S. 2008. *The stuff of thought.* Harmondsworth: Allen Lane.
Ricoeur, P. 1976. *Interpretation theory: Discourse and the surplus of meaning Fort Worth.* Texas: Christian University Press.
SCAA (Schools Curriculum and Assessment Authority). 1994a. *National Model Syllabus I.* London: SCAA.
SCAA (Schools Curriculum and Assessment Authority). 1994b. *National Model Syllabus II.* London: SCAA.
Walford, G. 2008. The nature of educational ethnography. In *How to do educational ethnography*, ed. G. Walford, 1–15. London: Tufnell Press.
White, J. 2003. Five critical stances towards liberal philosophy of education in Britain. *Journal of Philosophy of Education* 37, no. 1: 147–84.

More purpose than meaning in RE: a response to James Conroy, David Lundie, and Vivienne Baumfield

Christina Osbeck

Center for Didactic Research in the Social Sciences, Karlstad University, Karlstad, Sweden

> In their essay 'Failures of meaning in religious education', James Conroy, David Lundie, and Vivienne Baumfield report findings from their recent project 'Does Religious Education Work?', during which ethnographic studies in 24 British schools were conducted. In this response I first highlight the importance of the character of RE for considering what 'works' and describe the kind of RE that the authors discuss. Secondly, I point to findings and conceptualisations which I consider important. Thirdly, I comment on factors which, the authors maintain, are important regarding failures of meaning in RE. I conclude with my interest in further empirical findings resulting from the rich material of this project.

What kind of religious education?

The authors mention how colleagues criticised the original main question – does Religious Education (RE) work? – as being impossible to answer. The answer depends on how 'work' is defined. Nevertheless, the researchers seem to have left the question of defining 'work' aside, as they started to look for themes emerging from the empirical material, i.e. elements in RE that seem not to work that well. One of these themes was the failure of meaning in RE.

The authors do not mention whether any of their colleagues commented on how unclear the notion of religious education is. However, reading Conroy, Lundie, and Baumfield's (2012 in this collection) essay from a Swedish perspective, this lack of clarity strikes me as being important here. As Schweitzer (2004) has pointed out, it is hard to compare different forms of RE. Even when there is a general or national curriculum, which – I understand – is not the case in the UK, a subject is both a product and a process, changing over time (Ongstad 2004). In Sweden, for example, RE in the 2011 curriculum moved towards a subject which is more clearly dominated by learning-about-aspects in relation to learning-from-aspects (Grimmitt 1987). The Swedish RE curriculum expert Sven-Åke Selander (2011) has described this change as a move from ultimate questions, ethics, and reflection towards society, knowledge, and analysis. This coincides with the implementation of a more differentiated grade system, greater stress on specific learning outcomes, and the launch of more national tests, including tests in RE. Therefore, it is important to be clear about what RE in a certain context is or, looked at from a normative perspective, what it should be. The essay by Conroy, Lundie, and Baumfield describes, in relation to the Ofsted subject report *Transforming RE*, '"meaning" as a central, perhaps the central, feature of religious education'. A distinction is made between RE and RS (Religious Studies), where 'the purpose may be one of enhancing understanding of the phenomena. One is not required to have a meaningful encounter with the beliefs under scrutiny; in religious education, one is (at least theoretically)'. 'Meaning' and 'meaningful' are, however, not defined. On the contrary, meaning is said to have a 'characteristic slipperiness' and therefore cannot be grasped. At the same time, meaning in RE is related to religious experience:

> If RE is to distinguish itself from other educational entailments, it does so surely on the grounds that it brings something different – religious experience – to bear in the educational space. Of course, religious experience makes steep demands; it invites the enquirer to enter a space which is the property of neither the atomised individual nor the community as a structurally closed static phenomenon, a space which belongs to the Ultimate. In this context, the individual – pupil and teacher – ought to be brought face to face with the incompleteness of their condition, their 'enstranged' self.

This quotation gives us an idea of what kind of RE the authors have in mind. Whether this kind of RE 'works' is, of course, a different question from the question whether another kind of RE works. The kind of RE which is discernible in the above quote would be impossible in Sweden, due to the requirement that RE be neutral. While the main thesis of the essay – that there is a lack of and a need for meaning in many RE classrooms today – is correct and important to state, I would have found it easier to agree with the authors' message if the RE they have in mind did not include the dimension of religious experience.

Illustrative examples and fruitful conceptualisations

The authors present empirical material as 'particular instances' with no other claim than 'that they highlight important tropes in the experiences and practices of the subject in secondary schools'. They suggest that their validity could be tested by further studies which replicate theirs. Another way of discussing validity in qualitative studies is 'generalisation through recognition of patterns' where the reader discovers something that s/he has not seen that clearly before and the pattern is also recognized in other cases (Larsson 2009). This means that, despite the fact that it is unclear how the examples in Conroy, Lundie, and Baumfield's essay are related to the material as an entity, validity is shaped in my reading of their text. I recognize similar patterns in previous studies and also in some of my own observations which are yet unpublished. The authors describe, mainly in reference to interviews with students about the way they experience RE, how meaning is lost when the experience of religion at home and the descriptions of religion in school become two different things – an issue which is especially frustrating for religious young people (see e.g. Moulin 2011). Generally, in these situations, it is the school perspectives that count (see e.g. Arweck and Nesbitt 2011; Buchardt 2007). In the end, the school decides what will come up in exams and what will pass as good answers. In the examples given by Conroy, Lundie, and Baumfield, school perspectives are characterised as rather descriptive and superficial. In a practice where standard formulations are supposed to be expressed, there is little space for dialogue and collectively negotiated meanings. How common this is, we do not know, however (see e.g. Fancourt 2007).

The examples given in the essay also show how the subject can be understood as mainly being about expressing one's personal feelings and private opinions. These kinds of activities tend to make communication artificial. Opinions are expressed but perhaps not seriously discussed with an expectation of negotiations of meaning. When conversations become artificial, a mocking atmosphere which risks affecting both subject and religion as a phenomenon (see e.g. Osbeck and Lied 2012) may arise. Swedish students, too, have described artificial conversations as the greatest threat in school (Risenfors 2011, 112).

In order to conceptualise these two kinds of problems – standardising performatives and declarations of private opinions, both of them artificial communications – 'silence' seems very fruitful. There is silence, despite some noise, when people do not reach each other. In this way RE risks being caught between these two kinds of silence: the performative silence and 'the mythical silence of the incommunicable and irreducible self'.

Factors which contribute to failures of meaning in RE

Conroy, Lundie, and Baumfield's essay points to factors that may help explain the possible lack of meaning in RE. The authors describe in an interesting way how purpose and meaning can be mixed up with each other. Purpose sometimes seems to be a substitute for meaning. Perhaps in order to provide the subject with a clear purpose, the subject has been given more, but also more disparate, tasks. Further, the emphasis on examinations can be understood as a way of making the purpose clearer, since exams highlight what can be considered to be important facts. But this does not necessarily mean that more meaningful education will take place. The authors actually imply that it might be the other way around. It seems to me that this is a really important conclusion for Swedish schools and for RE as a subject of today. Not even if the national test results rise in the future will we know that pupils are involved to a larger extent in existential discussions which mean something to them and allow them develop as human beings.

Another reason for the lack of meaning in RE may be, according to Conroy, Lundie, and Baumfield, the subject's two competing impulses: the epistemological and the ethical impulse, which are often called 'learning about' and 'learning from' religion(s). However, this point is not that straightforward, because I do not believe that the two impulses are competing with one another. In fact, I regard them as interdependent in RE. It is hard to value or relate anything to one's own life, if one does not have anything substantial to use as one's point of departure. I also think that it would be almost reductionist – considering the object of study, namely religion – not to move beyond information to existential reflection. Consequently, I do not understand how these perspectives can be in competition with one another and I do not see how meaning – the central feature of RE, according to the authors – can be developed without a combination of learning-about and learning-from perspectives.

In summary, both the essay and the project which the authors report are very interesting and important. I look forward to reading more about this project when perhaps more of its rich empirical material is presented. This essay has shown how RE can fail in its task to establish meaningful existential discussions and to interpret and negotiate meaning collectively. As some of the empirical examples indicate, further analysis will allow other important themes besides failures of meaning to emerge from the material.

References

Arweck, E., and E. Nesbitt. 2011. Religious education in the experience of young people from mixed-faith families. *British Journal of Religious Education* 33, no. 1: 31–45.

Buchardt, M. 2007. Teachers—and knowledge and identity technologies around 'religion': Discursive and other social practices in the religious education classroom. *Researching RE teachers: RE teachers as researchers*, ed. C. Bakker and H.-G. Heimbrock, 17–36. Münster: Waxmann.

Conroy, J.C., D. Lundie, and V. Baumfield. 2012. Failures of meaning in religious education. *Journal of Beliefs and Values* 33, no. 3: 309–23.

Fancourt, N. 2007. The 'dialogical' teacher: Should teachers express their commitments in the classroom? In *Researching RE teachers: RE teachers as researchers*, ed. C. Bakker and H.-G. Heimbrock, 53–67. Münster: Waxmann.

Grimmitt, M. 1987. *Religious education and human development*. Great Wakering: McCrimmons.

Larsson, S. 2009. A pluralist view of generalization in qualitative research. *International Journal of Research & Method in Education* 32, no. 1: 25–38.

Moulin, D. 2011. Giving voice to 'the silent minority': The experience of religious students in secondary school religious education lessons. *British Journal of Religious Education* 33, no. 3: 313–26.

Ongstad, S. 2004. Fagdidaktikk som forskningsfelt [Subject education as research field]. *Kunnskapstatus for forskningsprogrammet KUPP: Kunskapsutvikling i profesjonsutdanning og profesjonsutövning* [Knowledge level in the research project KUPP: Development of knowledge in education of professions and practice of professions], ed. Norges forskningsrad, 30–53. Oslo: Norges forskningsrad.

Osbeck, C., and S. Lied. 2012. Hegemonic speech genres of classrooms and their importance for RE learning. *British Journal of Religious Education* 34, no. 2: 155–68.

Risenfors, S. 2011. *Gymnasieungdomars livstolkande* [Life interpretations of young people in upper secondary school] Göteborg: Göteborgs universitet.

Schweitzer, F. 2004. Comparative research in religious education: International – interdenominational – interreligious. In *Towards a European perspective on religious education*, ed. I.R. Larsson and C. Gustavsson, 191–200. Skellefteå: Artos & Norma.

Selander, S.-Å. 2011. Från livsfrågor, etik och reflektion till samhälle, kunskap och analys [From ultimate questions, ethics and reflection to society, knowledge, and analysis]. *Religion och livsfrågor* 2: 18–21.

Seeing and seeing through: forum theatre approaches to ethnographic evidence

David Lundie[a] and James C. Conroy[b]

[a]Faculty of Education, Liverpool Hope University, Liverpool, UK; [b]School of Education, University of Glasgow, Glasgow, UK

> Ethnographic findings from a large qualitative research project on Religious Education in UK secondary schools uncovered contested meanings for the subject as a social practice. In order to bring to the fore some of the ways these contested meanings manifest themselves as confusions in the classroom, a performance ethnography was conducted, making use of Augusto Boal's forum theatre approach. This involved distilling ethnographic evidence into dramatic vignettes, performing these in front of an audience of pupils, and asking the pupils for feedback on the experience. The feedback enabled the research team to triangulate their findings, by inverting the ethnographers' gaze, allowing pupils to co-construct the meanings which the ethnographers had elicited from the data. The method is discussed in detail, as are the ways in which resource and examination pressures in the Religious Education classroom can obscure opportunities for authentic exploration of religious meanings in pupils' lives and the contribution of the forum theatre and pupils' reflections on how to remedy these distortions.

Introduction

As discussed in Conroy, Lundie, and Baumfield (2012, in this collection), the ethnographic findings of our study revealed multifarious failures of meaning in a broad array of classroom contexts. To understand these processes, we must consider how 'meaning' is created, constructed, and conveyed. This is no straightforward task, since there is more than one answer to the question 'what does X mean?'. In an attempt to distil the complex findings emerging from classroom ethnographies in 24 sites of enquiry, conducted in the course of the project 'Does Religious Education Work?' the research team opted for a reflective forum theatre approach.[1] This involved a team of students specialising in drama at the University of Glasgow choreographing a series of vignettes in collaboration with the ethnographers, which drew on sample dialogues of the ethnographic observations. The vignettes were designed to provoke debate about meanings and intentions in religious education (RE). They were performed in front of an audience of educational professionals and 16- to 18-year-old pupils from local schools at the launch of the project's findings conference, held at the University of Glasgow on 1 March 2011, with iterative feedback on recognition of key themes from the audience.

In posing the question 'what does education mean?', we may refer to not only the intentions, but also the processes and the resulting outcomes or entailments. The differing claims about the particular meanings of education emanate from its status as a flaccid designator – a place-holder for a plurality of accounts which are situated in particular cultural, intellectual, political, and material contexts. As Heubner states:

> The educator participates in the paradoxical nature of language. He wishes to talk about language, but must use language for his talk. He infers that meanings exist, but has only language, or other symbol systems as a vehicle for his inference. (1968, 8)

If education presents a conundrum as to language and meaning, the realm of the religious and spiritual, in particular where it intersects with public life and public policy, is still more deeply contested. For Berger (1970), the spiritual is about the exploration of metaphysical questions about life and existence; in some approaches to spirituality in the curriculum, the spiritual need not engage with metaphysics but includes 'anything which might be regarded as a source of inspiration' (Mott-Thompson 1996, 77); in some traditional Christian understandings, spirituality is first and foremost a 'preparation for death' (Liguori 2009). The religious domain is itself a highly contested field, with no single enumeration of measures adequately defining its boundaries. Most religious and spiritual traditions, however, attempt to convey meanings: on the personal level, about the moral meaning of life itself and life in the world; on the interpersonal level, with regard to communities of faith and the general inter subjective experience of living in the community; and on the transpersonal level, which is related to mystical experience, wonder, and the experience of transcendence (Lealman 1996, 13). Such meanings are further communicated within the context of socio-religious communities which differ in aim and practice from the ascriptions of meaning given by the polity and its educational institutions.

The nested nature of religious education as a social practice (Conroy and Lundie forthcoming) and its complexity are clearly shown in recent European studies which have refocused attention on the treatment of the religious dimensions of public education. A recent collection (Ziebertz and Riegel 2009) illuminates the complex and controversial political picture of religious education in twenty-first century Europe. The liminal identity of RE in UK schools involves a negotiation of meaning between the norms and processes of the educational enterprise as pursued in the early twenty-first century and the norms observed within communities of religious practice; for this reason, the recognition of the reporting of religious belief and practice by religious communities themselves is of vital importance to the effective communication of meaning (Jackson 2004), but despite the appreciation of this dual complexity, it is unsurprising that such recognition is often lacking in the actual materials which are in regular use (Jackson et al. 2010). Faced with a bewildering plurality of contested definitions, the temptation to elide all controversy in order to create a consensus of definition can at times lead to evacuations of meaning. Pedagogically, this is often manifested by an obsession with content knowledge, the enumeration of details of religious practices or terminology, without exploration of their significance in the life of the believer – a pedagogy which may be described as professionally embarrassed:

The characteristic principle of the embarrassed is a particular kind of tolerance, a tolerance that is tolerant of all 'nice' things, that treats all world religions, for example, as being about the golden rule (do unto others…), and there are no real differences except for the names of the buildings and the dates of the holidays. The politics of embarrassment pushes all questions of truth into the personal and private worlds of individuals, leaving public spaces free of truth but implacably tolerant. (Stern 2007, 24)

Methodology

The data which inform this essay are drawn from 240 days of ethnography carried out by five researchers in schools across Scotland, England, and Northern Ireland. Employing a linguistic framework which takes account of the complexities of language in intersubjective contexts, the tracing of meanings from intention to practice and the personal, social, and spiritual entailments in the pupils' experience requires a trans-contextual analysis, including an appreciation of the 'absent presence' (Lefstein and Snell 2009, 22) of language and practices outside the classroom – those contextual factors which influence the role and culture of curriculum, teacher, and pupil over a course of time, beyond the observed and reported encounter. While it is true of all educational ethnography that it is limited by the classroom experience, this is particularly significant in the case of religious education because of the diversity of experiences which forms pupils' frames of reference for the meaning making in the personal, interpersonal, and transpersonal spheres. To that end, the complexity of contexts and sources cannot be overestimated and the reader must beware of extrapolating from these generic vignettes an accurate picture of the totality of RE.

Far from intending to lampoon a systemically dysfunctional curriculum area, we sought to distil consensus about the need for effective practice by juxtaposing effective practice with typical examples of its opposite. Pollock (2006) draws attention to the potential of performance ethnography to manifest and subvert the power relations of ethnographic data-gathering. In the case of our study, by inviting pupils in our audience to comment on the authenticity of our representations, the ethnographers' critical gaze was inverted, turning the subjects of our research into co-creators, into both constructors and conveyors of meaning. In so doing, we did not intend to parody or elide the sincere efforts of teachers or to present an 'aesthetic of objectivity', as Snyder-Young (2010) criticises, but to recognize that our constructions of others' constructions of reality (Geertz 1993) would be further developed by the reflexive constructions of our research subjects.

The possibility that anything within a given context has meaning for its inhabitants beyond the merely descriptive or mechanistic implies the possibility of failures of meaning. Following Tomlinson and Engelke (2006, 2) and Conroy et al. (2012, in this collection), we suggest that failures of meaning in a given social practice offer novel opportunities for re-imagining that social practice and the features of social and cultural life that inhere therein. Such recognition avoids any essentialising tendency within education and acknowledges that pupils and teachers need not be caught in a rigid system that constrains them, but that can enable them to weave their own tapestry or tapestries. The tapestry is never blank at the outset, being formed by the cultural domain which pupils inhabit prior to their engagement with RE. An aspect of the meaningfulness of such a tapestry is that it can have holes, areas where the negotiation of meaning falls flat; the tapestry can unravel when core values and beliefs fail to withstand the testing of life in the world; the possibility of the failure to make meaning renders meaning possible on a normative level, beyond the purely descriptive. Meaning allows for the imagined and the normative to have a place within culture, for the intersubjective paradigm to retain its ethnographic closeness to the language and identity of the subjects. As Bornstein (2006, 91) illustrates, moments of meaninglessness which participants experience may be both pedagogically and ethnographically meaningful. Such moments open the possibility of seeing things afresh. The analytic and pedagogic possibilities of these gaps can emerge from the displacement of the 'normal' institutional frames of reference.

In displacing frames of reference from their specific contexts and institutional cultures, we decided to employ Augusto Boal's *forum theatre* approach to the presentation of our findings. More than a medium for presentation, the forum theatre – and the audience which responded to it – offered an additional lens for the analysis and triangulation of key findings, a tapestry of the researchers' creation. In such a deliberate displacement, which involves displacing or eliding aspects of the cultural domain, material is disjointed from the realm of its ordinary meaning making, 'something is *made* invisible' (Battaglia 1997, 233). However, the use of such sources without a clear understanding of the domain and representational conventions which operate within the ethnographic site may obfuscate as much as elucidate the meaning of the data. In presenting visual data in photographic format, a displacement occurs which transforms the context by 'freezing an image for contemplation', separating an object from the experiential conditions in which meaning is intersubjectively constructed (Morphy and Banks 1997, 16). The photograph of a classroom display in a scholarly paper is not the same as the display in the classroom, as the latter is turned from an aspect of the learning environment to an artifact for analysis. In the case of the RE classroom, a double displacement may occur, in which an artifact is first displaced from its sacred use within the cultural domain of religious worship and transformed into an ambient or pedagogical use in the classroom, then further displaced from the classroom environment to serve as an illustration of the attitude to religious practices in a particular school for the purposes of ethnographic analysis.

In order to address the threat to validity by displacing visual and multi-modal findings from the cultural domain, we can consider several correctives. Triangulation of visual data with linguistic and other ethnographic data is essential to demonstrate the validity of assertions made with reference to the meaning of visual sources, situating these within the broader context. Boal (2006, 35) identifies three levels of perception which are at work in the course of aesthetic judgments:

Information – the receptive level … information … inter-relates…with the other senses…

Knowledge and Tactical Decision Making – the more active level … [in which] the individual relates the new information to similar or complementary information…

Ethical Consciousness – the human level … [which] consists of giving meaning and value to the decisions we take. I interrogate myself. This is the level of doubt and of ethically justified choice. (emphasis in original)

In the course of our work, we were concerned with the production, re-production, and interrogation of meaning and value through the evaluation of the de-contextualised performance. Pupils themselves were to triangulate our performative findings, bringing to bear their own ethical consciousness as experienced *connoisseurs* of schooling, offering insightful comments on whether our findings cohered with their lived insider perspectives of the cultural domain of RE. Names, in Boal's understanding, 'are polysemic signifiers that, when perceived by their receiver, lose a large part of the meanings which motivated their sender and acquire new meanings according to each receiver' (2006, 14) – in displacing the performances (examined below) from their contexts, the acquisition of a new intersubjective context permitted the central themes of the data to be evaluated in a perspective consciously shorn of many of its contextually specific meanings.

It is necessary to consider the ethics of our methods of presentation. In consenting to participate in the project, schools and teachers remained in control of the aspects of school life which they opened to us. Schools sometimes chose to keep aspects of their work away from the ethnographers' gaze, by managing the process of data collection, and teachers often asked the ethnographer to focus on a particular element, such as classroom management or pupil engagement, and give feedback to help improve the curriculum. This process enabled schools to interpose their own values on the way they conveyed their corporate aspects in our data. Regarding findings, schools were offered the opportunity to review and comment on the ethnographers' field notes, which allowed us to receive further feedback on our constructions, in line with the linguistic model the team had adopted. Regarding the material presented in the vignettes, many teachers were present at the conference and thus able to provide feedback on our representations.

Recognizing the liminal role which RE plays in schools, in rhetoric as well as practice, often challenging the accepted performative directions of the curriculum, we considered that Boal's forum theatre – which acknowledges that the conventions of the theatre as social practice are created habits (Boal 1979, 167) in need of 'joker' characters or tricksters to subvert them – provided a companion methodology for the representation of our findings. The trickster affords clear sight of the rules of a given site of culture by breaking them, by momentarily exposing everything the rules exclude and conceal (Hyde 1998, 295). Tricksters appear as characters in theatre and mythology, not with unmediated access to a metaphysical realm, but involved in processes of meaning making which include access to culturally excised or concealed realms and involved in re-making meaning with the awareness of imperatives beyond those of the accepted social practice. By inviting pupils to re-make the world of our representations, this ludic and liminal method revealed significant insights into the coherence of pedagogical approaches to meaning in religion with meanings in the pupils' lived cultural domain. In her play *The Seer* (2006), the Scottish playwright Ali Smith uses the device of her antagonist's awareness of stage and audience to destabilise an otherwise closed culture – the encroachment of the audience on the scene establishes the seer, despite this distinctiveness, as part of the insider group, a fellow character, but also a door-keeper. Smith draws on the tradition of the Scottish seers who claimed access not to prediction or prophecy, but to 'sight' or 'truth' in the raw (Sutherland 1974, 157). However, the teacher as trickster, a pedagogical model (Conroy 2004; Conroy and Leitch 2010) frequently observed in the course of our empirical work (Lundie 2011), is not the subject of our deliberations here; instead, the researcher/playwright as trickster comes to the fore, subverting cultural commonplaces in order to return to fundamental questions of meaning and value.

In the creation of their vignettes, the drama students focused on a range of practices and conversations which, they considered, made manifest themes that resonated with their own experiences. They foregrounded and accentuated practices that, in their ludic representation, raised questions of meaning as well as questions about how advisable it is to harness the impulses of popular culture for the pedagogical imperatives of communicating meaning and understanding.

The drama students met with the ethnographers over a period of four months to identify key themes for the vignettes. The ethnographers began with nine themes which had emerged from the first phase of the ethnographic work in 2009 and which formed the basis for coding over a million words of field notes. As the students identified themes which they were interested in investigating, the ethnographers further interrogated the data, providing the students with numerous sources which related to the themes, including classroom observation notes, recordings and transcripts of pupil and teacher focus groups, photographs, schemes of work, and teaching materials. These were initially presented to the drama students in their raw state. In the first case noted below, the students worked on a pedagogical appropriation of the TV game-show 'Who wants to be a Millionaire?'.

Key themes

'Millionaire': normative and descriptive meanings

In the opening of the vignette 'Millionaire', the purpose – examination success – is foregrounded to signify a number of engagements observed in the research. Figure 1 illustrates the centrality of examination success in marketing RE, which subsumes a range of other moral, spiritual, and philosophical aims under the external performative agenda. While students recognized common aspects of the teachers' practice across the curriculum, it was in the performance of the vignette, as questions of

Figure 1. Corridor war display in one school encouraging students to take full-GCSE Religious Studies.

meaning and value were displaced within the purpose of examination success, that the power of forum theatre to elicit reactions from pupils and teaching staff attained its significance.

The dichotomy between methodology and value, as performed in the vignette, had parallels in the pedagogical practices in several schools. The codes and repertoires represented by the TV game-show 'Who Wants to be a Millionaire?' – with its emphasis on individual performance, high stakes on financial rewards, and use of pressure and stress to heighten audience interest – formed a stark contrast to the Gospel narrative presented in the questions. Moreover, the performance of 'Millionaire' drew attention to significant patterns of confusion and conflation between various levels of meaning. On the level of normative and descriptive meanings, the imperatives of examination success often elide the normative, reducing questions of meaning making to mere definitions. At times pupils fail to grasp a coherent account of the frame of reference to which religious education alludes or to see through facile constructions with only purposive or eccentrically constructed frames of reference.

Furnishing RE with a frame of reference which delineates the religious on its own terms is a complex task, given the ambiguities of the religious domain discussed above. A difficulty may be observed in mistaking the unconscious fears which accompany the development of childhood spirituality (Lealman 1996) with an authentic and mature openness to transcendence, making it far easier to construct a lazy, psychological, and spiritually disengaged pedagogy than to encourage genuine engagement with mystery and transcendence. Such confusions are constitutive of many instances of failures to explicate a sense of progress in RE (Ofsted 2010). For a similar reason, Copley (2005) expressed some wariness of the concept of spirituality in RE, seeing it as an agenda to separate religious practice from religious belief, a dismemberment of subjective worlds of faith as social practice from serious consideration of the possibility of metaphysical realities. Nonetheless, the articulation of the distinction between personal, supra-personal, and transpersonal allows for identifying many of the causes of confusion in RE and proposing solutions. Regarding the personal and transpersonal, particular questions can be raised about the role of religious education in teaching about sex and relationships, a core aspect of several examination syllabuses.[2] While one school, with an explicitly Christian character, sought to locate teaching about sex and relationships within a transpersonal framework, noting key Bible texts in a set of introductory worksheets before expounding their application in different church communities, another school, also based on a Christian foundation, presented religious worldviews with reference to the personal as the dominant narrative; pupils were asked to rank (from 1 – I agree strongly to 5 – I do not agree at all) the following statements which had no explicit reference to religious arguments:

(1) People should live together before they get married.
(2) People should have sex together before they get married.
(3) Marriage is a waste of time.
(4) The minimum marriage age should be raised to 21.

Between the transpersonal, which is concerned with religious experience, and the interpersonal, similar confusions can be noted in the curriculum, with concepts drawn from religion which function as ciphers for broader moral and social entailments or with broader social entailments which frame religious discourses; however, the relationship between the two, whether analogical, contextual, allusive or doctrinal, is not clarified in either the teachers' or the pupils' understanding. An example is a scheme of work on Moses and the slavery of the Hebrews, which begins with a UNICEF report on child slavery today and then 'discusses' questions such as:

(1) Why is slavery bad?
(2) How do the stories make you feel?
(3) Is there anything we can do about slavery?

By making an important context an emotional issue, such approaches fundamentally misrepresent the transpersonal, specifically religious, significance of the Exodus narrative which conveys meaning in the Jewish tradition. Conversely, in a Muslim majority school, a scheme of work on *zakah* or *zakat* (Islamic practice of donating 2.5% of one's income) is introduced with the implicit aim to discuss broader social obligations to charity; while this scheme of work contains significant levels of descriptive meaning (who pays *zakat*, who it is paid to, how much is paid), little attention is paid to normative meaning. In one teacher's introduction, the significance of *zakat* is presumed on the basis of the authority of the following narrative:

> the Prophet left ... was forced out of Mecca to live in Medina, and whilst he was there, he began creating the perfect ideal society, and one of the things that he did whilst living in that community was introduce the idea of Zakah to help the community, so that's what we're looking at today.

Between supra-personal meanings – concerned with creativity and the making of personal meaning – and transpersonal meanings, further confusions may be observed. The invitation to journey and the intended destination are presented as self-evident by recourse to the Prophet's authority (Carless and Douglas 2010) and at the same time pre-judging the destination. A scheme of work at S2 level (Year 9) aimed to help pupils understand the symbolic dimensions of religious language; the pupils at one school studied, among other myths and parables, the Vikings' belief in Valhalla. Instead of interrogating the question symbolically, by asking 'what does it tell us about these people that they believed this?', the pupils immediately found problems with the story, which suggested a failure to communicate an appropriate framework for meaning making. Here is an extract from field notes, describing the situation:

> The teacher becomes impatient with a lot of trivial questions ... how do warriors get severed limbs back, etc. One pupil asks the teacher, 'Do you believe it?'. The teacher replies with barely disguised sarcasm, 'Do I believe in Valhalla? – No.'

The difficulty pupils encounter in understanding the purposes of RE are illustrated by such examples – sometimes the subject introduces concepts which are proposed for belief, sometimes it presents concepts for moral evaluation, sometimes it uses symbolic language which is to be interrogated. All these are valid domains for study within RE, but they need to be understood within a normative evaluative framework which is clearly communicated and shared.

At times, teachers made great efforts to explore the normative dimensions of religious experience, reflexively commenting upon the uses to which religion is put in school and wider society. In one school in Northern Ireland, which emphasised bridging the sectarian divide between Protestant and Catholic communities, which had increased during the years of the 'Troubles' in the period of the 1970s to the 1990s, in its social and religious curriculum, a teacher exemplified such a normatively reflexive pedagogy with his AS level (age 16–17) class, as the following extract from field notes shows:[3]

> Mr Clive reflects on the shallow use of the parable of the Good Samaritan in the lower school; he says the parable 'is the RE teacher's dream … you do this in junior school and you get Celtic and Rangers … but I kind of think they miss the point of the story … "and who is my neighbour?" … the guy who asked the question is a teacher of the law, almost certainly he's a priest [or] a Levite… Jesus is having a dig at the man that asked him the question' – he goes on to point out that the story is told to a crowd, not on a page, says it is over-used by politicians, most notably by Margaret Thatcher.
>
> To this, Shane responds, 'I hate Margaret Thatcher', and there follows a brief discussion on Thatcher's legacy in Northern Ireland, interrupted by the end-of-period bell.

The ways in which Mr Clive's discourse draws attention to the subversive dimension of Jesus' message in its original context adds a further layer of liminality, removing the parable from the ownership of now settled patterns of ritual performance within the context of the school, the now familiar discourse of 'The Good Rangers Supporter' [sic].[4] In taking the story out of the hands of the 'teacher of the law', Mr Clive executes precisely the kind of subversive levelling with regard to his status as teacher which is characteristic of the trickster pedagogy alluded to above. Mr Clive's reference to Margaret Thatcher's infamous and idiosyncratic interpretation of the parable before the Church of Scotland's General Assembly (e.g. Gilchrist 2009) opens the discussion to normative claims regarding the use of religious language; in turn Mr Clive is willing to permit Shane to present a community's perspective on this. In the liminal encounter, the familiar is presented in unfamiliar context (Turner 1967), a familiar discourse, a linchpin of anti-sectarian religious education is de-centred and presented for criticism in a forum within which pupils' own normative values are respected.

'Avoiding difficult questions': representation without explanation

As well as failing to see the framework for RE, another common difficulty was pupils 'seeing through' superficial or purposive models of religious education. In these examples, pupils were fully aware of the aims their teachers pursued, but these failed to cohere with the pupils' own deeply held worldviews.

In the vignette 'Avoiding difficult questions' the teacher acts as the representative of an official discourse, which is drawn from the textbook, seeking to impart knowledge from a position of presumed ignorance. Perpendicular to the official discourse runs a heated discussion among pupils, through which they seek to make sense of known religious concepts and misconceptions in their cultural domain. Islam, terrorism, denominational schooling, and individual rights circulate in unstructured discussion, as the teacher increasingly vacates the space of encounter.

Understanding the linguistic culture of an ethnographic encounter and understanding the categories employed by participants in meaning making allows for understanding the site of encounter as *place*. Place in this context denotes more than physical location. The linguistic and multi-modal streams of ethnographic analysis illuminate and validate one another, particularly in the interconnectedness of *place* and *voice*. Place 'means the ... position ... from which one may speak to important issues ... without being challenged about identity or the right to engage in dialogue' (Gerhart 2003, 117). Actors, voices, artefacts, texts, and images in the site all speak to the domains of educational and religious culture from within a particular place. In sites of religious and cultural meaning making, language may reveal an imagined place as much as a concrete location (MacDonald 2003, 2). At the level of purpose-led knowledge and tactical decision-making, the pupil perceives what is proposed, but there is a failure of meaning making at the level of ethical consciousness, as the teacher paints on a canvas which is different from the one to which the pupils pay regard. In this process:

> [t]he visible frees itself for itself, as contrary to the consciousness that perceives it, since in fact the gaze understands very quickly, in front of the canvas, 'that there is nothing there to see' (Marion 1996, 17).

For example, in a scheme of work for Year 9 about the attributes of God, which was taught at a school in East London, one teacher's well-meaning approach to controversy, reported in an extract from field notes below, illustrates what is meant by the dullness as to detail. The representation and discussion of a collection of unevaluated concepts, shorn of their meanings within particular cultural domains (the Christian significance of God as the 'father of Jesus' was reduced to a universal notion of fatherhood), failed to find traction with the pupils who continued to make meanings in their own social worlds.

Ms F: You can be as controversial as you like.

Audrey: What does that mean?

Ms F: It means you can say anything you want.

...

Jack: What about the father of Jesus?

Ms F: I'm just gonna put 'Father' [on the board].

> There are a lot of group discussions arising from the pupils' ideas; this is generating background noise in what is intended as a whole-class discussion; Ms F sits at the front desk, with her arms folded, she looks fed up. 'Is it possible to have a discussion with you lot?'

The elision in this encounter, not only of the Christian narrative in Jack's comment, but also of the spontaneous discussion which arose (including the comment of a girl who argued vocally that God was a murderer because of the apparent commands of genocide in the Old Testament), represents an exercise of teacher authority in the service of 'coverage' – the determination to cover the syllabus by the end of the lesson. Pupil feedback suggests that this pattern – of pupils having meaningful conversations with one another, while teachers ignore these because they either find it professionally embarrassing to engage with controversy or are determined to achieve pre-defined outcomes – is common in many RE lessons. To transcend this temptation is a challenging task for any teacher, particularly when constrained by time and examination requirements.

The audience feedback on 'Avoiding difficult questions' singled the teacher out for specific criticism. While the teacher in 'Millionaire' could at least be seen to advance the purpose of shared values (success in important public examinations), the teacher in 'Avoiding difficult questions' sought to ignore or silence criticism of the official discourse, without trying to engage with the pupils' cultural domain. Subtle invitations to participate in narratives of explanation were offered by teachers and pupils (more subtle in the ethnographic observations, less subtle in the performance of the vignette), but rejected by both sides.

At times, representation or description was presumed to satisfy demands for explanation, as in the case of an S1 level (Year 8) group task, in which a group made use of objects from the 'Articles of Faith' collection of religious and devotional objects, which is based on the work of Hull (1984). While Hull's pedagogies were rooted in personal exploration of phenomenological *numina*, the unstructured use of the objects in the group presentation suggested a naïve reliance on the presence of the *numen* to communicate its significance to the learner. During one group's presentation, the field notes recorded the following:

> Ewan has an Islamic prayer mat on the floor, he is wearing two sets of prayer beads around his wrist. Unable to find the Muslim prayer cap, he is wearing a *yarmulke* [Jewish prayer hat]. His task in the group is to demonstrate how Muslims pray. He says to the class, 'they go down, and then they come back up', making a prostration on the mat, 'and then they go down again, and that's it, basically, and the beads, I think, are just to help them concentrate'.

The conflation of descriptions of phenomena with the way they are understood is further illustrated by one pupil focus group which took place following a number of examination-driven lessons. The pupils expressed boredom with the lesson content and a desire to study 'more exotic religions'. When asked what 'more exotic religions' were, one pupil suggested 'cannibalism'. Teachers' concern to represent religions from a position of presumed neutrality – many teachers expressed anxieties about communicating their own faith commitments to pupils – at times risked reducing religions to descriptive banalities which do not cohere with pupils' worldviews and fail to excite their imagination.

If there is no Archimedean point for religious meanings, the presumed neutrality which many teachers espoused must give way to either a distorted view of religion or an explicit commitment to a pluralistic worldview. Commitment remains a contested area within the professional community; despite the demise of the 'Sunday School' confessional model of religious education as a place between school and church, this topic still stands apart, on the threshold between school and another imagined place. In some cases, that other place is a space for multicultural discourse, in others an imagined community or communities of religious practice. Articulating that sense of place is essential to equipping pupils with an understanding of a subject, which transcends triviality.

Discussion and conclusions

Just as the possibility of meaning includes the possibility of failure of meaning, the possibility of 'seeing' clearly entails the possibility of deception – 'the possibility of false prophecy means prophecy is mediated by imagination, and that the listener needs at least to be conscious of imagination itself if he or she is not to be deceived' (Hyde 1998, 296). The distinction between *seeing* – the visual – and *listening* as an interpersonal activity at times obscures awareness that visual imagination is no less interpersonal and in need of conscious excavation if misrepresentations are to be avoided. The dangers of representation without explanation have been illustrated above. That the teacher's frame of meaning finds coherence with the ethical consciousness of the pupil in his/her lived experience is essential if a framework for meaning is, firstly, to be seen and, secondly, to have value, not to be seen through. The educator within the culture of education points a pupil to the *habitus* of that culture, the limits of imagination (Bourdieu and Passeron 2000), but the effective religious educator also stands in the liminal place between this and the culture of religious knowledge and practice, where meanings can effectively translate across institutional cultures; the teacher thus also functions as seer, pointing to the limits of hope (Kant 2008), opening possibilities for meaning making on a level beyond the literal. To do so effectively, s/he must approach religious texts and practices as well as theological and ontological claims with a hermeneutic openness that is not constrained by the sceptical eye of late modernity, which, ironically, has a tendency to foreground the naturalistic. The teacher must be prepared to allow religious claims their own space, even where they do not appear to hold meaning for the pupil. The teacher should also consider how pupils are to do their own meaning making in complex engagement with the texts and traditions under scrutiny (Vermeer 2010). Pupils bring their own meanings to bear anyway; the challenge is to understand how these should interact with the historically inscribed meanings which are etched into the textual and doctrinal fabric of religious traditions.

Notes

1. The project was funded by the Religion and Society Programme of the Arts and Humanities Research Council (AHRC) and the Economic and Social Research Council (ESRC).
2. e.g. Christian Belief & Lifestyle at GCSE level for AQA (Assessment and Qualifications Alliance, one of four private bodies licenced to award GCSE and A-Level public examination grades in England and Wales) and Making Moral Decisions at Intermediate 2 level for SQA (Scottish Qualifications Authority, the statutory public examination body for Scotland).
3. All the names used in the extracts from field notes are pseudonyms.
4. This is the title of a story-board written by a Year 8 pupil, which was displayed in a classroom in the school.

References

Battaglia, D. 1997. Displacing the visual: Of Trobriand axe-blades and ambiguity in cultural practice. In *Rethinking visual anthropology*, ed. M. Banks and H. Morphy, 216–39. New Haven, CT: Yale University Press.

Berger, P. 1970. *A rumour of angels: Modern society and the rediscovery of the supernatural*. Garden City, NY: Anchor.

Boal, A. 1979. *Theater of the oppressed* (Trans. C.A. McBride, M.O. McBride and E. Fryer). London: Pluto Press.

Boal, A. 2006. *The aesthetics of the oppressed* (Trans. A. Jackson). London: Routledge.

Bornstein, E. 2006. Rituals without final acts: Prayer and success in World Vision Zimbabwe's humanitarian work. In *The limits of meaning: Case studies in the anthropology of Christianity*, ed. M. Engelke and M. Tomlinson, 85–104. New York: Berghahn.

Bourdieu, P., and J.C. Passeron. 2000. *Reproduction in education, society and culture*. 2nd ed. London: Sage.

Carless, D., and K. Douglas. 2010. Performance ethnography as an approach to health-related education. *Educational Action Research* 18, no. 3: 373–88.

Conroy, J. 2004. *Betwixt and between: The liminal imagination, education and democracy*. New York: Peter Lang.

Conroy, J., and R. Leitch. 2010. From the prosaic to the Promethean: The teacher as trickster. Paper presented to the European Conference on Educational Research. Helsinki August 23–27.

Conroy, J., and D. Lundie. forthcoming. Does religious education work? In *Nested identities: New methods in the study of religion*, ed. L. Woodhead. Oxford: Oxford University Press.

Conroy, J., D. Lundie, and V. Baumfield. 2012. Failures of meaning in religious education. *Journal of Beliefs and Values* 33, no. 3: 309–23.

Copley, T. 2005. *Indoctrination, education and God: The struggle for the mind*. London: SPCK.

Geertz, C. 1993. *The interpretation of cultures*. London: Fontana.

Gerhart, M. 2003. Who is Hildegard? Where is she? On Heaven. In *Experiences of place*, ed. M.N. MacDonald, 115–46. Cambridge, MA: Harvard University Press.

Gilchrist, J. 2009. Thatcher 30 years on. *The Scotsman*, 2 May. Available at: http://thescotsman.scotsman.com/politics/Thatcher-30-years-on.5228881.jp.

Heubner, D. 1966. Curricular language and classroom meanings. In *Language and meaning*, ed. J.B. MacDonald and R.B. Leeper, 28–38. Washington, DC: National Education Association.

Hull, J. 1984. *Studies in religion and education*. Lewes: Falmer Press.

Hyde, L. 1998. *Trickster makes this world: Mischief, myth, and art*. New York: Farrar, Straus and Giroux.

Jackson, R. 2004. *Rethinking religious education and plurality*. London: RoutledgeFalmer.

Jackson, R., J. Ipgrave, M. Hayward, P. Hopkins, N. Fancourt, M. Robbins, L. Francis, and U. McKenna. 2010. *Materials used to teach about world religions in schools in England: Research report* DCSF-RR197. Coventry: Department for Children, Schools and Families and University of Warwick.

Kant, I. 2008. *The critique of judgement* (Trans. J.C. Meredith). Available at: http://ebooks.adelaide.edu.au/k/kant/immanuel/k16j/.

Lealman, B. 1996. The whole vision of the child. In *Education, spirituality and the whole child*, ed. R. Best, 9–19. London: Cassell.

Lefstein, A., and J. Snell. 2009. Linguistic ethnography in action: Initial, illustrative analysis of a literacy lesson. Paper presented to the 'Ethnography, language and communication' seminar, 22 May, North University of Glasgow.

Liguori, A. 2009. *Preparation for death: Considerations on death, judgment, heaven and hell*. London: TAN Books.

Lundie, D. 2011. The other in the curriculum: Ethnographic case studies on the spiritual, moral, social and cultural dimensions of religious education in sites of value commitment and contestation in the UK. Unpublished PhD thesis, University of Glasgow.

MacDonald, M.N., ed. 2003. *Experiences of place*. Cambridge, MA: Harvard University Press.

Marion, J.-L. 1996. *The crossing of the visible* (Trans. K.A. Smith). Stanford, CA: Stanford University Press.

Morphy, H., and M. Banks. 1997. Introduction: Rethinking visual anthropology. In *Rethinking visual anthropology*, ed. M. Banks and H. Morphy, 216–39. New Haven, CT: Yale University Press.

Mott-Thompson, K. 1996. Experience, critical realism and the schooling of spirituality. In *Education, spirituality and the whole child*, ed. R. Best, 75–92. London: Cassell.

Ofsted (Office for Standards in Education). 2010. *Transforming religious education*. Manchester: Ofsted.

Pollock, D. 2006. Marking new directions in performance ethnography. *Text and Performance Quarterly* 26, no. 4: 325–9.
Smith, A. 2006. *The seer*. London: Faber & Faber.
Snyder-Young, D. 2010. Beyond 'an aesthetic of objectivity': Performance ethnography, performance texts, and theatricality. *Qualitative Inquiry* 16, no. 10: 883–93.
Stern, J. 2007. *Schools and religions: Imagining the real*. London: Continuum.
Sutherland, E. 1974. *The seer of Kintail*. London: Constable.
Tomlinson, M., and M. Engelke. 2006. Meaning, anthropology, Christianity. In *The limits of meaning: Case studies in the anthropology of Christianity*, ed. M. Engelke and M. Tomlinson, 3–19. New York: Berghahn.
Turner, V. 1967. *The forest of symbols: Aspects of Ndembu ritual*. London: Cornell University Press.
Vermeer, P. 2010. Religious education and socialization. *Religious education* 105, no. 1: 103–16.
Ziebertz, H.-G., and U. Riegel. 2009. *How teachers in Europe teach religion: An international empirical study in 16 countries*. Münster: LIT-Verlag.

'We're all in this together, the kids and me': beginning teachers' use of their personal life knowledge in the Religious Education classroom

Judith Everington

Warwick Religions and Education Research Unit (WRERU), Institute of Education, University of Warwick, Coventry, UK

> In the context of international debates about teachers' knowledge, this essay reports a study of how and why a cohort of English trainee teachers of Religious Education used their personal life knowledge in their teaching. Four possible reasons for their commitment to this practice are examined. A belief in the value of openness, a desire to motivate and engage their pupils, and a need to create 'bridges' between the pupils' worlds and those of religions are considered. The possibility that trainees used their life knowledge to bridge a 'gap' between their personal and professional lives is also discussed. The findings of Communication and Teacher Effectiveness research are used to indicate the potential benefits of the practice and the works by Aldenmyr and Furedi are drawn upon to highlight potential dangers. The author concludes that the sharing of teachers' life knowledge can benefit pupils, but that teachers need to reflect on the dangers and further research is needed to support this.

Introduction

This essay focuses on a cohort of English trainee teachers of Religious Education (RE) and the role that their personal life knowledge played in their teaching and understanding of the relationship between the RE teacher and his/her pupils. The research discussed below is the latest in a 10-year series of qualitative studies of beginning RE teachers' personal and professional lives that I have undertaken in my role of teacher educator–researcher (e.g. Everington and Sikes 2001; Everington 2005, 2007, 2009). The perspective provided by these studies has led to an interest in the changes that have taken place in trainee teachers' interests, concerns, attitudes, and values.

In 2009, a resurgence of international research interest in teachers' knowledge (Ben-Peretz 2010) and the English government's enquiry into beginning teachers' subject knowledge (TDA 2007, 2008) prompted a study of the kinds of knowledge that the trainees attending my one-year post-graduate teacher training course were using in their planning and teaching. This indicated, without any direction or expectation on my part, that they were making greater use of their personal life knowledge than previous cohorts and that they had a greater commitment to doing so. For example, when teaching about reasons for not believing in the existence of God or explaining differing perspectives on suffering, there appeared to be more widespread and frequent reference to the teachers' personal knowledge of these matters, in relation to their own lives and those of family and friends. This development appeared to be worthy of further investigation, for several reasons.

Firstly, very little attention has been paid in research to the knowledge used by RE teachers and the study of teachers' professional lives, at both national and international level, has neglected RE teachers (Baumfield 2012; Van der Zee 2012). Mujis and Reynolds (2011) note the general neglect of British teachers in research on teacher effectiveness – again, teachers of RE are not represented in the research literature.

In the English RE context, there has been debate about teacher 'neutrality' since the 1970s (Copley 2008; Hulmes 1979). Although this has not been well supported by empirical research, philosophical studies have highlighted the need for religiously committed teachers to explore the relationship between their beliefs and the teaching of multi-faith RE and to create a theological 'bridge' between these (Cooling 2002, 2007). Life-history research has indicated the need for beginning RE teachers to reflect on their biographies and recognize the ways in which their life experiences influence their understanding of and priorities for RE as well as their day-to-day planning and teaching (Sikes and Everington 2001; Everington 2005, 2007). An international study of RE teachers found that a failure to recognize the influence of personal experiences on professional matters prevents teachers from making professional judgements about when and how to draw on these experiences for the benefit of pupils (Van der Want et al. 2009). Previous research thus indicated that there is reason to view an increase in beginning teachers' use of their personal life knowledge as potentially problematic and as a development requiring investigation.

A second reason for researching this matter is that it raises interesting questions about the teacher's role and relationship with pupils and the kinds of knowledge needed to meet the demands of these. Changes in UK and US education policy have led to renewed interest in these questions (Furedi 2010). For example, in 2010 and in the context of revising selection criteria for initial teacher training, the government of England and Wales sought to define 'good' teachers primarily in terms of their academic attainment and subject knowledge (DfE 2010, 20–21). This implies a particular view of the teacher's role and relationship with pupils. As discussed below, the extensive classroom use of the teacher's personal life knowledge suggests a different view of this role and relationship and of the relative value of academically derived subject knowledge.

The issues outlined above led to a decision to extend my initial one-year study to a second year in order to investigate trainees' use of personal life knowledge. The following report and discussion focus on the second phase.

Definition of terms, research questions, and methods
Definitions
During the first-year investigation into knowledge used in planning and teaching, a pre-determined definition of knowledge was avoided. The intention was to allow the trainees to offer a free response to two research questions: 'What kinds of knowledge do you think teachers of RE need?' and 'What kinds of knowledge did you use or draw on in your planning and teaching?'. In the second-year study of

trainees' personal life knowledge, the first-year data, together with insights from previous research, were used to arrive at a loose definition of knowledge.

In teacher-focused research, the term 'personal knowledge' is used in differing ways and can refer to knowledge primarily acquired or developed in the course of teachers' professional lives (e.g. Loughran and Northfield 1996). I use the term 'personal life knowledge' to refer to the kind of knowledge that teachers have acquired and continue to acquire in their personal lives. This includes knowledge acquired during childhood and adolescence and from family and schooling. For some teachers, membership of a faith community will have provided personal knowledge of the religions that are taught, as they are 'insiders' to a particular community and its wider context (Nesbitt 2004). Life knowledge used in the classroom might also be related to significant events and experiences such as illness, bereavement, parenthood, and gaining or losing a religious faith. There is also an ongoing 'everyday' kind of knowledge of, for example, the media, youth culture, and local events.

Second-year research questions and method

The research addressed three key questions: what kinds of personal life knowledge are the trainees using in their planning and teaching? How are they using this knowledge? Why do they use this knowledge? The entire cohort of 14 trainees participated in the study. According to their self-designations, there were three Muslims, one Sikh, three Christians, and two Atheists. Five described themselves as either Agnostics or 'undecided'. One trainee had a degree in Sociology, two were Philosophy graduates, the remainder had degrees in Theology or Religious Studies, three in combination with other Humanities subjects. Most of the group were aged 21–30, but three trainees were in their late 30s, all with school-age children.

At the beginning, mid-point, and end of the course, the trainees were asked to participate in a group discussion and to complete written responses to questionnaires or, at the mid-point, directed reflections. During the Autumn and Spring/Summer term school placements, I observed all trainees teach and data were gathered from observation notes and the scrutiny of lesson plans. In between the two placements, trainees were invited to participate in one-to-one semi-structured interviews of 45–60 minutes' duration. Ten trainees accepted the invitation. Group discussions and interviews were recorded on a digital MP3 player and transcribed. A reflexive journal (Lincoln and Guba 1985) was used to record thoughts and impressions and reflect on how my dual role as researcher and tutor might influence the research process and outcomes.

The collection of data through staged questionnaires/reflections and group discussions and through interviews and lesson observations made it possible to build a picture of recurring themes and patterns and opportunities to collect data at different times and in different ways provided a means of methodological triangulation (Cohen and Manion 2000; Denzin 2006). The interviews were intended and proved to be valuable in enabling participants to expand on group discussion comments in a situation where peer pressure could be minimised. The school-based research provided an opportunity to consider the relationship between trainees' reports of their practice and observations of what was happening in classrooms.

Analysis involved close interpretative reading of the data in order to identify categories, themes, and patterns (Denzin and Lincoln 2000, 633–43). Analysis of data obtained during the autumn term suggested themes and questions that were used to guide the spring-term interviews and spring/summer-term group discussions (Woods 2006). Data from all three terms were then analysed and the themes and patterns identified were examined in relation to a range of theoretical perspectives and published research findings.

Key findings

Although they were not required or expected to do so, all the trainees made regular use of their personal life knowledge in their teaching. All believed this to be a valuable, even necessary practice in RE. However, they used their knowledge in differing ways and recognized differing 'purposes' for using it, which appear to reflect the trainees' own 'theories' of teaching and learning in RE. Some viewed the use of their life knowledge as an important aspect of their teacher identity and as contributing to their sense of professional fulfilment. The trainees appeared to have an intuitive understanding of when and how to use their life knowledge in the classroom but recognized that there were dangers in doing so. They were able to identify potential problems and suggest solutions.

The research provided trainees with carefully sequenced opportunities to explore and reflect on their personal life knowledge as well as its use in the classroom. These opportunities were valued and appear to have led to positive developments in trainees' thinking. Trainees without degrees in the study of religions were no more inclined than those with such degrees to make use of personal knowledge, indicating that this was not a substitute for academic knowledge that was lacking. In the following sections, these findings will be considered in more detail, with the three research questions serving as headings.

What kinds of personal life knowledge did the trainees use in the classroom?

Analysis of the data suggested two categories of life knowledge. Some of this knowledge had a strong factual element but was based on the teachers' personal experience, making it different from the kind of knowledge gained through academic study. This is identified below as Category 1. Other life knowledge, Category 2, had a strong experiential dimension but included factual knowledge.

Category 1: knowledge with a strong factual element but based on personal experience

Knowledge of:

- a religion/religions – the trainees' own and other people's
- secular positions, such as agnosticism or atheism
- political ideologies and movements, including Human Rights
- cultures within the UK, including minority ethnicity and social class
- other countries and cultures
- interfaith encounters and projects
- the media, especially popular TV programmes, films, and music
- youth culture

Category 2: knowledge with a strong experiential dimension but including factual knowledge

Knowledge of:

- challenging life experiences, such as bereavement, divorce, and serious illness
- adolescent experiences, such as feeling inadequate, bullied, and rebellious
- racism, sexism, stereotyping, discrimination
- spiritual experiences, e.g. of 'the numinous'
- 'everyday experiences,' such as resisting temptation, self-discipline/sacrifice, love, and friendship

How was personal life knowledge used?

The most common use of life knowledge involved the teacher deliberately sharing his/her knowledge and experiences with pupils during a lesson. This was often planned, although a number of trainees reported spontaneous use of their knowledge, for example, when they felt that pupils had not understood a point and wanted to provide an example or illustration.

A related but distinctive way of using life knowledge was in response to the 'truth questions' that pupils directed at the teacher, for example, 'Do *you* think that God exists?'. Most trainees reported that they responded by revealing their own beliefs and some had given reasons related to personal experiences. In doing so they may not reflect general practice among English RE teachers (Hampshire 2011), but support evidence that newer generations of such teachers are more likely to share their religion-related beliefs with pupils (Everington 2009).

As the study proceeded, participants were asked more and less directly about the 'pros and cons' of using their life knowledge in the classroom and they were encouraged to reflect on how they made judgements about what to use and when. There was agreement that teachers should take great care in how they talk about personal life knowledge, as this might influence pupils' opinions or offend individuals. Ideally teachers should plan ahead what to say and when and even consider the tone of voice to be used so that this would not be too strident. In group discussions, a key principle emerged: teachers should know pupils well before deciding what, how, and when life knowledge should be used. It was pointed out that it took time to get to know individuals and this prompted a more general and agreed age-related principle: while 11- to 13-year-old pupils were receptive to knowledge that does not relate to 'everyday life', older pupils were less receptive and the teacher's use of life knowledge could be crucial in engaging this age group. Nevertheless, there was recognition that 'distancing' strategies may be needed for all pupils. One interviewee explained how she deliberately chose examples from her life that related to her girl friends rather than her boyfriend, to avoid revealing too much of her private life; for the same reason, another spoke of changing an example so that this was presented as relating to friends rather than people closer to her.

Why was personal life knowledge used?

I first present the analysis of trainees' own understandings of the purpose of using personal life knowledge and then explore this question from the researcher's point of view. Trainees were asked the 'why question', with varying degrees of directness, in questionnaires, group discussions, and interviews. The data were examined in order to identify 'purposes' that were presented by three or more participants. Each identified 'purpose' is headed by an illustrative quotation.

'You've got to make religious stuff real and relevant for them – to get them involved and interested'

Most of the trainees spoke of drawing on their personal life knowledge to offer the kind of lively examples and illustrations that would draw pupils into a topic. Some recognized that they were 'trading on' pupils' fascination with teachers' personal lives.

'You open up yourself so that they will open up'

Some trainees used terms such as 'opening up' to describe how they used examples from their lives to encourage pupils to volunteer their own ideas and experiences. One purpose of this was to generate interest in a topic and model the kind of responses that the teacher was seeking from pupils. More often, however, the intention was to create an atmosphere of trust and openness and to break down barriers between pupils and between teacher and pupils, so that there could be an open sharing of personal matters. Here the emphasis was on the relationship between teacher and pupils; as one trainee explained, 'It's not me and them. We're all in this together, the kids and me.'

A desire to create a classroom atmosphere of trust and openness was found to be a common theme in the responses of RE teachers from six European countries who participated in a study of teaching about and in situations of diversity (Van der Want et al. 2009; Everington et al. 2011). This suggests that, despite different national understandings of the subject, there may be a particular need in RE to decrease traditional teacher–pupil 'distance'.

'If they know you're on their side, they're less hostile to RE, less defensive'

I have examined the challenges presented to trainee teachers by pupils who are hostile to religion and RE in previous research (Sikes and Everington 2001; Everington 2005). In the study reported here, some of the agnostic and atheist trainees who were working with anti-religious pupils described revealing aspects of their own secular backgrounds and views in order to counter pupils' negative views of RE and RE teachers. The potential dangers of this strategy are considered below, but there were less controversial examples of teachers attempting to combat pupil negativity. When working with Muslim pupils, two of the Muslim teachers used their personal knowledge of pupils' attitudes, reference points, and language to challenge their negative views of religions other than Islam. Both regularly quoted from the Qur'an and Hadith and one spoke of encouraging pupils to use the term 'non-Muslim' rather than *kuffar*, a term she translated as 'disbeliever' and understood to have negative connotations.

'They didn't understand the numinous until I talked about my sunset photos and then they got it!'

Many of the trainees described using personal experiences to help pupils understand or interpret a religious concept or belief. In such cases, the teacher aimed to use his/

her own experience as a bridge between the pupils' world and that of the religion studied. The quotation above is taken from an interview account of how the agnostic trainee had struggled to convey the concept of the numinous to her a-religious class before deciding to use holiday photos of an experience that had conveyed a sense of the numinous to her. This had been successful and confirmed her belief in the value of using her life knowledge and experiences as a teaching aid.

'They thought all religious people were aliens until I told them how I celebrate Christmas the same way they do' (Sikh trainee)

Two of the younger religiously committed trainees – a Sikh and a Muslim – who wore clothing signifying their religious identities, gave accounts of their use of personal life knowledge in largely a-religious classrooms. These suggested that they were not simply creating, but personifying a bridge between the secular world of their pupils and the religions studied. Both trainees felt at ease in living in religious and secular worlds and wanted to use their personal knowledge and experience of this to address pupils' misconceptions and help them appreciate the similarities between the pupils' lives and those of many religious people.

The 'purposes' outlined above can be viewed as reflecting or expressing the trainees' emergent theories (Afdal 2010; Kessels and Korthagen 2001) of the relationship between RE teachers and pupils and of the teaching and learning process that can and should occur in their interaction. These matters will be considered in the following section. The implications of enabling trainees to develop such theories will be discussed in the conclusion.

Discussion of some key findings

From a researcher's point of view, this section addresses two questions: why might these beginning teachers have a belief in the value of using their life knowledge in the RE classroom and a commitment to doing so and what issues does this raise? I examine perspectives on this practice which highlight potential dangers and benefits for pupils, before considering the value of the practice in relation to teachers' personal–professional development.

The dangers and benefits of intimacy, openness, and relevance

When asked to reflect on the reasons why she and her colleagues believed in the value of using their life knowledge in the classroom, one interviewee responded that sharing personal experiences and feelings is part of 'normal everyday life' for pupils and younger teachers. As the majority of the participants in this study were in their 20s, it is perhaps unsurprising that they viewed intimacy and openness as cultural norms, reinforced on a daily basis by reality TV shows, 'Facebook,' and 'Twitter' (Van Manen 2010). The analysis of the trainees' written and interview reflections also suggested that many, including some with a commitment to a particular religious faith, had a post-modern view of faith and belief (Wright 2004; Erricker 2010): they had a personal openness to the potential truth and value of differing beliefs and perspectives on life and a desire for their pupils to develop this. Thus 'openness', with others and to 'the other', appeared to be a key theme in the trainees' discourse. However, how should this be viewed from a professional perspective?

Drawing on Sennett (1993), the Swedish researcher Aldenmyr (2010) draws attention to the potential dangers of teacher–pupil 'openness' and the 'tyranny of intimacy'. She argues that teachers are drawn into abandoning the proper 'distances' of a professional role and into relationships with pupils that require strict authenticity, emotional expression, and intimate bonding. When teachers interest themselves in pupils' personal lives, present themselves as 'equals', and use themselves as examples, there is a danger that pupils will be denied privacy and lose the sense of security that should be provided by an 'objective' professional who is entirely focused on their learning.

The participants in this study wished to avoid the danger of influencing pupils' views and some felt the need for distancing strategies to protect their own privacy. However, they did not wish to be or be viewed by pupils as 'objective professionals' or view a relationship based on mutual sharing of personal knowledge and experiences as inappropriate, regarding pupils' privacy, security or otherwise. Moreover, they were convinced that the benefits of this relationship for pupils outweighed any potential dangers.

While Aldenmyr's research raises some important questions about these trainees' practices, they may have demonstrated an intuitive grasp of the key factors in pupil motivation and effective teaching/learning identified in teaching-related research. Research on teacher effectiveness has drawn attention to the crucial role played by a positive teacher–pupil relationship (friendly, understanding and caring of personal situations) and classroom climate (warm and supportive) in pupils' motivation, ability to contribute, and achievement (Mujis and Reynolds 2011, 127–38).

A summary of Communication Studies research (Richmond and McCroskey 1992, 101–19) highlights that the greater students' liking for or affinity with the teacher, the more likely they are to enjoy the subject, learn from it, and pursue it. Teachers who use techniques to enhance affinity create greater pupil motivation, their teaching is more effective, and pupils' learning is enhanced. When identifying techniques which enhance affinity, Daly and Kreiser (1992, 133) include the technique of 'Equality/Homophily' by which the teacher reduces the sense of teacher superiority and creates a sense of 'similarity' between pupils and teacher. The 'teacher image' thus created can set the tone of the classroom culture, increase the teacher's credibility, and enhance the effectiveness of his/her teaching. The technique of 'Openness' involves teachers disclosing information about their backgrounds, interests and views, and sometimes feelings.

Research on this kind of self-disclosure indicates that college students value teachers who share personal knowledge, experiences, and views and are more motivated to learn from them than from teachers who do not self-disclose (Cayanus 2004; Cayanus and Martin 2008). Two studies of self-disclosure by college teachers of Religious Studies/Theology (Kuiper 1975; Ejsing 2007) arrive at similar conclusions but recommend that teachers exercise caution and sensitivity to avoid influencing students' views and manipulating their emotions.

The 'techniques' referred to above appear to describe accurately some of the ways in which the trainee teachers in this study used their life knowledge in the classroom and the research findings support some of the reasons they gave for what and how they shared with pupils. An awareness of negative images of RE caused some trainees to be concerned about their 'teacher image' and 'credibility' and pupil motivation was a key theme in all trainees' reflections on their practice. However, as noted above, one of the trainees' theories was that sharing life knowledge motivated pupils because it makes unfamiliar ideas relevant to them – in this respect there is reason to question their belief in this practice.

In recent work, which refers to the UK and US, Furedi (2010) launches a scathing attack on the 'pedagogy of motivation' and what he views as the current obsession with making the curriculum and teaching relevant to young people's lives and interests. This he attributes to a deep societal suspicion of authority, in particular, the authority of knowledge that transcends everyday life and of teachers who provide such knowledge.

Cast in the role of facilitators and deliverers of the policies of social engineers, teachers are unable to engage in the 'inter-generational conversation' that is 'an essential component of education' (Furedi 2010, 3). When the teacher–pupil relationship is viewed as a 'learning partnership', teachers are denied the opportunity to act as guides to the important truths and insights, which have been acquired throughout history, truths that have emerged in attempts to find answers to many of the deepest and durable questions facing humankind (41). Moreover, a pre-occupation with pupils' emotional lives and the adoption of 'therapeutic' techniques has led to the manipulation of pupils' emotions as a substitute for a more honest, authoritative direction of their attention and behaviour. The primary school practice of 'circle time', in which pupils are invited, or – in Furedi's view – expected, to share their personal problems and feelings, is given as an example of how teachers have been drawn into training feelings as a form of control (2010, 186–7). The result of the many factors that have contributed to a view of education as anti-intellectual/ academic is teaching that fails to challenge pupils, pose the kind of questions that direct their attention beyond everyday experience or enable them to begin to appreciate how the wisdom of the past is crucial to an understanding of and reflection on the present and future.

In relation to the practices and views considered in this study, Furedi's critique raises important issues. His concern that a preoccupation with pupil motivation leads to teaching that sacrifices subject content to relevance requires particular attention. RE teachers who believe in the value of using their life knowledge to illustrate the 'everyday' relevance or meaning of religious beliefs, or use their knowledge to create analogies between secular and religious concepts, might consider whether this practice dominates lessons in terms of time and emphasis. More crucially, they might consider whether this practice results in an over-simplification or even distortion of spiritually profound and intellectually challenging 'truths' that pupils could and should benefit from encountering directly (Wright 2004). RE teachers who use their life knowledge and experiences to encourage pupils to share their own might consider whether this is a necessary or valuable step in a learning process, rather than simply a motivational strategy, and if they have established a relationship and classroom culture that does not emotionally pressurise pupils to publicly share personal matters.

While Furedi's critique offers a valuable perspective on the practices and views of participants in this study, the findings of this study and the nature of the subject that is their context present a challenge to some of his accusations. Despite changes to the RE curriculum over the past six decades (Copley 2008), its subject content has remained the six 'world religions' (QCA and DfES 2004). RE is thus fundamentally concerned with the kind of knowledge, truths, questions, and answers that Furedi views as pupils' rightful inheritance and crucial in providing them with the existential security that they need to deal with an insecure world

(2010, 50). However, the ongoing challenge for RE teachers has been, as Furedi recognizes, to make such knowledge accessible to pupils and to engage them in its exploration. One solution has been for the teacher to act as a mediator between young people's worlds and the worlds of religions and to create an interaction between these that might be viewed as a three way 'conversation' between teacher, pupils, and religions.

Given Furedi's criticism of 'child-centred' approaches to teaching and learning, it is ironic that his call for the 'inter-generational conversation' that is 'an essential component of education' echoes the view of Loukes (1965), often viewed as the 1960s originator of 'child-centred' approaches to secondary school RE (Copley 2008): 'At root religious education is a conversation between older and younger on the simple question what is life like?' (Loukes 1965, 148).

Since the 1960s, RE classes have become increasingly secular or religiously diverse (Copley 2008) and the task of mediating between the worlds of young people and the religions studied has become increasingly complex. Contrary to Furedi's claim that there has been little pedagogic interest in attempting to reconcile the rigorous teaching of subjects with the need to engage pupils (2010, 183), this has been a key concern in the development of 'RE pedagogies' for four decades (Grimmitt 2000). In the research reported here, the trainees did not make reference to these pedagogies. However, it appears that they used their life knowledge to create bridges between religious beliefs and concepts and their pupils' lives and interests and to launch 'inter-generational conversations' in which, as relatively young, religiously literate adults, they could create interaction between youth culture, 'everyday adult wisdom', and the 'wisdom' of ancient religious traditions. While the dangers of using personal life knowledge have been recognized, I argue that this practice can help teachers avoid the more significant danger identified by Furedi: of denying pupils access to spiritually profound and intellectually challenging 'questions and answers', because these are judged to be too remote from their lives and interests.

I now turn to a final response to the question why the participants in this study had a commitment to using their life knowledge, focusing on the value of this practice for the teacher rather than for pupils.

Trainees' use of personal life knowledge and the development of teacher identity

In the individual and group responses to the research questions, many trainees expressed the view that the teachers' personal and professional selves should not be separated. Some felt that bringing their personal selves into the RE classroom was the most important and fulfilling aspect of their teaching: 'I do take my whole self into the classroom and, if I didn't, I'd always be questioning what I'm doing, if I'm not wholeheartedly there.'

Teacher development research suggests that many beginning teachers experience difficulty in adopting the social role and identity of the teacher and view this as eclipsing or diminishing their personal identity (Lacey 1977; Sikes, Measor, and Woods 1985). However, all teachers can experience a discomforting 'gap' between their personal and teacher identities and the need to create a bridge between these (Sikes and Everington 2001). It is possible that at least some of the trainees who participated in this study experienced or wished to avoid such a 'gap' and used their life knowledge in RE lessons as a means of creating a bridge between their personal and professional selves.

The spring term interviews enabled participants to articulate and explore their life knowledge and the ways in which they used it in their teaching and to begin to create a narrative that 'connected' aspects of their personal and professional lives. As an (older) interviewee explained, 'Since the interview I've been thinking a lot about how everything in my life connects up – it's been really good and I'd like to do more.'

Conclusion

At present there appears to be very little research on RE teachers' use of personal life knowledge and on the role that this plays in their relationships with pupils. The study reported here attempts to address this neglect. Although small in scale, the study draws on research undertaken in Europe and the US to indicate that the issues it raises are of international interest within and outside the field of RE and it presents findings that appear to be fruitful areas for further, ideally comparative, research. Among the findings that have implications for initial teacher education, the following appear to be particularly worthy of further investigation.

The study suggests the need to provide trainees with opportunities to reflect on the practice of sharing life knowledge with pupils, in relation to their own views and experiences of this and the kind of research cited in this essay. There appears to be a particular need for beginners to become aware of the importance of using their life knowledge to promote pupils' learning, rather than their own credibility or class control, and of the dangers of encouraging an unprofessional relationship in which teacher or pupil 'sharing' is of a highly personal nature and/or involves manipulation by either party.

The study indicates that the opportunity to reflect on and 'explain' their practice enabled the trainees to begin to develop their own theories about the RE teacher's role and the relationship between RE teachers and pupils. In a training context, opportunities to recognize and develop such theories may be of value, especially if practice-based and context-bound theories could be related to what Loughran refers to as the kind of 'Theory with a big T' (episteme) that transcends particular contexts and provides new perspectives on and insights into practice (2006, 63).

Finally, the study and discussion provide some evidence that RE teachers' use of their personal life knowledge can be important for pupil motivation, effective teaching and learning, and access to subject content that pupils would otherwise find very difficult. The value of such knowledge is not recognized in the definition by the current English government of 'the good teacher' or the policy of selecting beginning teachers on the basis of their academic capabilities and the 'relevance' of their degree level subject knowledge. In the US this approach to selection has been challenged (Nieto 2006) and there is a need for a research-based challenge in the UK. This is especially important in the case of RE teachers who, I argue, need to possess the kind of broad life knowledge and outlook on life that enables them to move between and bridge many different personal, social, cultural, and religious worlds.

In his conclusion Furedi declares that 'It is time for society to have a grown up conversation about what we mean by a teacher' (2010, 97). In this essay and the further development of the research, I hope to promote and contribute to such a conversation.

References

Aldenmyr, S.I. 2010. Teacher identity and the marketised society: Discursive constructions in teacher discussion groups. *Journal of Social Science Education* 9, no. 3: 68–76.
Afdal, G. 2010. *Researching religious education as social practice*. Münster: Waxmann.
Baumfield, V. 2012. Understanding the wider context: Meaning and purpose in religious education. *British Journal of Religious Education* 34, no. 1: 1–4.
Ben-Peretz, M. 2010. Teacher knowledge: What is it? How do we uncover it? What are its implications for schooling. Available at: http://dx.doi.org/10.1016/j.tate.2010.07.015.
Cayanus, J.L. 2004. Effective instructional practice: Using self disclosure as an instructional tool. *Communication Teacher* 18, no. 1: 6–9.
Cayanus, J.L., and M.M. Martin. 2008. Teacher self disclosure: Amount, relevance and negativity. *Communication Quarterly* 56, no. 3: 325–41.
Cohen, L., and L. Manion. 2000. *Research methods in education*. 5th ed. London: Routledge.
Cooling, T. 2002. Commitment and indoctrination: A dilemma for religious education. In *Issues in religious education*, ed. L. Broadbent and A. Brown, 44–55. London: Routledge-Falmer.
Cooling, T. 2007. The challenge of passionate religious commitment for school education in a world of religious diversity. *Journal of Education and Christian Belief* 11, no. 1: 23–34.
Copley, T. 2008. *Teaching religion: Sixty years of religious education in England and Wales*. Exeter: Exeter University Press.
Daly, J.A., and P.O. Kreiser. 1992. Affinity in the classroom. In *Power in the classroom: Communication, control and concern*, ed. V.P. Richmond and J.C. McCroskey, 121–43. Hillsdale, NJ: Lawrence Erlbaum.
Denzin, N., ed. 2006. *Sociological methods: A sourcebook*. 5th ed. Chicago, IL: Aldine Transaction.
Denzin, N., and Y. Lincoln, eds. 2000. *Handbook of qualitative research*, 2nd ed. Thousand Oaks, CA: California, Sage.
DfE (Department for Education). 2010. *The importance of teaching: The schools White Paper*. London: The Stationery Office.
Ejsing, A. 2007. Power and caution: The ethics of self disclosure. *Teaching Theology and Religion* 10: 235–43.
Erricker, C. 2010. *Religious education: A conceptual and interdisciplinary approach for secondary level*. Abingdon: Routledge.
Everington, J. 2005. Adolescent attitudes to 'the other': Citizenship and religious education in England. In *Religion, education and adolescence. International empirical perspectives*, ed. L.J. Francis, J. Astley, and M. Robbins, 235–61. Cardiff: University of Wales Press.
Everington, J. 2007. Freedom and direction in religious education: The case of English trainee teachers and 'learning from religion'. In *Researching RE teachers: RE teachers as researchers, religious diversity and education in Europe*, ed. C. Bakker, H.-G. Heimbrock, R. Jackson, G. Skeie, and W. Weisse, 111–25. Münster: Waxmann.
Everington, J. 2009. Individuality and inclusion: English teachers and religious diversity. In *Teachers responding to diversity in Europe: Researching biography and pedagogy*, ed. A. Van der Want, C. Bakker, I. Ter Avest, and J. Everington, 29–41. Münster: Waxmann.
Everington, J., and P. Sikes. 2001. 'I want to change the world': The beginning RE teacher, the reduction of prejudice and the pursuit of intercultural understanding and respect. In *Towards religious competence: Diversity as a challenge for education in Europe*, ed. H.-G. Heimbrock, C.T. Scheilke, and P. Schreiner, 180–203. Münster: LIT-Verlag.
Everington, J., I. Ter Avest, C. Bakker, and A. Van der Want. 2011. European religious education teachers perceptions of and responses to classroom diversity and their relationship to personal and professional biographies. *British Journal of Religious Education* 33, no. 2: 241–56.
Furedi, F. 2010. *Wasted: Why education isn't educating*. London: Continuum.
Grimmitt, M. 2000. *Pedagogies of RE: Case studies in the research and development of good practice in RE*. Great Wakering: McCrimmon.
Hampshire, D. 2011. Does it matter by degrees: The impact of the academic backgrounds of teachers on their teaching of religious education. Unpublished research for MA dissertation. Coventry, UK: University of Warwick.
Hulmes, E. 1979. *Commitment and neutrality*. London: Chapman.

Kessels, J., and F.A.J. Korthagen. 2001. The relation between theory and practice. Back to the classics. In *Linking practice and theory: The pedagogy of realistic teacher education*, ed. F.A.J. Korthagen, J. Kessels, B. Koster, B. Lagerwerf, and T. Wubbels, 20–31. Mahwah, NJ: Lawrence Erlbaum.

Kuiper, H.P. 1975. *Teacher self disclosure and advocacy compared to neutrality: Their effect on learning with reference to religious studies*, EDd. Practicum. Fort Lauderdale, CA: Nova University. Available at: http://www.eric.ed.gov.

Lacey, C. 1977. *The socialisation of teachers*. London: Methuen.

Lincoln, Y.S., and E.G. Guba. 1985. *Naturalistic inquiry*. London: Sage.

Loughran, J. 2006. *Developing a pedagogy of teacher education: Understanding teaching and learning about teaching*. London: Routledge.

Loughran, J., and J.R. Northfield. 1996. *Opening the classroom door: Teacher, researcher, learner*. London: Falmer.

Loukes, H. 1965. *New ground in Christian education*. London: SCM Press.

Mujis, D., and D. Reynolds. 2011. *Effective teaching: Evidence and practice*. 3rd ed. London: SAGE.

Nesbitt, E. 2004. *Intercultural education: Ethnographic and religious approaches*. Brighton: Sussex Academic Press.

Nieto, S. 2006. Solidarity, courage and heart: What teacher educators can learn from a new generation of teachers. *Intercultural Education* 17, no. 5: 457–73.

QCA (Qualifications and Curriculum Development Agency) and DfES (Department for Education and Skills). 2004. *Religious education: The non-statutory national framework*. London: QCA.

Richmond, V.P., and J.C. McCroskey. 1992. Increasing teacher influence through immediacy. In *Power in the classroom: Communication, control and concern*, ed. V.P. Richmond and J.C. McCroskey, 101–19. Hillsdale, NJ: Lawrence Erlbaum.

Sennett, R. 1993. *The fall of public man*. Cambridge: Cambridge University Press.

Sikes, P., and J. Everington. 2001. Becoming an RE teacher: A life history approach. *British Journal of Religious Education* 24, no. 1: 8–20.

Sikes, P., L. Measor, and P. Woods. 1985. *Teachers' careers: Crises and continuities*. Lewes: Falmer.

TDA (Training and Development Agency). 2007. *Developing trainees' subject knowledge for teaching*. London: TDA.

TDA (Training and Development Agency). 2008. Guidance to teacher educators attending consultation meetings on subject knowledge for trainee teachers. Unpublished.

Van Manen, M. 2010. The pedagogy of Momus technologies: Facebook, privacy and online intimacy. *Qualitative Health Research* 20, no. 8: 1023–32.

Van der Want, A., C. Bakker, I. Ter Avest, and J. Everington, eds. 2009. *Teachers responding to diversity in Europe: Researching biography and pedagogy*. Münster: Waxmann.

Van der Zee, T. 2012. Inspiration: A thought provoking concept for RE teachers. *British Journal of Religious Education* 34, no. 1: 21–34.

Woods, P. 2006. *Qualitative research*. Available at: http://www.edu.plymouth.ac.uk.

Wright, A. 2004. *Religion, education and post modernity*. London: RoutledgeFalmer.

Teachers only stand behind parents and God in the eyes of Muslim pupils

Jenny Berglund

School of Gender, Culture and History, Södertörn University, Stockholm, Sweden

> In the course of reviewing a recent quantitative survey of approximately 1300 Swedish youths on subjects like religion and leisure activities, I came across a finding which seemed intriguing to me: some 50% of those identifying themselves as Muslims reported that they confided in their teachers (compared to only 5% of non-Muslims) for help with personal problems. Supplementing this finding with several studies as well as my own interviews, I explore its possible meanings and examine its implications relative to such matters as the value of relational skills in teaching, the content and direction of teacher training, the importance of the teacher–student relationship, and the potential of teachers to facilitate integration.

Introduction

My aim in writing this essay is to explore the possible causes and implications of a particular statistical finding that, at least at first sight, suggests the positive contribution of Swedish teachers to the process of integrating Swedish Muslims, which points to an area of educational research that appears deserving of more scholarly attention. However, it should be stated that one statistical finding of a survey does not, and should not, establish a general fact, rule or principle. When one such finding is sufficiently unexpected or counter-intuitive, however, it can stimulate new directions of thinking and alert us to areas that have so far not been considered. This is, in fact, precisely what occurred in the case of my finding.

The process began when I was asked, in my capacity as researcher of Islam in Sweden, to review and interpret the responses of the Muslim participants in a survey which aimed to determine the place and meaning of religion in the lifestyles, activities, and existential outlook of Sweden's younger population.[1] While carrying out this review, I found the following question: 'Who do you talk to when you are concerned or worried about something?' The question had the following response options, from which respondents were permitted to select five: (a) a parent or step-parent; (b) a sibling; (c) another relative; (d) a teacher; (e) a counsellor, school nurse or other adult working at my school; (f) a friend; (g) a boyfriend/girlfriend or spouse; (h) a leader of an organisation of which I am a member; (i) BRIS[2] or some other hot-line; (j) a youth centre; (k) a priest, imam or other religious representative; (l) an Internet meeting place/social network; (m) God; (n) no one. During the quantitative analysis of the responses to this question, I found that, compared to only 5% of the rest of the respondents, some 50% of those identifying themselves as Muslim indicated that they confided in their teachers for help with personal problems; indeed, in terms of response frequency, they placed their teachers in third position, only after parents (70%) and God (58%).

The remainder of this essay consists of a discussion of the possible reasons for this somewhat surprising statistic, which is supplemented by examples from my own recent interviews with young Swedish Muslims. The essay concludes with a broader analysis of the finding and an examination of its implications in terms of such matters as the content and direction of teacher training programmes, the value of relational skills in teaching, and teachers' potential contribution to the process of European integration. However, before I begin this discussion, I shall provide some information about Sweden's Muslim demographics and the survey's more noteworthy comparative results.

Based upon twentieth-century country-by-country migration of workers and refugee statistics as well as the estimates of the Swedish Muslim community, the current number of Muslims living in Sweden is usually cited to be about 400,000; another, and perhaps more reasonable, way of presenting this figure is to say that it ranges between 250,000 and 450,000, which refers to the lowest and highest estimates found in the literature (Roald 2009, 62). Of these, approximately 110,000 are thought to be formal members of Islamic communities and approximately 100,000 are thought to be of school age or younger (Otterbeck and Bevelander 2006, 8).[3] However imprecise these various estimates may be, it is incontestable that Sweden's Muslim population represents a diasporic minority that must to some degree shape its religious identity in relation to a secular, post-Protestant social majority. The Muslim population comprises a diversity of individuals from different cultural, ethnic, educational, and social backgrounds, some of whom can be considered active practitioners of Islam, while others can be considered 'cultural Muslims' with a more or less secular approach to life.

Regarding the survey's significant findings, it revealed hardly any major differences between the Muslim and non-Muslim respondents regarding their general habits and priorities in life. Both groups emphasised, for example, the importance of good health, family, and high self-esteem and reported that they spent their leisure time relaxing, earning extra money, exercising, and/or 'hanging out' with friends. One notable distinction between the two groups is that only some Muslim respondents reported that they spent leisure time with members of the opposite sex. As might be expected, when the responses of young Muslims were compared to the responses of those who identified themselves as active Christians, the statistical difference in this category was significantly reduced. This is hardly surprising since those who are actively involved in either religion tend to approach pre-marital relations with a great degree of caution (Zackariasson 2011). Another difference between Muslim and non-Muslim respondents is that a far higher percentage of the former considered 'belief in something' to be an important aspect of their lives.

As to the question of religious commitment and/or participation, two-thirds of the Muslim respondents reported that they came from homes that were 'very' involved in Islam. In connection with this query, the questionnaire included an option which allowed respondents to indicate *why* they felt a sense of belonging regarding the religious tradition of their choice. Approximately the same percentage of Muslim and Christian respondents stated that they considered their particular religious tradition to be either a 'fairly' or 'highly' significant part of the culture to which they had belonged from birth. However, the survey results also revealed some differences between the two groups. For example, three-quarters of the Muslim respondents, as opposed to a little less than two-thirds of the Christian respondents, indicated that the decision to adhere to their given religious tradition was a 'personal choice'. Moreover, a clear majority of Muslim respondents, as opposed to only one-third of those who identified themselves as Christians, stated that their religious affiliation 'shows who they are' as individuals (Berglund 2012; see also Roald 2001; Waardenburg 2003).

Possible explanations for the finding

To re-state the finding under discussion: response frequency in the *Religion som resurs?* survey indicates that young Swedish Muslims place their teachers in third place, after parents and God – they are inclined to confide in their teachers when they have problems, concerns, and worries. When compared to non-Muslim respondents, only 5% of the latter claimed that they would turn to their teachers for help in such matters, placing teachers almost to the bottom of the list of possible responses.

In attempting to explain why Muslim respondents allocate teachers such a high place as possible confidants, one must ask questions about both teachers and pupils – what is it about Swedish teachers and/or their teaching that inspires this degree of confidence among the Muslim respondents to the survey? What is it about the Muslim respondents and/or their cultural backgrounds that makes them far more likely than their non-Muslim counterparts to confide in teachers when they face problems?

Regarding the question about the teachers, their capacity to establish and maintain relationships of trust between themselves and their pupils seems to be an important factor. In this regard, Frelin (2010) has demonstrated that whether they are aware of it or not, teachers are continuously involved in establishing, negotiating, and maintaining interpersonal relationships with their pupils, an essential ingredient of which is the negotiation of trust. Frelin has further noted that relationship-building should be regarded as an essential aspect of a teacher's *'task perception'* because building tutorial relationships with pupils is beneficial not only with respect to pupils' emotional well-being, but also with respect to their ability to learn – and the teacher's ability to teach. Within this framework, *pupil confidence in teachers* is considered to be an important component: the teachers whom Frelin studied viewed building confidence as an important aspect of their job. Apart from the fact that relationships of trust help to create learning conditions that are conducive to education, it is likely that they also contribute to a view of the teacher as a trusted adult – an adult to whom a young Muslim might be inclined to turn in times of trouble. However, the suggestion that Muslim pupils' confidence in Swedish teachers can be *wholly attributed* to the relational skills of the teachers themselves is mitigated by the fact that only 5% of the survey's non-Muslim respondents expressed an inclination to confide in teachers. Other factors must also be at work.

It could be, for example, that many of the young Muslim respondents came from families whose original national and cultural traditions incline them to hold 'the teacher' in much higher esteem than Swedish society is presently inclined to – in fact, the current status of teachers is generally quite low in Sweden (Ohrlander 2009). It is well known that, historically, Islam has placed great emphasis on the value of knowledge, education, and learning, which might also have a bearing on teachers being appreciated by Muslim families (Günther 2007). Here, the suggestion is that when parents display a high regard for the societal role and status of the teacher, the children will follow suit and thus be more inclined than their non-Muslim counterparts to confide both the small and the big troubles in their lives in their teachers.[4]

Another possible explanation for the relatively high level of confidence in teachers among Muslim respondents is related to the potential for generational conflict within 'migration families'.[5] When the younger generations of such families begin to view their elders as being out of touch with the social, cultural, and practical realities which they encounter as members of a minority in a modern Western society, they may also begin to view their elders' counsel as being less helpful than that of a known and trusted teacher who is perceived to have a better grasp of the challenges they face and the adjustments they are called upon to make (Jonker and Amiraux 2006, 11). However, the weight of this argument is greatly reduced – although not nullified – by the fact that over two-thirds of the same Muslim respondents indicated that they would turn to their parents for help with their problems (their most frequent choice). The high degree of confidence in parents, which this finding conveys, challenges the widely held assumption that there are major generational conflicts within migration families, but it does not necessarily negate my argument that it is the perception of Muslim elders being 'out of touch' which inclines Muslim youths to rely on their teachers instead. It is possible that, although both parents and teachers are frequently approached about problems, the types of problems and the reasons for approaching the teacher rather than the parents are different.

Teachers as trustworthy adults, not 'buddies'

In an attempt to shed more light on this matter, I conducted qualitative interviews with young Swedish Muslims, focusing on their relational experiences with previous teachers as well as on their level of confidence and trust in the teachers they encountered. Relevant selections from two of these interviews will be briefly discussed in the following sections.

Alia was a 20-year-old university student at the time of the interview; her recollection of a particular elementary (primary) school teacher (from the fourth to the sixth grade) confirmed the Muslim pupils' trust in teachers as expressed in the survey described above. Alia's impressions of this person and her view of the time she spent in school were generally positive:

> Because my parents often left early in the morning for work, this particular teacher was the first adult I encountered every day … and, of course, I turned to her when I had problems. She always took time to listen while I helped straighten the room after class or during her own breaks.

Alia also pointed out that this particular teacher clearly indicated when she had time to chat and when she had other things to do – she 'was not one of those "buddy" teachers'. This somewhat pejorative statement describes a teacher who becomes so much of a peer during breaks that she undermines her own authority and ability to teach during class; or, as Alia put it, someone 'who could be cool during breaks, but to whom no one listens in class'. She encountered this 'buddy' type of teacher mostly during her secondary school years – the type a girl might turn to for advice on make-up or fashion, but not for advice on more serious matters.

While Alia spoke positively about the trustworthiness of teachers she had encountered at both secondary and high school level, none of them appeared to have equalled the elementary school teacher in terms of her ability to inspire confidence and trust. Now a young adult, Alia noted that she was more inclined to turn to friends than teachers when she felt the need to confide in someone, although friends were not always the most trustworthy confidants due to their inability to keep secrets. She also mentioned 'God' (the second most frequently cited choice of the Muslim respondents in the survey), musing that she ought to turn to 'Him' more often than she did.

Joseph, a 22-year-old journalism student, recalled that he often stayed behind in primary school after lessons:

> Sometimes we stayed to play football and at other times I simply remained in the classroom with my teacher, who was generally there for an hour or two after class, marking papers and preparing for the next day's lessons. She was aware that it was crowded and hectic at home with all my little brothers and sisters; I myself preferred staying on as long as possible, because it was less tiring than being at home.

Joseph further noted that while there, he sometimes did his homework or helped with tidying up the classroom. Nor was he the only pupil who stayed:

> ... there were several of us, and as long as we weren't a nuisance, she [the teacher] didn't seem to mind. If we talked too much, she would tell us to leave – or, as I remember it, rather than telling us to leave, she simply looked at us and nodded towards the door; then we knew it was time to go.

When I asked Joseph whether he remembered this teacher as being very strict, he answered that she was not so much strict as fair and just:

> She did not seem to have 'favourites'; I sometimes thought that I was one of her 'favourites', but if I misbehaved, I was put in my place like everyone else. As I remember her, she was not the type to help you tie a shoe-lace or give you a hug; she showed that she cared by other means – actually by being just and strict, now that I think of it.

Significantly, Joseph noted that his mother also appreciated this teacher: 'She used to say that [this teacher] was one of the few who really trusted her as a parent and did not treat her differently because she wore the veil.' Regarding this teacher's approach to the matter of religious practice, Joseph recalled that 'fasting was never problematic for her, unlike for some of the other teachers I encountered. She simply discussed the matter with my mother and together they decided that I should fast on Fridays and weekends.'

Both of the above accounts show that it was the teacher's fairness, justness, and professional interest that inspired the appreciation, trust, and confidence of the Muslim pupils – and also, at least in Joseph's case, of the parents. Moreover, both Alia and Joseph indicated that they felt drawn to associate with their teacher beyond the regular teacher–pupil interactions of the classroom – during breaks and/or after school, which suggests that she had become important to them as a trusted and reliable adult figure in their lives.

While we need to avoid attributing too much probative value to what is, after all, one comparative statistic from a Swedish survey, we can venture to make the following tentative assessment: that teachers were the third most frequent choice – after parents and God – as persons in whom Muslim respondents confided suggests that the teachers themselves must be credited with having built effective (and affective) relationships with their pupils; on the other hand, that teachers were among the least frequent choices of the non-Muslim respondents in the survey suggests that both positive and negative factors on the pupils' part also account for this result. Thus, as with many questions in academic research (e.g. the question of nature vs nurture), the most reliable answer probably lies somewhere in between – the place where both aspects can be seen to be significantly influential. In the present case, the interview material makes it clear that teachers with developed relational capacities (a topic I shall return to below) are able to connect with Muslim pupils on a level that transcends the strict confines of the classroom, thus inspiring admiration, interpersonal confidence, and trust. But what are we to make of the big statistical difference between the Muslim and the non-Muslim respondents? Apart from the suggestions offered above, one could certainly venture any number of educated guesses. In a recent interview, a Swedish teacher noted, for example, that:

> There are certain things about which [Muslim] youngsters [in particular] are hesitant to ask their parents [because they think the matter might be forbidden according to Islam]... And since they themselves are not always able to determine how others [Muslims and non-Muslims] perceive their words and actions, they feel the need to test the waters with us teachers first, to see how we react. They learn quite quickly that these conversations are kept strictly confidential and that we do not gossip about them with their parents.

Yet another possibility is the likelihood that in their search for acceptance and admittance in Sweden's social, cultural, and economic spheres, Muslim youths – as members of a minority – may feel more needy, insecure, and vulnerable than those who belong to the majority culture; under these circumstances, a teacher who is part of the majority society and appears as an interested, accepting, and trustworthy adult might naturally become an important confidant and role model in their lives – perhaps more so than in the lives of those that are non-Muslim Swedes.

Concluding discussion: implications for teacher training

Ultimately, of course, the reasons for the comparative difference will not be better understood by mere guesswork; rather it will require further empirical research, in Sweden and in other European countries, although this may not be the most significant question for researchers to pursue. Irrespective of the disparity between the Muslim and non-Muslim responses in the survey, the fact remains that Muslim respondents did indicate a high degree of confidence in their teachers and this may have some bearing on one of the most pressing current questions: what more can European countries do to facilitate the peaceful and harmonious integration of their burgeoning Muslim populations?

Immigrant young people, including those of the second and third generation, sometimes feel like 'strangers in a strange land' – a feeling that can be either reinforced or mitigated by their encounter with the majority society and its various social, cultural, political, and economic institutions. The teacher is undoubtedly one of the prime representatives of Western society that immigrant young people (as well as their parents) encounter upon arriving in Sweden. Thus the teacher's ability to make immigrant pupils (and their parents) feel welcome, respected, confident, and included may be of significant societal value at this particular time. The interviews discussed here make it clear that at least the young people in question felt safe, secure, and accepted in the presence of their teachers and had an extremely positive experience of Swedish society. Joseph's recollection that his mother also liked his teacher because she was inclusive and accepting of Muslim cultural differences is significant, indicating that a teacher's potential to promote integration extends beyond the pupils to the adult immigrant community. For those that can appreciate the importance of this kind of contribution, the question naturally arises what can be done in terms of teacher training and continuing educational programmes to prepare teachers better so that they can forge trusting and meaningful relationships with their Muslim pupils and their parents. Therefore, I shall discuss two suggestions in this regard: (1) the introduction of teacher training and continuing educational programmes that include courses on Islamic traditions, practices, and cultural requirements; and (2) the introduction of teacher training and continuing education in form of discussion groups and workshops that focus on the relational dimension of teaching.[6]

Similar to other times throughout history, the character and complexion of European culture are currently undergoing significant transformation – largely as a result of globalisation, mass communication, and the influx of Muslim and other immigrants. Also, the manner in which Europe's social institutions respond to these realities is closely linked to whether the transition involved is smooth or difficult. As the formal education system constitutes one of the most encompassing of all social institutions – a societal sphere that requires the participation of every young person and parent – it continues to be an area of great opportunity, in terms of being able to contribute to a successful outcome of these processes. However, in order to take advantage of this opportunity, the primary representatives of that institution – the teachers – must be prepared appropriately. In my view, one way of addressing this is to include courses in teacher training that provide specialised knowledge about Islam and the lifestyles, values, habits, and unique requirements of the diverse Muslim communities. Such programmes are of particular relevance at a time when the media portrayal of Muslims is often misleading and the phenomenon of 'Islamophobia' is becoming more widespread. Some Swedish universities have begun to offer further education courses for teachers interested in increasing their understanding of Islam and comprehending the unique challenges that Muslim pupils face. In August 2011, I interviewed a primary school teacher who had attended such a course. This teacher noted that special courses in Islam were necessary for teachers today and explained why at some length:

> As a teacher you cannot afford to turn a blind eye to reality and today's reality is that there are Muslim pupils in almost every class you teach... Thus the more you know [about Muslim traditions], the better you can respond to your [Muslim] pupils and their parents... When teachers lack a basic knowledge of Islam, they have no choice but to accept whatever pupils or parents say, no matter how out of place it may seem... Fear of being accused of racism or 'Islamophobia' can cause [an uninformed teacher] to submit to everything: to stop-gap solutions, un-scheduled absences, exclusions from standard activities, etc. [On the other hand] if you have read the Qur'an ... and understand that both it and the Hadiths can be interpreted in various

ways, depending on who you are and where you come from ... and that Islam does not require one to follow everything that is mentioned in the Qur'an, you can then respond to both pupils and parents in a much better way... Of course, I don't claim to know everything simply because I attended one course; but I now know enough to feel comfortable to discuss or question things. [I have found that] when I show myself to be somewhat knowledgeable and interested, I win parents' confidence and this is absolutely necessary! If I sit like a fool with no understanding or ability to question, I tend to lose trust and may also lose respect – and that can become a serious problem.

In other words, if teachers have no knowledge of Islam and the differences that exist within Islamic traditions, they may feel that they have no basis for discussing with Muslim parents how their children might participate in particular lessons, activities, and extra-curricular events. The teacher cited above makes an important point about respect and confidence, which applies to both the Muslim pupils and their parents. When a society makes a point of educating its teachers about Islam and Muslim traditions, enabling teachers to be knowledgeable, sensitive, and able to discuss Muslim-related issues, it forms teachers who are better able to educate and nurture their *Muslim pupils*. This also leads to a set of teachers who are more able to earn the approval, trust, and respect of *Muslim parents* who will be impressed that their child's teacher has taken the time and trouble to learn about Islam and that the host society has seen the need for this kind of cultural training. All of this is an obvious advantage with regard to the overarching goal of European societies to facilitate the successful integration of their immigrant Muslim populations.

The teacher quoted earlier continued by relating an incident that highlighted for her the significance of the training about Islam that she had received:

During a meeting with the father of one of my Muslim pupils, I was informed that Qur'anic law forbade that his daughter participate in swimming in public... When I replied, 'no, this is not specifically mentioned in the Qur'an, which was revealed at a time when there were no schools or swimming or PE' ... he simply stared ... and [then] said that the Qur'an did not allow girls to swim in the company of boys... I then inquired whether it was really the swimming that was the problem ... and he replied that it was not so much the swimming than the idea that his daughter was not properly dressed with the boys present... When I told him that his daughter could wear whatever she liked for the swimming lessons ... he agreed that she could swim [with the rest of the pupils] if she was properly covered; he also mentioned that he would tell the other parents at the mosque about this solution. Had I not taken the further education course on Islam at the university, I would probably not even tried to say a word and acquiesced in this father's wishes immediately, as most other teachers do.

This teacher's anecdote makes it clear that teacher training and continuing educational programmes would benefit from including courses that convey a basic knowledge of Islam.

Regarding the relational dimension of teaching, a number of researchers have turned their attention to the importance of *relational practices* (teaching practices that involve the establishment of meaningful and trusting relationships with pupils). Increasing teachers' relational skills, or at least making them more aware of the relational dimension, would certainly enhance their ability to interact positively with and gain the trust and confidence of pupils – both Muslim and non-Muslim. According to Frelin (2010, 6), 'teachers' relational practices consist of actions with the (sometimes single) purpose of establishing, maintaining and/or enhancing relationships that are beneficial for education, or aimed at preventing the opposite: relationships that impede or obstruct students' educational possibilities'. She concludes that 'there are times in which relationships in schools are in need of conscious attention and rigorous work on the part of teachers in order to be (or become) educational' (187). She further notes that many of the informants in her study 'were quite explicit about the positive influence that they want[ed] to have on their students – an influence [that] extends to the whole person and not just the learning of a given subject' (192). Grossman and McDonald reinforce this point, noting that:

> Any framework of teaching practice should encompass [its] relational aspects ... and identify the components of building and maintaining productive relationships with students. *Such an understanding might be particularly useful in preparing teachers who can work effectively with students who differ from them in terms of race, ethnicity, socioeconomic status, and language.* (2008, 188; emphasis added)

This raises the question whether the relational dimension of teaching can be actually taught or, as Frelin puts it, whether 'teachers' professional practice [can] be turned into educational content within teacher education' (2010, 197). I propose that the most effective way of doing this is *not through* teaching specific relational techniques, *but through* forums such as workshops and discussion groups that place a teacher's relational work with pupils centre-stage, so that they can be demonstrated, reviewed, and assessed. Such forums might also facilitate the development of 'a practice-based theoretical language that furthers understanding and stimulates discussion relative to the relational dimension of a teacher's work' (2010, 6).

In conclusion, I argue that apart from researching the relationship of trust that seems to exist between many Muslim pupils and their teachers, we should encourage further research into the relational dimension of teaching as well as the implementation of Muslim-specific courses in teacher training and continuing educational programmes. Research into these areas, and the practical educational improvements that are likely to result from this, could do much to enhance the ability of all teachers – at whichever level and of whatever type – to have a positive influence on the successful integration of Muslim populations, not only in Sweden, but also in other European countries.

Notes

1. Known as *Religion som resurs?* (Is Religion a Resource?) and funded by the Church of Sweden, the survey was conducted between 2007 and 2010 by Lövheim and Bromander (2012). It consisted of a questionnaire that was randomly mailed to 4000 Swedish citizens, aged 16–24, in municipalities known to have high concentrations of active Christians as well as Muslims. Among the 1300 individuals that participated, approximately 10% (or 131) identified themselves as Muslim. Once the responses had been received and the basic statistical data had been compiled and quantitatively assessed, various specialists were asked to assist with further analysis of the material. As a scholar specialising in the area of Islamic Studies, with a focus on Islam in Sweden, I was called upon to review the findings of the survey which related specifically to Muslims and to interpret their significance in the light of my own knowledge of the field.
2. BRIS stands for 'Barnens Rätt I Samhället' or 'Children's Rights in Society'.
3. The estimate for the communities is derived from the Swedish Commission for Government Support to Faith Communities (SST).

4. A related question is the significance of individuation and individualistic values in Western European societies and in different Muslim majority countries where such processes are also occurring. Although important, a discussion of this goes beyond the scope of this report (but see Berglund 2012).
5. A 'migration family' is understood here as a family where either the entire family or the parents have migrated to Sweden.
6. Given Sweden's multi-cultural situation, it is relevant that teacher training and further education programmes include courses not only on Islam but also on other minority cultures.

Interviews

Primary teacher, 9 August 2011.
Alia (pseudonym), 3 May 2010.
Joseph (pseudonym), 13 May 2010.

References

Berglund, J. 2012. Islamic identity and its role in the lives of young Swedish Muslims. *Contemporary Islam.* 6, no. 3 DOI: 10.1007/s11562-012-0191-1.
Frelin, A. 2010. *Teachers' relational practices and professionality.* Uppsala: Uppsala Universitet.
Grossman, P., and M. McDonald. 2008. Back to the future: Directions for research in teaching and teacher education. *American Educational Research Journal* 45, no. 1: 184–205.
Günther, S. 2007. Be masters in that you teach and continue to learn: Medieval Muslim thinkers on educational theory. In *Islam and education myths and truths*, ed. W. Kadi and V. Billeh, 61–82. Chicago, IL: University of Chicago Press.
Jonker, G., and V. Amiraux, eds. 2006. *Politics of visibility: Young Muslims in European public spaces.* Bielefeld: Transcript Verlag.
Lövheim, M., and J. Bromander, eds. 2012. *Religion som resurs? Existentiella frågor och värderingar i ungas liv.* Skellefteå: Artos & Norma.
Ohrlander, G. 2009. *Den gudarna älskar: Om konsten att överleva som lärare.* Sundbyberg: Optimal Förlag.
Otterbeck, J., and P. Bevelander. 2006. *Islamofobi: En studie av begreppet, ungdomars attityder och unga muslimers utsatthet.* Stockholm: Forum för levande historia.
Roald, A.-S. 2001. *Women in Islam: The Western experience.* London and New York: Routledge.
Roald, A.-S. 2009. *Muslimer i nya samhällen.* Göteborg: Daidalos.
Zackariasson, M. 2011. Gamla förbud eller levande värderingar? Attityder till alkohol och sex hos ungdomar i frikyrkan. *Religion som resurs? Existentiella frågor och värderingar i ungas liv*, ed. J. Bromander and M. Lövheim, 287–310. Skellefteå: Artos & Norma.
Waardenburg, J. 2003. *Muslims and others: Relations in context.* Berlin: de Gruyter.

Keeping the faith: reflections on religious nurture among young British Sikhs

Jasjit Singh

School of Philosophy, Religion and the History of Science, University of Leeds, Leeds, UK

> Although young Sikhs are regularly accused of not attending *gurdwara* and not being interested in Sikhism, many young Sikhs are now learning about Sikhism outside traditional religious institutions. Using data gathered as part of a research project studying the transmission of Sikhism among 18- to 30-year-old British Sikhs, this essay explores how young Sikhs are learning about Sikhism in their pre-adult life stage. Examining the influences of the family and the school environment and the various methods used in *gurdwara*s, this essay offers a retrospective look on the ways in which young Sikhs are nurtured and socialised into Sikhism, providing an understanding from the perspective of young Sikhs themselves about which methods actually work and why.

Introduction

As a young Sikh growing up in the UK I often heard statements from *gurdwara* (Sikh place of worship, literally 'the Guru's door') stages, which lamented that young Sikhs were not interested in Sikhism. Speakers complained that young people did not attend *gurdwaras*, were not interested in learning Punjabi, and failed to keep the Sikh identity, with parents – particularly mothers – being blamed for not educating their children about their faith. Those who did attend *gurdwara* regularly were praised and highlighted as good examples to the rest of the congregation, although I remember wondering why this was the case, given that I understood that going to the *gurdwara* every Sunday was the normal practice for all Sikhs.

On reflection, it is clear that my upbringing in a family in which all the male members wear turbans and in which regular *gurdwara* attendance is the norm has been a key influence in leading me to undertake research into the British Sikh community. Although there were few opportunities to learn about Sikhism formally as I was growing up in the 1980s, I had a good knowledge of Sikh history compared to most of my peers, because my parents had ensured that my bookcase was readily stocked with books and comics about the lives of the Sikh Gurus. I first experienced formal learning about Sikhism at the Sikh Missionary Society camps (Singh 2011) which I attended from 1985 to 1989 and where I demonstrated my knowledge by winning the competition for best historical essay four years in a row.

This essay presents data gathered as part of a wider research project which explored how 18- to 30-year-old British Sikhs learn about Sikhism. The focus is on how young Sikhs reflected on their religious upbringing during the pre-adult life stage, the period of life which is divided into childhood (up to 13 years old) and adolescence (13–18 years), with – as many scholars have observed – a decline in religious adherence from childhood to adolescence (Roberts and Yamane 2011, 97). As the majority of today's 18–30 year olds grew up in the 1980s and 1990s, recent technological innovations such as the Internet did not play as large a role in their religious socialisation as they may play in the lives of young Sikhs today. This essay is therefore mostly concerned with the role of the family, schools, and *gurdwaras*.

Methodology

In undertaking this research, a qualitative methodological approach was taken, using a variety of sources as part of the investigation (Denscombe 2007, 37). The main methods included: semi-structured interviews with 30 18- to 30-year-old British Sikhs who had attended and participated in events organised for young Sikhs; a self-selecting online survey of young British Sikhs; focus groups with Sikh students; and participant observation at events organised for young Sikhs, including Sikh camps and university Sikh society events. The fieldwork was undertaken throughout 2009–2010, with the online survey running from November 2009 to July 2011. The survey elicited 645 responses in total; it had been advertised on discussion forums relating to Sikhism and Bhangra[1] and on Facebook pages belonging to *gurdwaras*, Sikh camps, university Sikh societies and Bhangra groups in order to reach to as wide a range of respondents as possible. As there is currently no means of obtaining a random sample from all young British Sikhs and as young people are a difficult population to study – they tend to be very busy and mobile (Denton and Smith 2001, 2) – survey respondents were self-selecting and consequently respondents are likely to be young Sikhs with a strong commitment to Sikhism. This is justified by the fact that this research examined how and why young Sikhs engage with their religious tradition and therefore sought the views of young Sikhs who would respond to an online survey relating to the Sikh tradition. Rather than aiming to gather the views of young Sikhs from one or all of the various groups in the Sikh community,[2] I examine here the socialisation of young Sikhs from a variety of sectarian and ideological backgrounds.

Families and schools

Sociologists of religion recognize the role of the family as the primary agent of religious socialisation throughout the life course and as the main influence on individuals' religious choices (Sherkat 2003, 151–8). Indeed, Zuckerman concludes that 'ultimately, religious identity and conviction aren't generally so much a matter of choice or faith or soul-searching as a matter of who [sic] and what one's parents, friends, neighbours and community practice and profess' (2003, 51). It can be argued that of these factors the family is the most important in religious socialisation, as it determines the types of friends, neighbours, and community to which individuals are exposed to in early life.

According to Werbner, most accounts of Sikh families in the popular media, including Gurinder Chadha's *Bend it like Beckham* (2002), tend to focus on 'the struggles of a younger, British-born generation against arranged marriages imposed by authoritarian, coercive, gerontocratic elders' (2004, 901). References to religion in these accounts usually relate to issues about keeping long hair and the turban, with Sathnam Sanghera in his *The boy with the topknot*[3] explaining that despite the other male members of the family not keeping long hair, his mother had 'found God before she had me and decided to raise me as a religious experiment' (2008, 27). Sanghera comments on the 'haphazard nature' of the way he was instructed in Sikhism, stating, 'all that Punjabi classes on Saturday mornings had taught me was how to write "the camel went to the well" in Punjabi' (197), and he describes his struggles with keeping long hair; he wanted to 'get rid of my long hair because: (i) I was fed up of being teased about my topknot; (ii) I hated the way my topknot restricted my freedom...; (iii) I LOATHED the way it made me look' (198). Sanghera's account highlights some of the issues young Sikhs face regarding the effectiveness of religious instruction, the impact of family identity practices, and the difficulties they encounter between the family and school environment.

As Alexander (2006, 259) explains, the idea of young Asians being 'between two cultures' remains the dominant paradigm for understanding Asian youth identities, although British Asian communities have been established for over 40 years in Britain. She observes that:

> the notion of 'the second generation' remains intact in the popular and sociological imagination [carrying] with it ingrained ideas of an originary/parental culture and of a 'next' generation trapped between this ancestral homeland and the 'host' country – between old and new worlds. (271)

Ballard rejects the idea of cultural conflict in favour of viewing young Asians as 'skilled cultural navigators' who have a 'sophisticated capacity to manoeuvre their way to their own advantage both inside and outside the ethnic colony' (1994, 31). Instead of actively navigating, Jackson and Nesbitt (1993, 174) view these young people as having 'multiple cultural competence', able to use culture as a 'toolkit of resources', employing whichever aspects of their culture they require at a particular time (Vertovec 2009, 72). Although much of the subsequent work on Asian young people bears the traces of the earlier 'between two cultures' approach (Alexander 2006, 265), the focus is now on 'continuity and change' and on the growth of a 'new culture which is a synthesis of the "old" and the "new"' (Anwar 2002, 189).

Diversity

Above all, as Brah argues, it is important not to assume that there are discrete British and Asian cultures which necessarily 'clash' (1996, 41). Although Sikh families may share some elements, many have their own unique way of expressing and practising Sikhism influenced by their migration experiences, caste, political affiliation, economic status, and the extent to which they are committed to the Sikh faith (Hadwen 1995, 72). In addition, many families may align themselves to particular charismatic individuals (*Sants*) or particular ideological groups (*Akhand Kirtani Jatha, Damdami Taksal, Guru Nanak Nishkam Sewak Jatha*)[4] or belong to other sectarian groups (*Namdharis, Nirankaris, Radhasoamis*).[5]

According to Singh and Tatla, 'the distinctive social pluralism that pervades Sikh society is to be found not along the familiar cleavages of region, language, ethnicity or class, but in caste distinctions' (2006, 27). Although the concept of caste is generally used uncritically in discussions relating to the South Asian traditions, as Nesbitt explains, the term 'caste' obscures the crucial distinction between a *varna* (the four *varna*s being Brahmin, Kshatriya, Vaishya, Shudra) and a *jati* (*zat* in Punjabi) (2004, 100). Among Sikhs, it is *jati* rather than *varna* which has become the main distinction, with the *Jats* at the top rung, being landowners, followed by the artisan castes of the *Ramgharias* (carpenters), *Chhimbas* (tailors), *Julahas* (weavers), *Nais* (barbers), *Jinwars* (water carriers), and *Ghumars* (potters) (Singh and Tatla 2006, 28). Ballard explains that *jati* influenced the occupational base of Sikh migrants, as 'Jats were largely concentrated in physically demanding manual work and the Bhatras in small business and market trading, while many Ramgharias had taken advantage of their traditional skills as blacksmiths and carpenters to become craftsmen in the building trade' (1994, 110).

Although caste may influence religious socialisation in terms of *gurdwara* attendance, this is not as clear-cut as it is often presented, with many *Jats* attending the *Ramgharia gurdwara* in Coventry (Nesbitt 2009, 43) and, similarly, many *Ramgharias* can be observed attending a primarily *Jat gurdwara* in Leeds. Rather than considering caste *per se*, it is important to consider how migration history affects religious socialisation, as speaking the Punjabi language and visiting the Punjab are integral to Sikh children's nurture (Nesbitt 2000, 242) and are factors which are clearly influenced by migration history. Those who have relatives or contacts in India, regardless of caste, are more likely to visit the Punjab as children and consequently to visit sites of Sikh history, including the Golden Temple. For Sirjit,[6] a 23-year-old male from south England, visiting the Golden Temple at a young age had an important impact on the rest of his life as a Sikh:

> I was born in the UK – and my family were not particularly religious ... but when I was six or seven, I went to *Harimandir Sahib* [the Golden Temple] with my family ... and then when the golden throne of *Guru Granth Sahib* [the Sikh scriptures regarded by many Sikhs as a living Guru] was coming out, my Grandfather got my hand and touched the *palki* [palanquin] – and basically after that experience on that day at the age of six and a half, everything changed. I used to have cut hair, couldn't speak Punjabi very well, I didn't know anything about *bani* [sacred writings] ... and then on that day I bought four books on Sikh history, which I've still got to this day ... and I used to read them every day – everyone thought it was a phase, like me keeping my hair, giving up certain things to eat, getting up early in the morning ... but eventually after a few months, when things didn't stop, then everyone realised that actually he's taking it for real. (interview, August 18, 2010)

Although it is not possible to generalise about the impact of migration history, Takhar notes that 'the majority of East African Sikh migrants to Britain are on the whole more religiously inclined than other zats coming directly from India' (2005, 42). Whereas many direct migrants removed their turbans on arrival in the UK (Ballard 1994, 111), male members of East African families tended to keep their turbans on arriving in the UK, having already experienced migration to Africa (Takhar 2005, 42). Survey responses to questions about identity reveal differences between Sikh families according to parental migration history, as Table 1 shows.

The details in Table 1 highlight that, firstly, the percentage of females wearing turbans in East African households is lower than that in other categories and, secondly, while the percentage of male turban wearers with full beards is similar across all categories, there are differences between males outside this category. In East

Table 1. External identities of survey respondents by migration history.

	Total	Both parents from India	Both parents from East Africa	Both parents born in UK
No of respondents	645	322	48	28
Male Turban + Full Beard	27.0%	29.8%	27.1%	17.9%
Male Turban + Trim Beard	10.4%	9.3%	25.0%	7.1%
Male with Haircut	18.6%	20.2%	6.2%	39.3%
Female wearing Turban	4.3%	4.7%	0.0%	3.6%
Female Uncut Hair	13.5%	11.5%	8.3%	14.3%
Female Haircut	26.1%	24.5%	33.3%	17.9%

African families, the percentage of male turban wearers with trimmed beards (25%) is roughly equivalent to the number of males with cut hair in other Sikh households, indicating that for males in East African households the most common identity outside the category 'male with full beard' is 'turban with a trimmed beard'. This indicates that Sikh children born in East African households generally are more likely to grow up in households in which turban wearing among males is the norm.

The fact that children born in East African households are generally more likely to encounter turban wearers may have an impact on their religious socialisation in various ways. Although ideas of *izzat* or family honour are regularly discussed in ethnographies of South Asians (e.g. Baumann 1996, 103), there is little if any discussion about how issues of *izzat* might affect religious transmission. As *izzat* affects individuals' standing in the community (Jhutti-Johal 2011, 67) and 'following religious "tradition" increases and maintains one's identity and *izzat*' (116), it follows that families in which male members wear turbans generally have higher status in the community than those who do not. That members of East African families are viewed as being religious may help explain why so few East African females wear turbans. If an East African family has a number of turban wearers and is therefore viewed as being religious, there is little need for female family members to express their religiosity explicitly, as they are 'included' in the males' maintenance of the family's honour. On the other hand, female members of families who do not have this religious status are compelled to express their religiosity explicitly by wearing turbans, as only keeping the hair uncut indicates the same level of commitment as that of a turban wearer (Singh 2010, 215). However, it is important not to assume that only those who keep the normative Sikh identity are engaging with the Sikh tradition. Mandeep, a 26-year-old young male from the Midlands who regularly speaks at camps and Sikh societies, explained:

> My dad was a *mona* [had his hair cut] ... but I remember from a young age that he knew Japji Sahib, Rehras Sahib, Sohila Sahib [the daily Sikh prayers] off by heart. And if we were ever going anywhere in the car, my Dad would say 'it's evening time, let's do Rehras' [the Sikh evening prayer] – he wouldn't cover his head or anything, it was automatic – and all we knew was that you should do Rehras in the evening –

and in the morning my Dad would say, 'let's do Japji Sahib' [the Sikh morning prayer]. (interview, February 14, 2010)

Rather than simply using external identity as an indicator of a Sikh family's religiosity, it is important to examine other factors, including knowledge of Sikh history and prayer practices. Both have an impact on the religious socialisation of young Sikhs, as does the structure of the household, especially the question of whether the household supports a nuclear or an extended family. As Nesbitt observes, 'parents, grandparents, aunts and uncles contributed to the nurturing of young Sikhs in their faith tradition' (2000, 52), as 'many of the young people referred to hearing an older relative "doing a prayer"' (2000, 69).

Similarity

Many interviewees mentioned that, as children, they had been explicitly taught Sikh practices by their parents. The president of a Sikh society in the Midlands explained that he 'used to do *Mul Mantar*[7] from the age of 5 – every day ... that's what my mum had raised me to do'. A number of interviewees also noted that the family keeping the *Guru Granth Sahib* in the house had an important impact on their religious socialisation, presumably because hosting the *Guru Granth Sahib* in one's home is very labour- and time-intensive. As Nesbitt explains (2005, 39), 'most Sikhs do not have a complete hard copy of the scriptures at home, as this means setting one room aside as a mini-*gurdwara*, with family members ensuring that the Guru Granth Sahib is opened in the morning and laid to rest for the night.' For Narinder, a 39-year-old speaker at camps and Sikh societies, these reverential practices became part of her daily routine, acting as a daily reminder of her commitments as a Sikh:

> ... the house I grew up in with my parents, there was always *Guru Granth Sahib*. Ever since I can remember, my mum does *prakash* [the formal opening of the *Guru Granth Sahib*] before she does anything else. So I had a couple of ground rules as a child, [one of] which was you had to *mattha tek* [bow to the Guru] before you came downstairs. (interview May 8, 2010)

Although not all Sikh households are able to house the *Guru Granth Sahib*, many studies of young Sikhs highlight the importance of iconography; James notes, for example, that 'pictures of the Gurus, and of events in their lives and places associated with them, decorate the walls of nearly all Sikh homes ... they must be important elements in their developing imagination' (1974, 31). This is supported by my observations in Sikh households, as iconography was present in all of the households where interviews were conducted, ranging from pictures of the Gurus to pictures of notable martyrs in the Sikh tradition and framed translations of quotations of the *Guru Granth Sahib* on the walls. The impact of this iconography on religious socialisation is clear, as Santokh, a 33-year-old male from north England, described:

> ... my mum would have at least 15–20 photos of the Gurus' pictures in every room – there's probably more pictures of the Gurus and Gursikhs [respected historical Sikhs] than there are of us ... [so] if I come into a room and see the Guru's photo, I'd think they were watching me. (interview, March 9, 2010)

Whereas pictures of the Gurus, in particular Guru Nanak and Guru Gobind Singh, are found in a number of Sikh households, families who are inspired by *Sants* [charismatic leaders] or particular Sikhs from history often display pictures of these individuals in their homes. Nurture in families which follow *Sants* appears to be slightly different from that in families who do not, as *Sants* often have the status of a Guru. In their study of Sikh children's ideas of God, Nesbitt and Jackson note that in *Sant*-following families the elevated status of the *Sant* is encouraged by the use of language: 'not only is the same word [*Babaji*] used for all three (Guru, *Guru Granth Sahib* and living *sant*) but the actual living *Sant* (Babaji) is equated with both the Gurus and the *Guru Granth Sahib*' (1995, 115–18).

Besides iconography, Nesbitt notes that food played an important role in informal nurture, as young Sikh children were 'accustomed to receiving, distributing and eating food in culturally acceptable ways which were distinct from those current in the surrounding western society' (2000, 55). Apart from being distinct from Western society, food practices in the home can also reinforce group membership. As Sukhdev, a 23-year-old female Sikh from south England whose family follows a particular *Sant*, explained, vegetarianism had become an important identifier for her household, distinguishing the family from other households which did not conform to the 'basics of *sikhi*':

> Dad used to eat meat, whereas for Mum it was the complete opposite ... and Mum seems to have had the good influence and now they've all stopped ... so in that way this house is a house which has [the] basics of *sikhi* – no alcohol, no meat. (interview, May 18, 2009)

The interviews also highlighted the importance of stories in religious transmission. For example, Param, a 22-year-old Sikh society president, pointed out that:

> history means so much to me – when I hear about what some of the *shahids* [those martyred for the faith] have done – I get kind of emotional. I think it's magic. I'd love to do something for my religion – I'd love to live the life of a Sikh. (interview, October 22, 2009)

Similarly, Narinder highlighted how her 'Mum would read *sakhiyan* [stories] to me before I used to go to bed – and I just couldn't bring myself to cut my hair'. It is clear from these accounts that stories about key figures in Sikh history have an important impact on the religious socialisation of young British Sikhs, causing some to question their own identities when being made aware of the lives of Sikhs in the past. Navdeep, a 26-year-old male from south England, explained:

> The one thing that I do recall about my childhood is that my bedtime stories would always be about stories about Sikhs... And when I was in Year 2, about five or six years old, I looked in the mirror once and I said to my mum, 'you tell me these stories about all these people, about these great soldiers... This blood runs through my body as well – runs in my veins – so why am I a *mona* [a person with hair cut]?' I don't know what hit me – it was a simple thing, but I thought, 'why don't I keep my hair? If this is what I'm made of as well, then why can't I keep my hair?' (interview, May 12, 2010)

A number of scholars have noted the significant role of stories in religious socialisation, among them Roberts and Yamane who observe that – together with scriptures, moral codes, and the celebration of religious events – stories are important, as they become 'imbedded in the memory and meaning for youngsters' (2011, 95). That the role of stories was mentioned by a number of interviewees indicates that for young Sikhs, the stories of sacrifice made for the faith have left a long-lasting impression, most importantly because of the emotional impact of these accounts.

Stories may also contribute to young Sikhs' awareness of 'different degrees of Sikhness', a phrase coined by Nesbitt (1999) to illustrate how young Sikhs describe more visibly observant Sikhs as 'the English "proper Sikh" or "real Sikh", etc. and the Punjabi "*pagwala*" and "*amrit chhakia*" with a small minority applying "Sikh" only to those who were committed to the Khalsa code' (329). The idea that young Sikhs are socialised to be aware of different degrees of Sikhness may help explain religious intensification in later stages of life, when young Sikhs search for greater engagement and aim to become 'proper Sikhs' themselves. A number of the male interviewees who wore turbans while growing up explained that they were aware that removing the turban was not an option for them, especially as other family members acted as 'identity enforcers'; Gurpal, a 22-year-old from the Midlands, recalled this, commenting that 'they used to call my *chache* [Dad's younger brothers] if I threatened to cut my hair'.

School

As Sanghera's (2008, 197) earlier comments illustrate, school becomes the most important 'other' environment outside the family, an environment where young Sikhs encounter plurality and face questions about their tradition. This encounter can be seen as an important factor in motivating young Sikhs to learn about their tradition, as Santokh, the 33-year-old male from north England, suggested:

> When I was at school, there were loads of Muslims ... and there was one guy who was well into his Islam – and he used to give all the *salaam* to his friends – shake all their hands in the morning and never shake ours ... so I thought I need to learn about my own [religion] ... so I went to the central library and I found a book on the history of Sikhs... I remember that being the first book that I read properly.

Similarly, Narinder explained how an experience at her Catholic school led her to wanting to find out more about Sikhism:

> I was in the choir ... and I thought to myself, 'today I'll get the Holy Communion' ... so I had my hands in the right place ... and I knew from his eyes that the priest wasn't going to give it to me ... and he just said, 'Bless you my child'. I was so angry – I thought, 'I've done your *kirtan* [singing of religious compositions] for so many years and you don't give me *parshad* [blessed food]?' Then I thought, 'if these *gore* [white people] go to a *gurdwara*, they'll get *parshad* no matter what.' So from then on, every time we used to say, 'In the name of the Father, the Son and the Holy Spirit', I used to *mattha tek* [bow to the Guru] ... it was an internal rebellion – and I was like 'I'm going to *gurdwara*, I'm going to show my friends, I'm going to talk about Sikhism – I'm going to tell them why I don't cut my hair.'

These examples highlight the impact of a 'moment' when these young Sikhs felt they needed to learn more about their faith. As Hervieu-Léger (1998) explains, people identify with religious groups in four main ways: (1) communally, by using a 'set of markers (social and symbolic) that define the boundary of religious groups and that allows one to distinguish "those who are in" and "those who are out"' (219); (2) ethically, by having accepted the values attached to the religious message; (3) culturally, by having embraced 'the set of cognitive, symbolic and practical elements which constitute the heritage of a particular tradition' (220); (4) emotionally, through 'the emotional experience associated with identification' (220). Given the experiences quoted above, Hervieu-Léger's (1998, 220) following statement applies:

> what is new in modern societies is that this intense experience which produces the collective feeling 'us', is less and less a result of communal belonging ... [and] is more and more often – and particularly among the young – the moment at which a primary experience of belonging becomes established.

The interview data suggest that although there are various possible experiences and although these experiences need not be as dramatic as those described above, emotional moments are important in understanding why young Sikhs choose to engage with their faith.

The ethnic composition of a school was also important: while there may not be any religious socialisation in schools, interviewees who attended schools which had a number of Sikh pupils all indicated that they preferred to socialise with fellow Sikhs. Similar to the study of Jewish pupils by Sinclair and Milner (2005, 100) who observed that issues of kinship and connection and awareness of difference were the main factors relating to self-categorisation, Baldev, a Sikh female from the Midlands, explained that when at school, she had felt most comfortable in a kin group:

> I can get on with *gore*, but it does make a big difference – even when I was at school I've always had that circle of Sikh and Punjabi friends – I dunno, it's not a safety thing, but I feel more at home, more like able to talk about whatever I want to talk about. (interview, December 20, 2009)

Although Abbas (2002, 83–4) noted that 50% of the Sikh respondents in his study agreed with the statement, 'No, I have never experienced difficulties of any kind' (84), informal telephone interviews with the organisers of bodies which aim to assist young Sikhs[8] highlighted that young Sikhs do face issues at school, in particular bullying, due to racism. The issue of bullying has been discussed on a number of Sikh websites,[9] with the Sikh coalition, an organisation based in the US which formed in the aftermath of discrimination against Sikhs following the attacks of September 11, 2001, going as far as to produce a guide about bullying for schools.[10]

The sense of not fitting in is clearly one reason why some young Sikhs are attracted to Sikh camps and other Sikh youth events, as they provide a 'safe space' in which to be Sikh. Few survey respondents mentioned learning about Sikhism in Religious Education (RE) lessons, with one stating that 'we are unlikley [sic] to be taught about our history in British schools' and another noting that a problem with British society was 'that most other religions except sikhism [sic] is taught in schools'. Although the purpose of this essay is not to examine the teaching of Sikhism in British schools, it is clear that the amount and quality of education in Sikhism across the UK varies considerably: state schools are legally required to follow the RE syllabus set by the local authority, which generally states 'that the religious traditions of Great Britain are in the main Christian', but requires that RE should '[take] account of the teaching and practices of the other principal religions represented in Great Britain';[11] however, faith schools are free to make their own decisions regarding the form of their RE syllabus (Jackson et al. 2010, 10).

Although it is important to recognize that 'religious education contributes to the religious nurture of pupils from Sikh and other faith backgrounds' (Nesbitt 2001, 148), the extent of this contribution depends on the importance placed on teaching Sikhism by individual local authorities and RE teachers. Given the inconsistency in approach, it is not surprising that many survey respondents stated that they had not been taught Sikhism in school. This is also apparent whenever and wherever I teach Sikhism at degree level: for the past three years, before beginning my lectures on Sikhism for Theology and Religious Studies students at the University of Leeds, I have asked who in the audience studied Sikhism before. Of 100–120 students present, less than five usually indicate that they did. Although this evidence is anecdotal and may result from students not wishing to draw attention to themselves, it is clear that by the time young people reach higher education, many have not encountered Sikhism in school. Where Sikhism is covered in RE lessons, Jackson et al. observe, it receives 'a rather superficial, descriptive treatment focusing on the externals of the religion more than on the religion's power for transformation in the lives of the individual or its contribution to wider society' (2010, 6).

Gurdwaras

Therefore, it would be easy to assume that young Sikhs must learn about Sikhism in *gurdwaras*. Before examining the types of religious education which occur there, I need to point out that not all *gurdwaras* are managed in the same way. Singh and Tatla (2006, 77) distinguish between 'mainstream' *gurdwaras*, where committee and congregation belong to a variety of castes, and 'caste-based' *gurdwaras*, where committee and congregation belong to a particular caste group. Further, some *gurdwaras* are led by a charismatic individual (*Sant*) or by people entrusted by the *Sant* (this arrangement differs from that of a committee, as this usually involves a process of selection rather than election).

Regardless of type, many *gurdwaras* make efforts to transmit Sikhism to Sikh children (Nesbitt 2000), depending on available resources and the priorities of those in charge. According to Nesbitt (2000), *gurdwaras* generally use the following six methods to transmit the Sikh tradition to young Sikhs:

(1) Punjabi supplementary schools
(2) specially organised children's services
(3) teaching in the main *gurdwara* programme with a focus on children
(4) Sikh youth camps
(5) formal instruction in the harmonium or *tabla*
(6) provision of library facilities

It is important to note that the supplementary classes are not classes in Sikhism but classes which focus on the Punjabi language. This helps to explain Drury's (1991) observation that despite attending supplementary classes, many young Sikhs demonstrate ignorance about Sikh teachings. The classes do, however, play an important social role in transmitting Sikh ethnic consciousness to young Sikhs, as Gurdeep, a 23-year-old from the Midlands, explained:

> ... we used to go to Punjabi class ... 'cos our parents used to send us – we didn't used to want to go first, then we used to go every evening 'cos we wanted to see our mates ... we didn't really learn much, but the main reason we used to go was the social side.

Nevertheless, some *gurdwaras* organise classes in addition to Punjabi classes. Puran, a 22-year-old male, described how he spent his childhood attending '*tabla* class, *vaja* [harmonium] class, and Sikhism GCSE class at X [name of *gurdwara*], then on a Sunday Y [name of *gurdwara*] Punjabi school, then Z [name of *gurdwara*] for *Gatka* [a Sikh martial art]'. This demonstrates that Sikh parents may be increasingly willing to send their children to any *gurdwara* which offers the best provision, even if this means attending more than one *gurdwara* on the same day. As Puran further explained, the Sikhism classes were very important in influencing his decision to grow his hair and wear a turban:

> *Sikhi* classes were really influential ... for a young person like myself at the time, it was really welcoming and it was so basic that everyone could understand ... before the classes I didn't know anything about *sikhi* – I started to get inspired 'cos I started learning about Sikh history and I could see how much people had done for us to be able to stand here today as Sikhs ... so that's when I started to grow my hair.

Despite increased provision, interviewees highlighted issues related to the management of *gurdwaras* and the committee system, which offered little stability to young Sikhs' learning. Puran also referred to this:

> ... there was a new committee at the *gurdwara*, but they wanted to dominate ... they told ... [the teacher] that he can't teach any more. And it was like, 'why have you done this? You had so much *sangat* [congregation] coming' – and from then it's dropped ... now, it's just five or six people.

Puran points to a key issue regarding the religious transmission in *gurdwaras*: for organising classes for young Sikhs, much depends on the goodwill of volunteers who give up their time and have to curry favour with those in charge. The 'chop-and-change' nature of teaching makes little sense to young Sikhs and may be one reason why many events for young Sikhs are now organised outside *gurdwaras*. Hardev, a teacher of *kirtan*, explained that for many *gurdwaras* provision for young Sikhs was simply not an economic priority:

> All the experiences we've had with *gurdwaras* in terms of this kind of activity are very negative. And I'll tell you why that is: it's because this kind of activity doesn't generate any revenue for the *gurdwara*; the only revenue it generates is the people who come to *mattha tek* [bow to the Guru and give offerings] to attend the class. One of the committee members at one *gurdwara* was extremely supportive; he said to us, 'you don't even have to ask'. but he said, 'just be aware that if there's a wedding or *Akhand Paths*

[unbroken readings of the *Guru Granth Sahib*], they're generating £2000 whereas this is generating £30' – and I understand that. (interview, January 28, 2010)

Here, the distinction between the different types of *gurdwara* is important. Unlike mainstream and caste-based *gurdwaras*, *gurdwaras* where the management is based on selection rather than election, such as *Sant*-led *gurdwaras*, appear to offer more stability for young Sikhs, as teachers are generally not dismissed if they find themselves belonging to the 'wrong' party following an election. The need to address economic concerns seems paramount in the minds of most *gurdwara* committees, often to the detriment of providing classes for young Sikhs. It is therefore not surprising that many young Sikhs themselves have started to organise events outside *gurdwaras*, which they are free to shape as they wish.

Conclusion

This essay has highlighted some of the variety in religious socialisation which young British Sikhs encounter in their early lives. As the site of primary socialisation, the family sets out much of what follows, but there is great diversity within Sikh families, with caste and migration history being important points of difference. While caste had an influence on the occupations of the early Sikh migrants, given the variety of occupations in which Sikhs find themselves today, caste does not appear to determine occupation as much as it once did. It is also no longer predictable that members of a particular caste attend a particular *gurdwara*, as many Sikh parents now appear to send their children to *gurdwaras* which offer the best facilities.

The structure of the household also has an impact on socialisation, especially if grandparents live in the same household or close by. Migration history has been shown to be an important factor here, too, as there are clear differences in the identity practices of 'direct' and 'twice' migrants. Both factors are linked to the level at which Punjabi is spoken, which in turn influences the type of religious learning which young Sikhs engage with in later life. Further, geography has been shown to be important both for the opportunities of learning about Sikhism, which are open to the family, and for the composition of the classroom at school which young Sikhs attend.

Besides these differences, this essay has described a number of commonalities. Nesbitt's analysis of the idea of 'proper Sikhs' is important, as it helps to explain why many young Sikhs who appear not to be interested in Sikhism take on Sikh identity in later life, when they experience a process of religious intensification (Roberts and Yamane 2011, 123) rather than religious conversion. The encounter with pluralism in the school environment is another important factor, as young Sikhs experience emotional moments of both belonging and not belonging.

Finally, this essay has discussed the role of the *gurdwara* as a site which primarily offers young Sikhs an environment within which they can simply 'be Sikh'. As *gurdwaras* are not homogenous communities, the type they represent determines the stability and importance placed on religious transmission. It is clear that for many *gurdwaras* organising events for young Sikhs is not a priority, given the low economic return of these events. Formal transmission organised by the older generation is generally regarded as being of poor quality and appears to be far too unstable, being subject to personal grudges and factional politics, much of which young

British Sikhs do not understand or wish to engage with. For these reasons, many events organised by young Sikhs are now held outside *gurdwaras*, in activity centres, schools, and universities. If those in charge of *gurdwaras* are serious about teaching young Sikhs about their faith, they must ensure that the environment they present is both stable and nurturing.

Notes

1. Examples of these postings can be found at: http://www.sikhnet.com/news/phd-research-british-sikhs-18-30-currently-underway http://www.sikhsangat.com/index.php?/topic/48145-phd-research-into-british-sikhs-18-30, http://simplybhangra.com/forum/5-general-chat/271-phd-research-into-british-sikhs-18-30, http://www.bbc.co.uk/dna/mbasiannetwork/html/NF4154526?thread=7157509
2. For further details about some of these groups, see Takhar 2005.
3. Sanghera's *The boy with the topknot: A Memoir of love, secrets and lies in Wolverhampton*, published in paperback by Penguin in 2009, was originally published in 2008 by Viking in hardback as *If you don't know me by now: A memoir of love, secrets and lies in Wolverhampton*.
4. For further details about the *Akhand Kirtani Jatha*, see Nesbitt 2005, 51; for details about the *Guru Nanak Nishkam Sewak Jatha* and Namdharis, see Takhar 2005.
5. Many of these groups are regarded by many Sikhs as being heterodox (see Takhar 2005). For details about the Nirankaris, see McLeod 1984; for details about the Radhasoamis, see Juergensmeyer 1995.
6. All the names of interviewees used in this essay are pseudonyms.
7. The *Mul Mantar* is a statement found at the beginning of the *Guru Granth Sahib*; its translation is 'root formula'.
8. These bodies are the Sikh helpline, Sikh Sanjog (Edinburgh), and the Sikh Community and Youth Services.
9. See e.g. http://www.rajkaregakhalsa.net/literature/For Schools and Teachers/Helping Sikh Children Dealing with Bullying.PDF
10. See http://www.sikhcoalition.org/documents/DOE_Report.2.24.2011.pdf
11. For further details, see 'Religious education in English schools: Non-statutory guidance 2010. http://media.education.gov.uk/assets/files/religious%20education%20guidance%20in%20schools.pdf

References

Abbas, T. 2002. A retrospective study of South Asian further education college students and their experiences of secondary school. *Cambridge Journal of Education* 32, no. 1: 73–90.
Alexander, C. 2006. Imagining the politics of BrAsian youth. In *A postcolonial people: South Asians in Britain*, ed. N. Ali, V. Kalra, and S. Sayyid, 258–71. London: C. Hurst.
Anwar, M. 2002. *Between cultures: Continuity and change in the lives of young Asians*. London: Routledge.
Ballard, R. 1994. *Desh Pardesh: The South Asian presence in Britain*. London: C. Hurst.
Baumann, G. 1996. *Contesting culture: Discourses of identity in multi-ethnic London*. Cambridge: Cambridge University Press.
Brah, A. 1996. *Cartographies of diaspora: Contesting identities*. London: Routledge.
Denscombe, M. 2007. *The good research guide: For small-scale social research projects*. 3rd ed. Milton Keynes: Open University Press.
Denton, M.L., and C. Smith. 2001. *Methodological issues and challenges in the study of American youth and religion*. Chapel Hill, NC: National Study of Youth and Religion (NSYR). Available at: http://www.youthandreligion.org/sites/youthandreligion.org/files/imported/docs/methods.pdf.
Drury, B. 1991. Sikh girls and the maintenance of an ethnic culture. *Journal of Ethnic and Migration Studies* 17, no. 3: 387–99.

Hadwen, D. 1995. Contemporary religious nurture among the Sikhs in Bradford. Unpublished MPhil. Thesis, University of Leeds, UK.

Hervieu-Léger, D. 1998. The transmission and formation of socioreligious identities in modernity: An analytical essay on the trajectories of identification. *International Sociology* 13, no. 2: 213–28.

Jackson, R., and E. Nesbitt. 1993. *Hindu children in Britain*. Stoke-on-Trent: Trentham Books.

Jackson, R., J. Ipgrave, M. Hayward, P. Hopkins, N. Fancourt, M. Robbins, L.J. Francis, and U. McKenna. 2010. *Materials used to teach about world religions in schools in England. Research Report DCSF-RR197*. Coventry: Warwick Religions and Education Research Unit, Institute of Education, University of Warwick. Available at: https://www.education.gov.uk/publications/standard/publicationdetail/page1/DCSF-RR197a.

James, A.G. 1974. *Sikh children in Britain*. Oxford: Oxford University Press.

Juergensmeyer, M. 1995. *Radhasoami reality: The logic of a modern faith*. Princeton, NJ: Princeton University Press.

Jhutti-Johal, J. 2011. *Sikhism today*. London: Continuum.

McLeod, W.H. 1984. *Textual sources for the study of Sikhism*. Manchester: Manchester University Press.

Nesbitt, E. 1999. Sikhs and proper Sikhs: Young British Sikhs' perceptions of their identity. In *Sikh identity: Continuity and change*, ed. P., Singh, and N.G. Barrier, 315–33. Delhi: Manohar.

Nesbitt, E. 2000. *The religious lives of Sikh children: A Coventry based study*. Leeds: Department of Theology and Religious Studies, University of Leeds.

Nesbitt, E. 2001. Representing faith traditions in religious education. In *The fourth r for the third millennium: Education in religion and values for the global future*, ed. L.J. Francis, J. Astley, and M. Robbins, 137–51. Dublin: Lindisfarne Books.

Nesbitt, E. 2004. *Intercultural education: Ethnographic and religious approaches*. Brighton & Portland: Sussex Academic Press.

Nesbitt, E. 2005. *Sikhism: A very short introduction*. Oxford: Oxford University Press.

Nesbitt, E. 2009. Research report: Studying the religious socialization of Sikh and 'mixed-faith' youth in Britain—Contexts and issues. *Journal of Religion in Europe* 2, no. 1: 37–57.

Nesbitt, E., and R. Jackson. 1995. Sikh children's use of 'God': Ethnographic fieldwork and religious education. *British Journal of Religious Education* 17, no. 2: 108–20.

Roberts, K.A., and D.A. Yamane. 2011. *Religion in sociological perspective*. 5th ed. Thousand Oaks, CA: Pine Forge Press.

Sanghera, S. 2008. *If you don't know me by now: A memoir of love, secrets and lies in Wolverhampton*. London: Penguin.

Sherkat, D. 2003. Religious socialization: Sources of influence and influences of agency. In *Handbook of the Sociology of Religion*, ed. M. Dillon, 151–63. Cambridge: Cambridge University Press.

Sinclair, J., and D. Milner. 2005. On being Jewish: A qualitative study of identity among British Jews in emerging adulthood. *Journal of Adolescent Research* 20, no. 1: 91–117.

Singh, J. 2010. Head first: Young British Sikhs, hair and the turban. *Journal of Contemporary Religion* 25, no. 2: 203–20.

Singh, J. 2011. Sikh-ing beliefs: British Sikh camps in the UK. In *Sikhs in Europe: Migration, identities and representations*, ed. K. Myrvold and K. Jacobsen, 253–77. Aldershot: Ashgate.

Singh, G., and D.S. Tatla. 2006. *Sikhs in Britain: The making of a community*. London: Zed Books.

Takhar, O.K. 2005. *Sikh identity: An exploration of groups among Sikhs*. Aldershot: Ashgate.

Vertovec, S. 2009. *Transnationalism*. London: Routledge.

Werbner, P. 2004. Theorising complex diasporas: Purity and hybridity in the South Asian public sphere in Britain. *Journal of Ethnic and Migration Studies* 30, no. 5: 895–911.

Zuckerman, P. 2003. *An invitation to the sociology of religion*. London: Routledge.

Christian youth work: teaching faith, filling churches or response to social need?

Naomi Stanton

YMCA George Williams College, London, UK

> This essay explores the purposes of Christian youth work. It responds to Collins-Mayo et al.'s contention that youth work is an ineffective medium for faith transmission and building faith communities and to their affirmation of the church's role in this. The analysis is based on research with young people aged between early teens and early 20s, who are engaging with Christian activities in Birmingham. The discussion highlights young people's experiences of rejection by their churches, demonstrating that community membership is not always on offer. A model is presented that illustrates how youth work can be, but is not exclusively, a connecting influence between young people and church.

Introduction

It is no secret that Christian churches are struggling to attract and retain young people. The current generation of young people has largely abandoned the church or never known it as a significant part of their lives. The 2005 church census revealed that many churches have no young people at all in their congregations: around half have no 11- to 14-year-olds attending and well over half have no 15- to 19-year-olds (Brierley 2006). In recent decades, the rapid growth of Christian youth work programmes has emerged as a response to this decline (Church of England 1996; Green 2006; Pimlott and Pimlott 2008). The development and professionalisation of Christian youth work has coincided with a decline in statutory youth work which has been subject to both funding cuts and a re-focus on targeted rather than universal provision (Davies 2010; Wylie 2010). The space left by statutory provision has partly been filled by Christian youth work and many young people today engage in church-based youth work programmes.

Davie (2007) uses the concept of 'vicarious religion' to explain people's relationship with the church in a largely non-practising society. Collins-Mayo et al. (2010) have used this to argue that young people today view the church as believing and practising on their behalf. However, they assert that without church attendance, young people do not become part of faith communities and thus the Christian narrative is not passed on as in previous generations. Collins-Mayo et al. claim that youth work is an ineffective replacement for the Christian education provided in church. Much of their criticism of youth work stems from its inclusive nature, in allowing young people to engage as much with the Christian teaching as they choose, without catering exclusively for those who do engage with this teaching.

This essay argues that young people's relationship with church is often more problematic than a vicarious affiliation suggests and it provides a critique of Collins-Mayo et al.'s findings. The discussion below explores how young people have rejected or felt rejected by their churches, demonstrating that a sense of community is often not on offer. Issues of young people's 'choice and voice' is explored in relation to church and Christian youth work, challenging the popular idea that young people engage with religion as consumers.

Christian youth workers face tensions regarding the purpose of their role. The title of this article points to different, and often competing, purposes: firstly, youth work as 'teaching faith' through explicit Christian study groups; secondly, youth work as 'filling churches' by keeping young people from church families engaged with church and in some cases bringing new young people into church; and, thirdly, 'meeting social need' through the provision of open-access and inclusive youth provision in local communities. My research has found that youth workers manage these tensions by dividing their work into different domains, which I label 'social club,' 'cell group,' and 'Sunday service'. The first domain is where they offer open-access youth provision to local communities, in response to the need they have identified for this provision. The second is small Bible-study groups for young people who want to explore Christianity. The third is an attempt to facilitate young people's integration into the wider church.

In my research, some youth workers stated that their church placed little value on their work in and with the community; there were instances where young people regularly meeting in cell groups was not valued if they did not also attend church on Sunday. As acknowledged, the different domains are designed to meet different needs. Collins-Mayo et al. (2010) situated their research in the 'social club' domain, but looked for evidence for the transmission of the Christian narrative. This is more the purpose of cell groups than the social provision for meeting community need. Collins-Mayo et al. conclude that this social provision is ineffective in raising Christian consciousness, but for most youth workers, this is not its purpose. The discrepancy between Collins-Mayo et al.'s research and my own is largely not one concerning findings but interpretation. Collins-Mayo et al. (2010, 70, 88) do acknowledge the role of social provision as a key element in supporting the faith journeys of those who also access more explicit Christian activities. They also recognize the role of cell groups in the creation of faith communities (61, 87), as also observed in my research. However, my criticism is that their conclusion – that youth work is not effective for those accessing only the social provision – is flawed because it looks for evidence of faith transmission in a setting where this is not an objective. This social domain is effective in providing a service to the local community, where open-access youth clubs have been largely abandoned by statutory providers. The different domains Christian youth workers operate in represent different purposes and together present a model of Christian youth work that allows young people to access one domain or move between domains. Young people negotiate how much they engage with social activities, Christian teaching, and the wider church. Thus they may contribute to one or all of the multiple purposes of Christian youth work.

The essay has three sections: the first explores the claims of Collins-Mayo et al. (2010) and engages with other literature that both supports and challenges their arguments. The second challenges Collins-Mayo et al.'s findings based on my research with young people (aged between early teens and early 20s) who engage with Christian activities across different denominations in Birmingham and their youth workers. The final section illustrates a model of Christian youth work that has emerged from my research; it demonstrates how Christian youth work can be a connecting influence between young people and church.

Engaging with the literature
Young people and church

Davie's concept of 'vicarious religion' is useful for exploring contemporary religion because rather than considering believing and belonging as separate or inextricably linked, it allows for the analysis of a more complex relationship between belief in a particular religion and affiliation to its institutional body. Davie (2007, 22) defines vicarious religion as:

> ... the notion of religion performed by an active minority but on behalf of a much larger number, who (implicitly at least) not only understand, but, quite clearly, approve of what the minority is doing.

She claims that while the majority do not attend church regularly, many still view the church as acting on their behalf in both belief and religious practice. Collins-Mayo et al. apply this to young people's relationship with church and echo the dominant assumption that Western modernisation and individualisation have undermined the authority of the institutional church (2010, 11). They argue that the Christian 'chain of memory' (Hervieu-Léger 2000) has been broken for the current generation, leaving them without the means to reach any level of 'Christian consciousness' (Collins-Mayo et al. 2010, 14, 86).

Davie's notion of 'vicarious religion' is a development of her concept of 'believing without belonging', which suggested that people who had chosen to disengage from church often retained a residual belief in Christianity (Davie 1994). Believing without belonging may be a precursor to vicarious religion: while one generation of a family may reject church but maintain belief, the next may feel less hostile towards church but has learned less of its belief and is thus more inclined to view it as believing and practising on its behalf. Collins-Mayo et al. argue this for the young people in their study (2010, 85). However, Davie's evidence for vicarious religion is centred on people turning to the church for moments of celebration and mourning, through the ceremonies for baptism, marriage, and funerals. These occasions are usually arranged by adults rather than young people and it could therefore be suggested that people only develop a vicarious affiliation with the church once they get married and/or have children. Prior to this, as observed by Collins-Mayo et al., they are largely indifferent, reserving reflection for moments of crisis (2010, 110).

Collins-Mayo et al. (2010, 52) argue that contemporary youth work programmes foster only a passing interest in Christianity among young people. They build on their previous idea of young people's 'happy midi-narrative' (Savage et al. 2006) according to which young people seek happiness and fulfilment only for the present and near future. Similarly, in the US, Smith and Denton (2005) have suggested a 'moralistic therapeutic deism' for young people. Based on the National Study of Youth Religion, they argue that young people engage enough with the religious institution to feel a certain moral satisfaction, but their commitment is not based on any real belief conviction or reflected in their lifestyle. Dean (2010, 14) outlines the main beliefs of 'moralistic therapeutic deism', which are informed by religious belief but not specific to Christian theology: (1) there is an omnipotent God who is the world's Creator; (2) this God wants people to be nice to each other; (3) happiness is the purpose of earthly life, which ties in with Savage et al.'s 'happy midi-narrative'; (4) God has no direct involvement in individuals' lives unless they face a crisis, which links with Davie's (1994) 'vicarious religion' and its application to the young people in Collins-Mayo et al.'s study; and (5) all good people (as opposed to just believers) will go to heaven. Dean (2010, 6) suggests that American young people are *open* but not *committed* to religion and argues that churches are largely to blame because they fail to transmit the historical traditions of Christianity (29). This chimes with Collins-Mayo et al.'s argument of the broken 'chain of memory'. However, rather than pointing to a lack of church engagement as the reason, Dean states that in a culture where many young people are affiliated to churches, the chain of memory is not passed on: congregations transmit a diluted theology that is unlikely to last into adulthood (2010, 3). Given this failing within the church, Dean suggests that rather than being the 'relativists we make them out to be', young people may simply have not been offered a faith that is meaningful enough to commit to (193).

However, where young people have engaged more fully with Christianity, they are doing so with zeal. Roy Crowne, former Director of the national organisation Youth 4 Christ (Clayton and Stanton 2008, 112), has stated that in recent years there has been a diminishing significance of faith in most people's lives, which has led to fervour rather than apathy among those who are Christians. Dean (2010, 194) found that a significant element in young people developing what she describes as 'consequential faith' was engagement in a faith community that held this faith. This supports Collins-Mayo et al.'s assertion that faith communities are essential to nurturing faith choices, but it also supports my own finding that many churches simply do not offer this.

Mazabane (2009, 72) distinguishes between children attending and actually belonging at church and criticises the separation of children and adults during services. Collins-Mayo et al. argue that young people need to be part of the church 'community of faith' in order to develop continued engagement. However, it is questionable whether the institutional church is an accessible forum for young people, as many youth work programmes have emerged as a response to the church's inability to engage them. Pimlott and Pimlott (2008, 26) confirm that young people are not always welcome in church, citing a Midlands church where outreach work brought in a large number of unaccompanied local young people, but the congregation complained about them being a disturbance until the relationships were severed and the young people no longer attended. The rigidity of church can be seen in the unquestioned persistence of Sunday morning as the time for worship across the globe. While Pimlott and Pimlott recognize the origins of Sunday as Sabbath in the time of Constantine (2008, 14) and Greene (2011) explains that holding services mid-morning was to fit with milking times, the concerns of Christian young people today do not match those of Roman leaders or dairy farmers. Sports leagues, television programmes, and other recreational activities, together with weekend lie-ins, compete for their time on Sunday morning.

Sutcliffe (2001, 223) asks whether the decline in young people's involvement in organised Christianity means that they reject the Gospel or the institutional church. Based on their findings from the National Study of Youth Religion in the US, Smith and Snell emphasise that early adulthood (ages 18–23) is a time of transition and exposure to social and cultural diversity that can interrupt religious commitment (2009, 34, 75–76, 280). Their research found that 'emerging adults' are the least religious group in America (281). They suggest that cultural relativism and a fear of criticising others' beliefs have led young adults to view morals and beliefs as subjectively defined, which correlates with the findings of Collins-Mayo et al. (2010). Smith and Snell conclude that for young adults who are considering religion, the stakes are raised and previous social support for such choices is removed (2009, 283).

Shepherd (2010, 149) suggests that one reason why religious socialisation fails is because young people have a choice to believe. Young people from church families are aware that continued belief and engagement are a personal choice (152). Thus, while Collins-Mayo et al. (2010, 97) criticise the emphasis on choice in youth work settings, Shepherd (2010, 152) argues that belonging to a youth group nurtures faith choices. However, the differences between these findings are not as big as they might appear. Collins-Mayo et al. recognize that young people value choice in youth work settings and are likely to reject 'institutional authority in determining truth' (2010, 60). They also recognize the role of youth groups in supporting the continued belief of churchgoing young people (110). They distinguish between youth work and youth ministry, with open-access youth provision (in which they situate their research) being the former and more specific teaching groups for churchgoers being the latter (24). Collins-Mayo et al. acknowledge Brierley's (2003) assertion that youth ministry is a special branch of youth work, thus the 'cell group' domain is in both the special and the wider category. As Shepherd's research focuses on youth ministry, the two studies are, at least to some extent, in agreement. However, Collins-Mayo et al. (2010) look at open-access social provision in terms of faith transmission, which is not its purpose, whereas Shepherd (2009, 2010) focuses on participation in groups where faith nurture is an objective. Collins-Mayo et al.'s approach to separate the domains into one for non-churchgoing and one for churchgoing young people is somewhat simplistic; indeed, they suggest that 'Youth ministry is work with young people who are already part of the Church' (2010, 24). My research has found that young people from non-church backgrounds do in some cases engage with Christian teaching groups (although not necessarily with church services) and that young people who have rejected the church sometimes continue to nurture their belief in youth 'ministry' settings. Thus Collins-Mayo et al.'s distinction is too clear-cut, given that my research illustrates that 'youth ministry is [*also*] work with young people who are [*not yet* or *no longer*] part of the Church'. Youth ministry is not an entirely isolated domain from open-access 'social club' youth work but part of the youth workers' interconnected provision.

Shepherd (2009, 230–231) emphasises that successful youth groups are social, participatory, relational, experiential, and a place where faith is connected to real life. This is what the wider church setting often lacks for young people and why faith communities may be more easily nurtured in youth settings than in church services. Emery-Wright (2008) acknowledges the need for young people's participation in church and emphasises three key roles for young people for their engagement in collective worship in church: young people as theologians, interpreters, and liturgists, by relating scripture and tradition to contemporary life and culture, engaging in dialogue and finding a faith language that is relevant today, and encouraging contemporary expressions of worship, not just outdated traditions (5–25). Emery-Wright acknowledges that the traditional style of church as leader and followers is not effective in engaging young people and suggests a model of facilitator and active participants. He shows young people's frustration with the disconnection of church from real life.

While recent research emphasises that young people's engagement is often based on relationships and participation, these are not new ideas. Since the dawn of child-centred learning over a century ago, those writing about Sunday School, Christian Education, and Christian nurture have acknowledged these aspects of engagement with children and young people. They have simply never been widely implemented in churches (see Stanton 2011; Sutcliffe 2001).

The role of youth work

Collins-Mayo et al. (2010, 19; 33) use the notion of 'immanent faith' to represent the influences young people draw on in determining and validating belief in an individualistic society. They describe a 'secular trinity' of family, friends, and self and suggest that young people largely define their own beliefs, but look to others for validating them. They argue that youth work allows for and cements the process of validating self-defined belief, which thus fails to transmit the Christian narrative and tradition they assert as essential to faith building (61). They find fault with the liberalism of youth work and methods of informal education and believe its promotion of choice over 'truth' to be its downfall. They acknowledge young people's resistance to imposed religion, yet state that the 'downside' of giving young people a choice to participate in religious teaching is that 'many of the young people simply chose not to join in' (57–8). However, youth workers do not *give* choice – young people *have* choice; youth workers provide space for them to explore this within the 'cell group' domain. Collins-Mayo et al. found that the infrequent churchgoers in their study accessed youth clubs primarily to socialise rather than to engage with religion and that they viewed it as a place which enhanced their sense of belonging and identity (58). This reflects the purpose of the 'social club' domain and the youth workers' response to young people's self-identified needs should be appreciated, not exploited. Brierley (2003) celebrates the use of democratic methods of informal education in youth ministry: values such as equality of opportunity, voluntary participation, teaching through discussion, and promoting social justice are intrinsic values of Christian youth work; he suggests that Jesus himself used such methods while rejecting the religious institutions of his day (95). Collins-Mayo et al. state that young people seek an 'authenticity' that can only be found in situations where Christian teaching is explicit (2010, 27), but acknowledge that many young people can observe how their youth workers' behaviour and motivations are informed by faith.

Collins-Mayo et al. recognize that the emergence and growth of professional Christian youth work over recent decades occurred in response to the concerns of churchgoing parents who wanted to keep their children in church (2010, 23). However, a key aspect of youth work is starting where young people are – with their concerns and interests (Jeffs and Smith 2005). Thus, by employing professional youth workers, churches acquired individuals who were concerned with the needs of young people in their communities that extended beyond the church's definition of their spiritual need or even the need to fill the church. Ward's (1997) model of 'inside out' and 'outside in' youth work captures this tension. The former starts with the young people within the church and focuses on faith transmission, whereas the latter aims to engage young people outside the church, often with the aim of drawing them into church in some way. My research has found that most church-based youth workers employ both approaches. Collins-Mayo et al. (2010, 22) recognize that their research focused on the 'outside in' settings. Thus the starting point was likely to be more social than educative.

For Kandiah (2012), the reason why youth work has not been effective in stemming the decline of young people's church attendance is that the approach is not embraced by the whole church. He emphasises how churches have largely left engaging with young people to the youth workers and that they need to be 'desegregated' and become 'culturally relevant' to young people (15). For many of the young people in my research, their only formative relationship with an adult in church was their youth worker. However, youth workers attempted to integrate young people in the wider church through the Sunday service domain.

Young people as consumers

Many sociologists of religion chart a move from obligation to consumption in people's engagement with religion (Collins-Mayo et al. 2010; Davie 2007; Dunlop and Ward 2011). They suggest that young people's attitude to religion is 'what I can I get from this?'. Collins-Mayo et al. claim the church to be the 'antidote to individualisation' (2010, 94). However, consumerism is neither new nor incompatible with organised religion which thrives in the US where it operates as an 'open market' (Davie 2002). According to Luhr (2009, 24), Evangelicals have embraced consumer culture since the 1960s for engaging with young people, particularly through the promotion of Christian rock music, self-expression, and rebellion, but Dean (2010, 5) argues that a 'consumer-driven therapeutic individualism' has replaced a faith based on self-giving love.

While the literature mainly portrays a consumerist attitude towards religion, social action plays a large part in Christian youth work programmes (Pimlott and Pimlott 2008; Clayton and Stanton 2008). Kandiah (2012, 15) recognizes young people's desire to participate rather than just consume, stating that they are more likely to stay in church when given the 'opportunity to serve'. Emery-Wright (2008, 26) argues that young people in church need to not be 'sidelined as observers and consumers of something that might not feel authentic to them'. He emphasises their desire to 'explore and express their beliefs' in relation to their own culture and challenges 'the popular yet ineffective method of discipleship that tells participants what to think and do and how to behave' (2008, 26). Emery-Wright asserts that being involved rather than being consumers is how young people develop an authentic and meaningful faith identity. My research supports that young people's engagement with Christianity is a two-way process: their self-identified needs are met and they find ways to 'give something back'.

My research
Methods and sample

My research aimed to gather young people's narratives of their experiences, not to define beforehand what is significant in a list of pre-set questions. Thus a research method fitting this objective was chosen. Narrative inquiry technique was employed, involving open-ended interviews in which interviewees structure and control the conversation beyond an initial theme, with clarifying follow-up questions by the researcher when participants have presented their 'stories' (Bell 2005). My subsidiary questions were thus prompted by the young people's narratives rather than my questions shaping them. Three broad questions guided the interviews:

(1) how they came to be involved in Christianity and stayed involved;
(2) current experiences within churches and youth groups they attended;
(3) their relationship with the Christian organisation and perceptions of the wider church, particularly when they only accessed youth activities.

Youth workers were asked about their backgrounds, motivations, awareness of and involvement in institutional agendas, and their understanding of the relationship between youth groups and wider church. The interviews were analysed by coding and identifying themes in the transcripts (Braun and Clarke 2006).

The research was based in Birmingham. Young people who engage with Christianity (and their youth workers) were identified through youth groups and churches, resulting in an opportunity sample. I went where people were willing to be involved in the research, often relying on verbal recommendations from youth workers. I made no attempt to have a representative sample beyond ensuring access to a range of main Christian denominations. Interviews with 42 people took place, including 34 young people and eight youth workers. The denominations represented are Anglican, Methodist, Baptist, United Reformed, Catholic, Pentecostal, and a black majority church of no specified denomination. The interviewees belonged to eight different church-based groups. The young people were between 13 and 21 years old: seven between 13 and 17, 22 between 16 and 18, and five between 19 and 21. Regarding gender, 21 were male, 13 female; the gender balance was affected by: two groups being Boys' Brigades, young people's willingness to take part, and permission from adults. Three of the groups accessed had significant numbers of young people from minority ethnic backgrounds, who are represented within the sample. Two of the eight youth workers were female, six male; five were volunteers, three were employed by their churches.

Most of the youth workers had regular contact with non-churchgoing young people through open-access youth activities. The research involved both churchgoing and non-churchgoing young people. Around one third of the interviewees (12 of 34) were not brought up in churchgoing families; of these, half regularly attended church services at the time of the interview. Of those who regularly attended church, from both churchgoing and non-churchgoing families, many tended to attend monthly rather than weekly. Around a third of those from churchgoing families had only one parent attending church regularly. All the names used are pseudonyms.

Findings

The key themes emerging from this research that have implications for young people's engagement with Christianity are:

- the importance of relationships and social belonging for engagement;
- tensions between young people/youth workers and their churches;
- young people's desire to express 'choice' and 'voice.'

The findings correspond with those by Collins-Mayo et al. (2010) in that self, family, and friends influence young people's faith choices. Parental expectation and social belonging are the two most dominant reasons for young people's engagement. Lucy, aged 13, stated that her main reason for attending church was 'because my parents tell me to'. John, aged 18, who had moved to England with his adoptive mother after spending his early childhood in an orphanage in Africa, explained how the words of a nun with whom he had had a parent–child relationship encouraged him to stay involved:

> [T]here was an Italian nun who was pretty much my mum; she looked after me and I still speak to her now and she said to me before I came over, 'Don't lose your faith; carry on with church.' So that stuck with me and every time I'm down I remember that.

Social belonging was the most significant theme, occurring in most of the young people's narratives about their engagement with Christian youth activities. For the non-churchgoing young people, it was their primary reason for engaging.

A broken community?

Some of the youth workers expressed frustration about their efforts to support young people accessing church. Liam explained that church was sometimes reluctant to welcome young people:

> I've done it myself where I'm in a prayer meeting and some crackhead comes in and you're like 'I don't want you in here' – I'm just saying it in my head, but that goes on in churches. We think 'we don't want rowdy teenagers in here', but that's exactly what we do need.

Bill recognized that his church's traditions and rituals could be barriers to community engagement:

> [This church] is in a time warp, some of the sung responses and things like that are very, very high church ... and I think that they should be reaching out into our community a lot better than what they are and not portraying themselves as this high Anglican eunuch.

Many young people felt devalued or rejected by their churches. Tracey, aged 20, explained what happened when she tried to host a meeting of her regional Youth Executive at her home church:

> When we used to host the meetings at everyone's church, they asked me to host it the once ... Everybody else has got really friendly people who they can approach for funding or to ask them to run a meeting and I went to [the keyholder] and she was thinking about charging me for the rent of the room... And that's what I mean, it's like the older people there aren't in tune with it... [T]hat meeting never happened, but it's just the difficulties I face with it; I'm just like, why should I bother with it?

Tracey thus did not feel valued by her church and no longer attended regularly, although she was still fully engaged with the Youth Executive. John, mentioned above, did not feel accepted by his own church and its youth group:

> I'm not a member of the youth group over there, because I don't know them as much and I feel like an outcast because the church is more white... I didn't feel accepted in the Church ... because people kept themselves to themselves, which was another thing I found hard to get over ...'cos in Africa, where I'm from, everyone speaks to each other and everyone is friendly and ... knows everything about each other... [T]hey say there's a community, but it's not... And that definitely knocked me as well because churches are meant to be communities.

Given the multicultural nature of Birmingham's population, the white and middle-class character of most of the traditional churches in this study is notable. People from other backgrounds engage with Christianity, just not generally in these settings. The three churches which had significant numbers of young people from ethnic minority backgrounds were the least traditional settings. Perhaps Bill referring to his church as a 'high Anglican eunuch' emphasises the barriers that traditional churches present for those from diverse backgrounds. Hence John's criticism of the lack of community in his church. After having stayed away from church for a time, he found the sense of belonging he sought in the youth group of another church.

My research demonstrates that many churches are not accessible to young people. The social aspect of engagement is a major concern for those who seek a sense of belonging in the activities they access. While Christian youth workers often encourage a relationship between young people and church, this is only achieved where both church and youth workers support this. Some young people who engaged with church had (literally) had doors closed on them, as Tracey's request for a meeting room shows. Her engagement with Christianity might have discontinued altogether, had she not been involved in the Youth Executive, where she did feel part of a community. Many young people found a sense of belonging in their youth groups which they did not find in church. For those who engaged with the Christian teaching on offer, their youth groups appeared to become their 'faith community'.

Collins-Mayo et al. observed a vicarious affiliation to the youth worker among some young people (2010, 67). Engagement with Christian youth work and developing faith communities are very much based on relationships. Tracey's case illustrates the importance of this to youth work: her attendance at her home church and its youth group tailed off when her youth worker moved to Canada.

Positive experiences of church

The relationship between young people and their churches is complex. It is certainly not entirely negative. That many young people persist in engaging with church despite difficulties suggests that something keeps them connected. However, as discussed below, it is often when young people outgrow the youth work that their engagement with church breaks down. Where the social and relational exist in young people's relationships with the wider church, engagement is more sustained. Some youth workers emphasised positive relationships between church and youth work. This applied in the two least traditional settings and in one of the more institutional churches. Barry explained how his congregation viewed its young people:

> They love the young people ... they love it when they've come back from a youth camp and they get up and they'll tell a little story ... and they love the fact that most of the people get baptised at 15, 16, yeah, even 14/13-year-olds saying that 'God did this in my life'... And likewise I think the young people integrate well ... they interact really well.

Another youth worker talked about the youth group's connection to the wider church, stating that 'They feel part of church, because sometimes youth groups can be on a fringe... I think that the nice thing here is that they incorporate it a lot more.'

The young people in the two evangelical churches had the most positive experiences compared to those in other settings. Nancy, aged 18, felt accepted in her congregation, despite facing difficulties in other social contexts:

> Autism is very, very isolating. I've also had a lot of eating disorders as well and that's been isolating... If I've had a difficult day at college or I get bullied or something, then I can just come in here and know that no one's going to treat me differently, because there are people [who] have been in prison and they admit that and they know they won't get judged here and it's just the faith and just the Christian family, in general, here is just so strong.

Nina's (age 19) narrative demonstrates how belonging and belief go hand in hand in her engagement with church:

> I was in my first year of college, but there were three girls ... and we just clicked, so I spent a lot of time with them... Basically, Christianity was like the soul – it was the core of them really. It was something they were passionate about and that was something that I'd never seen before... So one day I said to her, I said, 'what made you become a Christian?' and she said, 'I'll show you.' So she brought me here... First time I came I wasn't interested, I was like 'uh uh!' ... it was like too friendly because you could tell people were really trying... But I came again on Sunday and ... I can't explain what it was, to be fair, but I think the Pastor was preaching about something that was going on in my life. And that really got me thinking. Then when I left church, the advice that he gave while preaching, I did it and the situation that I was in, which was like two years I was in that same situation, that day it just got solved. And that got me believing in God and then I started praying and reading my Bible... And then church is really like a family, so I couldn't leave, even if I wanted to, it just wouldn't happen.

Nina continued that, having lived in different foster homes and in a hostel, she found a 'family' through her church as she now lives with adults she met there. These positive experiences accentuate the significance of the relational aspect of young people's engagement with church. For those who felt welcomed and supported, Christianity felt more authentic than for those who did not feel valued.

Choice and voice

Recognizing young people's choice and promoting their voice are key elements in thriving youth work settings. Adam, aged 14, praised the opportunity to discuss everyone's opinions of Christianity, rather than being 'talked at':

> [W]e'll have a session where we discuss something from the Bible or discuss a topic about Jesus' life or something going on in the world and we all offer opinions, and it's good to hear different opinions.

Michael, a volunteer youth worker, explained that he understood Christian teaching as being one of the choices for young people: 'If you don't talk to them about it, someone else will; it's about inputting into the decision-making process, not deciding for them.' Lucy experienced great frustration until her church employed a youth worker, because her ideas for activities were often disregarded. The elders needed to discuss them at meetings over a long period, not getting back to her or telling her they were 'leaving them with God'. She felt she had more voice since the youth worker had been appointed.

Many young people found the 'authenticity' they sought in the youth worker, not in church. Many said they wanted to become youth workers; rarely did they aspire to be church leaders. The only one was Daniel who became a church deacon at the age of 20; his objective in this role was to help bridge the gap between church and young people.

The transition to adult church

While youth work is a supporting influence in accessing church for many young people in this study, their long-term involvement is not secured. My research involved older, and in some cases more fully engaged, young people than that by Collins-Mayo et al. (2010); the interviewees indicated anxiety about the impending transition to adult church. Many simply did not consider leaving the youth activities. Luke, aged 20, who had just moved into university halls, intended to travel back across the city for his youth group but not for church services. Claire, aged 19, explained why she had stopped attending church but still attended youth work activities:

> It was something that I have been part of since this started. And it's a lot more to do with people of my age and I enjoy doing more of this than sitting in a church service necessarily. I would rather go and talk to people and be more active and do things. I think it's a bit strange, the way the local church's ministers change and different people come and go... It seems to me, from my church, it's slightly less consistent than this is in a way.

Youth workers expressed concern about young people's transition into church – Theresa stated that it simply did not happen and Bill said that it happened rarely: during 30 years of youth work, 'Maybe three out of the endless amounts of kids that I've put through [confirmation], girls and boys, actually still go to church.' Some youth workers had developed ways to integrate young people with church adults. For example, when asked how the wider church viewed young people, Simon, aged 14, replied:

> I like to think the older people are proud of us because they like to see that we're growing in God... Adults in the church do talk to us; they don't shy away from us.

Simon's youth worker runs a programme that involves a range of activities, including social evenings, small teaching groups, and integration with adult services. There is no pressure on the young people to move through these phases. While the social activities are attended by a large number of local young people, the weekday 'cell group' attracts only some – those who want to learn more about Christianity. On most Sundays, there is a youth service running in parallel to the morning service, but the young people socialise with the congregation afterwards. They are also encouraged to attend the informal all-age evening service and many do. They get involved in church life, with some of them in the worship band, for example. In settings where youth workers had positive relationships with the church, young people were less anxious about the transition to adult church.

Interviews with older young people who had moved away from their home churches to attend university revealed that not finding a sense of community in the new churches was an issue, particularly for those from more traditional denominations. Amanda and Tim had both grown up in small traditional churches and, after moving away to university, attempted to integrate in churches of their affiliation rather than joining the student Christian groups which tended to be evangelical. However, the churches they attended in their university towns had no people of their age and they thus did not feel they belonged; this affected their motivation to attend regularly. Both retained a connection with the Youth Executive they served on, travelling back to their home region for meetings and fellowship. Several youth workers were concerned that moving to university was a factor in disconnecting young people from Christianity.

Social needs, consumerism, and social action

For some youth workers, church membership was not the primary concern of the youth activities they offered. Liam stated:

> It doesn't matter about this building. They can take what they've learned into later life ... it's about each individual and what they take away from this.

This causes tensions when youth workers are employed by churches. Some felt that their churches did not understand the purpose of the social aspect of their work if the young people were not integrated into church. However, as pointed out earlier, starting 'where young people are' is a key principle of youth work.

In a case study carried out in the US as part of my research, a church youth worker explained that her church valued the social aspect of her work so much that it built its own youth centre:

> There was a study done through the high school ... Families mentioned that they wanted a place where their children could hang out... There is a lot of families that are two-income families ... and they noticed a few years back a significant increase in drug use and alcohol use amongst young people... And then our church said, 'What if we were to build a youth space ... that anyone could come to and hang out in, not specifically, overtly Christian, it's just a safe place to be? What if we could offer that to our community?'

This highlights church-based youth work as a service to the community; the focus on meeting community needs emphasises a sense of purpose in engaging young people who may not become church attenders but in meeting identifiable social needs. The youth worker was quite clear about separating the various aspects, explaining that the youth centre did not contain Christian paraphernalia and that the social activities did not refer to Christian teaching. However, even such a seemingly ideal setting was not without tension: the youth worker mentioned difficulties in integrating churchgoing and non-churchgoing young people, with some churchgoing parents not allowing their children to attend the youth club for fear of exposing them to secular music and related influences.

The youth workers in my research viewed young people's engagement as being two-sided. Theresa expressed her frustration about her church's attitude which was that the young people should serve it, not the other way round:

> I don't think they're taking responsibility for the fact that they need to meet the needs of the young people. They don't think twice about the young people meeting their needs.

Particularly noteworthy is the number of young people engaged in Christian youth work programmes who become leaders or express their intention to become one. All the young people interviewed were involved in some social action or fundraising or volunteer activity through their youth work programmes. Maria outlined her voluntary work:

> On Sundays I steward, I'm a steward at church… On Sunday afternoons I do a dance class for the younger children… And then on the weekdays I work for a magazine and a website … I work for them as a journalist… [W]e put on events … so I'm part of the concert and the street team as well… I've tried to make sure that me being a Christian is not just for myself.

This reinforces assertions in the literature discussed earlier about young people's desire to participate. Those most engaged with church were in settings where this was possible. Young people in evangelical churches tended to have more opportunities through worship bands, stewarding, and children's activities. In more traditional denominations, roles tended to be more formal, but young people were involved in children's activities and on rotas for serving or reading in services. One young person's monthly attendance was determined by the serving rota. Some young people wanted to attend church more regularly than they managed to motivate themselves to.

Therefore, young people who choose to engage with Christianity today use their autonomy to do more than just consume – they are opting to 'give back'. The nurturing of choice, voice, and community is significant in this, but where this is lost in the transition to adult church, young people's enthusiasm is likely to wane. Many do not feel valued by their churches and disconnect as they reach adulthood. Churches themselves arguably act like consumers when they employ youth workers but do not engage in establishing relationships with young people beyond this economic investment.

A model for Christian youth work

A model of youth work emerges from my research that allows young people to engage in social activities and/or Christian teaching. Church-employed youth workers engage with young people from both church and non-church backgrounds. The main arena for initial engagement is through open-access social activities which are the most widely attended sessions, as they usually do not include explicitly Christian teaching. This is the Domain 1 in the model. The second is small group teaching, with sessions attended by fewer young people, involving Bible study and discussion-based Christian teaching, often with time for informal social interaction. My research has found no pressure for young people to engage in these sessions; they are mainly attended by young people from church families. Many young people access only Domain 1 and do so long-term. Domain 3 is church services: youth workers often provide an alternative to the sermon for young people. They also support young people's attendance of adult services. Young people either move through the model's domains (from social activities to teaching or from Sunday services to weekday activities) or remain in one domain (see Figure 1). Non-churchgoers tend to begin in Domain 1, while churchgoers start in Domain 3.

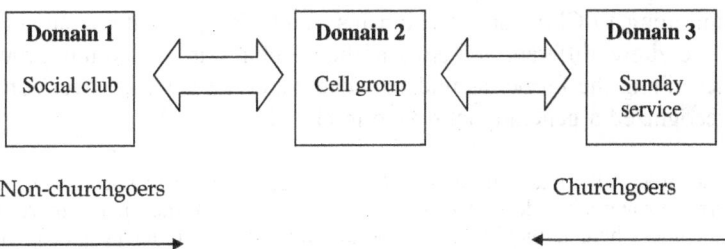

Figure 1. The three-domain model of Christian youth work.

Non-churchgoers who access the 'social club' first may move through the domains as their engagement continues, with some moving to the 'cell group' if they become interested in Christian teaching and some moving from there to attending church. By conducting their research entirely with infrequent churchgoers in the 'social club' setting, Collins-Mayo et al. (2010) cut themselves off from those who had chosen to become more engaged with Christianity. By focusing on one dimension of the social settings, they argue that youth work is ineffective in teaching the Christian narrative.

In my research, Matthew (aged 18) demonstrated how young people can move from the social activities of Domain 1 to Christian teaching in Domain 2 and then to engagement with the wider church through the development of social and faith communities in the youth work settings. He became involved with his youth group when he met the youth worker one night. He already knew her, as she worked in a school he used to attend. She invited him to one of the social evenings:

> I went along and then she told me about Friday night and then she told me about the Tuesday nights and then she eventually came on to the Wednesday group, which is the Bible group. And basically, I said, I was a bit apprehensive about coming ... but then I decided definitely to go and it was probably one of the best decisions of my life.

Matthew explained that the discussion-based approach helped him overcome his apprehension:

> I was thinking, 'Well, I haven't got a faith, so to go through, it would be weird because everybody will be talking about their faith and I won't be able to talk about it'.... But then there was an argument.' ... 'Go along, see what it's like because what [the youth worker] had said to me is that it's about the Bible and it was about being a Christian, that kind of thing ... in everyday life and having debates about it. And one thing for me is I love a good debate ... Because I just love that one person says one thing and then you say something and it just goes back and forth, back and forth ... that kind of drew me in and made me think, 'Well, I might enjoy it', and so I thought, 'Do you know what, I'm gonna give it a go.'

Matthew's reason for continuing with the Bible group was due to the sense of belonging he felt:

> As soon as I walked through those doors, it was like a sense of being welcomed. A sense of love that I felt was just 'Okay, I belong here' and it was that that initially made me keep on coming every week.

Since committing to Christianity within his youth group, Matthew attended church services. He drew differences between the teaching in the youth group and at church, describing the former as understandable and the latter as 'over-complicated'. He also recognized a generational divide in church:

> It does seem as if it's like you've got the young people and then you've got the adults ... There's always a divide... And it's like the adults think they know more than the young people when, if they'd go to talk to some of the young people, then they'd understand that they do know quite a lot.

Matthew's experience challenges Collins-Mayo et al.'s (2010) claim that youth work is ineffective in raising Christian consciousness, as many young people explore their faith through the youth work programmes they attend rather than through church. Many of those in Matthew's youth group did not attend church regularly, despite actively engaging in Christian teaching on a weekday evening. Another young person, Danni, aged 14, had attended church with her mother as a child, but had ceased attendance as a teenager because her hockey league took place on Sunday mornings. However, through engagement with her youth group, she maintained her connection with Christianity. In the first of two interviews with her, the reasons she gave for attending her group were largely social. Her attitude to faith reflected the indifference observed by Collins-Mayo et al.: she described herself as 'midway between a Christian and an Atheist'. Six months later, although still not attending church, she said that her faith had been renewed and that she was definitely a Christian.

When Christian youth work is viewed through the three-domain model, the links between youth club and church are clearer, as seen in the examples above. As Collins-Mayo et al. state, the Christian 'chain of memory' is broken for the current generation, but youth work within the model can create a new link in this chain. My research clearly shows that even where church relations are weak, many young people and their youth workers are establishing Christian communities within Domain 2 of the model. Although Collins-Mayo et al. (2010) criticise the lack of faith community in Domain 1, my research has found that the social community fostered in this setting is extremely significant for young people and for some it is the precursor to engaging with a faith community in Domain 2.

The determining factors for engaging with the domains, and for moving between them, have been shown in the research presented above. Choice and voice were found to be significant in young people's engagement with youth work programmes, in both social and spiritual domains. However, there is little room for autonomy and participation in church service structures, so engagement with Domain 3 is more problematic. In Matthew's case, the 'voice' factor was highly significant in his choice to engage with Domain 2, as he enjoyed discussion and debate. However, his sense of belonging was the significant factor in his continued engagement in Domain 2. His sense of acceptance did not extend to his experience of church in Domain 3. His case demonstrates that not just church structures inhibit young people's engagement with church services, but also, perhaps more significantly, church attitudes. Relationships and belonging were important features in all the young people's narratives. Relationships enable the formation of both social and faith communities. Acceptance into a social community in Domain 1 is likely to be a significant factor for young people to choose engagement with a faith community by moving into Domain 2. This certainly appeared to be the case with Matthew.

The positive examples of engagement with church presented here demonstrate that belief and belonging are interlinked. For Nancy and Nina, acceptance into the church community offered an authenticity that nurtured their faith choices. That many young people did not find acceptance or authenticity in their churches is the most significant reason why engagement with Domain 3 broke down. Thus the factors of choice, voice, relationships, and belonging are key elements in engagement with and movement between the domains. These factors are more supported in Domain 1 and 2, within the youth work provision. Relationships with Domain 3 remain problematic and often break down when young people outgrow the activities in Domain 1 and 2. Churches that consider their youth work programmes redundant if young people do not access church or that do not see value in other domains have a short-sighted view of youth work and the wider church's responsibility for young people's continued engagement with church.

My research cannot say how many people 'progress' through the model nor does it seek to do this. However, it demonstrates that while youth workers operate in different domains for different purposes, the domains are not isolated from each other, with many young people moving between them. Youth workers facilitate, but young people determine this process. Crucially, where movement does not occur, engagement is not meaningless because each domain has value in its own right – meeting community need in Domain 1, nurturing faith communities in Domain 2, the church's desire to see young people in church in Domain 3.

Concluding remarks

Many churches appear more concerned about filling pews on Sunday morning with a new generation of members than about looking for more appropriate and empowering ways of engaging young people. Young people's engagement with religion is a process of critical negotiation rather than an imposed obligation. Christian youth workers to some extent foster a participatory process, based on autonomous relationships between young people and church, where there is space to exercise both choice and voice. Youth workers recognize that the young people they engage are more than idle consumers and successfully provide opportunities to get them involved. The transition to adult church, however, is not smooth and it is at this point that many disengage. The traditional structure of services is not accessible or relevant to young people and thus does not foster community and belonging. Youth workers view their role as both meeting community needs and serving church interests – a balance between delivering universal and inclusive youth provision and Christian teaching. Collins-Mayo et al. (2010) largely ignore the social purpose of youth work and focus on youth work regarding faith transmission and facilitating young people's entry into church communities. Their and my interpretations differ in this area – hence a tension in our views of the purposes of Christian youth work, despite many of our research findings being comparable. While the key difference could be summarised with the question whether Christian youth work exists to meet church or community needs, recent research has found that churches that actively seek to respond to social needs in their community are more likely to grow (Christian Research 2012, 5).

References
Bell, J. 2005. *Doing your research project*. 4th ed. Maidenhead: The Open University Press.

Braun, V., and V. Clarke. 2006. Using thematic analysis in psychology. *Qualitative Research in Psychology* 3, no. 2: 77–101.
Brierley, D. 2003. *Joined up: An introduction to youthwork and ministry.* Carlisle: Spring Harvest Publishing/Authentic Lifestyle.
Brierley, P. 2006. *Pulling out of the nosedive: A contemporary picture of churchgoing.* London: Christian Research.
Church of England. 1996. *Youth a part: Young people and the Church.* London: Church House Publishing.
Christian Research 2012. A national survey of Church-based action to tackle poverty. *Quadrant* 31: 5.
Clayton, M.-A., and N. Stanton. 2008. The changing world's view of Christian youthwork. *Youth & Policy* 100: 109–28.
Collins-Mayo, S., B. Mayo, S. Nash, and C. Cocksworth. 2010. *The faith of generation Y.* London: Church House Publishing.
Davie, G. 1994. *Religion in Britain since 1945: Believing without belonging.* Oxford: Blackwell.
Davie, G. 2002. *Europe: The exceptional case (parameters of faith in the modern world).* London: Darton, Longman and Todd.
Davie, G. 2007. Vicarious religion: A methodological challenge. In *Everyday religion: Observing modern religious lives*, ed. N.T. Ammerman, 21–36. New York: Oxford University Press.
Davies, B. 2010. Straws in the wind: The state of youthwork in a changing policy environment. *Youth & Policy* 105: 9–36.
Dean, K.C. 2010. *Almost Christian.* New York: Oxford University Press.
Dunlop, S., and P. Ward. 2011. Migration and visual culture: A theological exploration of identity, Catholic imagery and popular culture among Polish young people. Paper presented to day seminar at King's College London, 25 January 2011.
Emery-Wright, S. 2008. *Empowering young people in Church.* Cambridge: Grove.
Green, M. 2006. *A journey of discovery: Spirituality and spiritual development in youth work.* Leicester: The National Youth Agency.
Greene, M. 2011. *Questions of Sunday sport.* London: The London institute for Contemporary Christianity.
Hervieu-Léger, D.L. 2000. *Religion as a chain of memory* (Trans. S. Lee). Cambridge: Polity Press/Blackwell.
Jeffs, T., and M.K. Smith. 2005. *Informal education: Conversation, democracy and learning.* Rev. ed. Nottingham: Educational Heretics Press.
Kandiah, K. 2012. It takes a whole church to raise a child. *Youthwork* 2, no. 15: 14–6.
Luhr, E. 2009. *Witnessing suburbia.* Berkeley, CA: University of California Press.
Mazabane, N. 2009. God welcomes children fully into the family of faith. *Children Matter* 1: 65–74.
Pimlott, J., and N. Pimlott. 2008. *Youthwork after Christendom.* Milton, Keynes: Paternoster.
Savage, S., S. Collins-Mayo, B. Mayo, and G. Cray. 2006. *Making sense of generation Y: The worldview of 15–25 year olds.* London: Church House Publishing.
Shepherd, N. 2009. Trying to be Christian: A qualitative study of young people's participation in two youth ministry projects. PhD thesis, King's College London, UK.
Shepherd, N. 2010. Religious socialisation and a reflexive habitus: Christian youth groups as sites for identity work. In *Religion and youth*, ed. S. Collins-Mayo and P. Dandelion, 149–56. Farnham, Surrey: Ashgate.
Smith, C., and M.L. Denton. 2005. *Soul searching: The religious and spiritual lives of American teenagers.* New York: Oxford University Press.
Smith, C., and P. Snell. 2009. *Souls in transition.* New York, NY: Oxford University Press.
Stanton, N. 2011. From Raikes' revolution to rigid institution: Sunday schools in twentieth century England. In *Reflecting on the past: Essays in the history of youth and community work*, ed. R. Gilchrist, T. Hodgson, T. Jeffs, J. Spence, N. Stanton, and J. Walker, 71–91. Lyme, Regis: Russell House.
Sutcliffe, J., ed. 2001. *Tuesday's child: A reader for Christian educators.* Birmingham: Christian Education Publications.
Ward, P. 1997. *Youthwork and the mission of God.* London: SPCK.
Wylie, T. 2010. Youthwork in a cold climate. *Youth & Policy* 105: 1–8.

Religious young adults recounting the past: narrating sexual and religious cultures in school

Sarah-Jane Page[a] and Andrew Kam-Tuck Yip[b]

[a]School of Languages and Social Sciences, Aston University, Birmingham, UK; [b]School of Sociology and Social Policy, University of Nottingham, Nottingham, UK

> Schooling can be a pivotal time in young people's formative experience when identities are negotiated and forged. However, contradictory dominant cultures can operate within the school context, making it very challenging for individuals to negotiate their religious and sexual identities within a sexualised and heteronormative space. This essay draws on interview data relating to 18- to 25-year-olds of diverse religious faiths in the UK, who recounted their secondary schooling experiences, and focuses on the formal and informal ways in which the school was constituted in relation to religion and sexuality.

Introduction

Schooling experiences can have far-reaching implications on an individual's life, having potential resonance many years later (Taylor 2007). The school can be a site of tension and conflict, especially if a student is stigmatised as different from others, for instance, in terms of ethnicity, sexual orientation or religion (Wilkinson and Pearson 2009). The school is a significant space for the production of identities, encapsulating a predominant normative universe for adolescents. In other words, their identity work is inextricably intertwined with school cultures. The present study, which focused on young adults from six different religious traditions, demonstrates that the school is indeed a salient space in which negotiations about sexuality and religion occur, significantly informing young people's formative experiences. For the young adults in the study, such negotiations, particularly in relation to sexuality, were undertaken at a time of fervent political and educational changes – most notably the abolition of Section 28 for England and Wales in 2003 (in Scotland, Section 2a was abolished in 2000), which had previously legislated that a local authority could not 'promote' homosexuality as a 'pretend' family relationship (Weeks 2007). This led to much confusion among teachers in approaching sex education and had an impact on how lesbian, gay, and bisexual (LGB) students were supported in the school context (Epstein, O'Flynn, and Telford 2003; Warwick, Aggleton, and Douglas 2001).

Massey has theorised 'space' as constituted by multiple trajectories based on interaction; it is not static – rather, 'it is always in the process of being made'

(2005, 9). The young adults in the study invoked the school as a formative space in which meaning making took place and used it as a lens through which they understood their current identity. However, the 'space' of the school became both fragmented *and* totalising, a bounded experience from the past, but based on uneven memory recall.

What the young adults described was their remembered experiences of particular school cultures. Allen refers to school culture as 'produced within daily schooling practices in which young people actively participate' (2009, 396) and although this can relate to formal processes (e.g. school policy on sexuality), it can also relate to materiality and spatiality, such as the layout of changing rooms for boys and girls, and informal incidents, such as couples holding hands. A number of researchers have heuristically divided school culture into two realms: the informal and the formal. For example, Warwick et al. specify 'formal' in terms of time-tabled lessons and 'informal' in terms of 'conversations, discussions, arguments and bullying that take place in classrooms and corridors, on playing fields, in gymnasia and during assemblies' (2001, 138). Kehily (2002) places specific emphasis on the way in which pupil interactions can contravene the ethos of de-sexualised school policy, where informal conversations are 'saturated with sex – through humour, innuendo, double-entendre and explicit commentary' (5). For instance, Kehily's (2002) study emphasised the informal sexualised banter that infused formal lesson time. Equally, teachers also used a sexualised lexicon in the staff room. It is therefore important not to reify the formal and the informal because the boundary between them is porous and continually re-constituted in time and space. This essay uses this heuristic device, stressing that in everyday school life, formal school processes and informal interactions inextricably intersect.

This essay addresses three themes: (1) religion and the school culture; (2) the school as a sexualised space; and (3) counter-normative sexualities and heteronormativity. Each theme explores the formal and informal levels that inform identity work within the school space. However, we first offer a brief methodological account.

Method and sample

The research was conducted between 2009 and 2011, investigating the negotiation of sexuality and religion of young adults aged between 18 and 25 in the UK, specifically those who identified themselves as Buddhist, Christian, Hindu, Jewish, Muslim, Sikh or mixed-faith (e.g. 'Muslim-Christian').[1] Participants also identified their sexual orientation. They were able to choose from a list which encompassed lesbian, gay, heterosexual, bisexual, and other identifications. We must stress, in line with contemporary sociological theorising, that religious and sexual self-identifications are not fixed, but flexible and continually evolving (Lawler 2008).

The research employed three methods: (1) an online questionnaire, completed by 693 participants; (2) in-depth interviews with a sub-sample of 61; and (3) video diaries with a further sub-sample of 24 participants, drawn from the interview sample (for more details, see Yip, Keenan, and Page 2011; Yip and Page forthcoming). All participants cited have been given pseudonyms to protect their identity.

This essay focuses exclusively on qualitative data drawn from interviews, as they illustrate most effectively how young adults recounted their schooling experiences in the context of faith and sexuality. The sample's age profile means that the oldest had secondary school experiences dating back to 1996. A small number of the youngest participants were still in school at the time of the interviews (2009–2010). The schools the participants attended were of a varied nature: public and private (e.g. international schools abroad), religious and secular, same-sex, and cross-sex.

In the interviews, participants invoked narratives of the past in identity construction. However, as Lawler (2002) argues, memory is not video playback; rather, events are chosen for their significance and importance and the part that they play in constructing individuals' biographical accounts. This involves a process of forgetting and re-remembering. Memory is used as a device of narration, where 'the past is interpreted in light of the knowledge and understanding of the subject's "present"' (Lawler 2002, 248). Hierarchies develop around what is worthy of remembrance and what is forgotten, often dependent on the significance these memories are given in wider culture and by significant others (e.g. parents and friends) (Halbwachs 1992; Lawler 2008).

Religion and the school culture

Formal level

In terms of the formal teaching of religion, there was a variety of experiences, with very different curricula encountered. Some emphasised an overly Christianised experience, while others highlighted that schools focused mainly on other religions. Some had specifically attended religious schools, where much emphasis was placed on religion-centred learning. Sabrina, a 21-year-old heterosexual Muslim who attended a school that primarily comprised Muslim students, said, 'I did find it quite odd that in Religious Studies we did cover Islam quite in depth… I would have liked to have learned about other religions.' Meanwhile, Charlotte, a Buddhist who chose not to define her sexual orientation, said, 'I think we only did Christianity and Judaism. They were the only ones that we studied. In Year 7^2 we did… the six major religions – but then [they were] never mentioned again.' School learning could be pivotal, however, in introducing new ideas, particularly for those who came from non-religious family backgrounds and a significant proportion of those who had converted to Buddhism had been introduced to Buddhism in the school setting. For instance, Rosamund, a 25-year-old bisexual Buddhist, said, 'I did Religious Studies for A level and there was a bit about Buddhism in there and, you know, I got an A and … [got] really into it.' Therefore, school was a significant marker and flashpoint for these young adults' later religious journeys. However, others resented the way their religion was portrayed:

> It wasn't brilliantly taught… Teachers would say things [like], 'All religions use symbols' and of course there are Quakers who pride themselves on not using symbols. And when I said this, I got, 'Who are the Quakers?' from my Religious Studies teacher. (Ellie, 23, bisexual Buddhist-Christian-Pagan)

> Religious Studies doing GCSEs was just Hindu stuff I'd never heard of, like I swear that's not how I live my life at all and I'm just like, 'What are you talking about?'; there's all these idols that people don't understand so they think, 'Oh you're the religion with many gods.' (Shalini, 22, heterosexual Hindu woman)

For some, formal school culture acted as a catalyst for future religious projects; for others, school was a time and space of negotiating misrepresentation.

Informal level

At the level of informal interaction with other pupils, participants were split between those whose religion had been positively welcomed and those who had experienced bullying on the grounds of their religion. For example, Parminder was the only Sikh in her predominantly 'white' school, but she said:

> The group of people that I went to secondary school with were the group of people that I've been friends with since I was four years old ... they know my culture ... so they are understanding and they respect it. (20, heterosexual)

Others, however, had more negative experiences:

> I was the only Buddhist in the school ... when they follow you around the playground and they won't stop doing it and when it gets abusive or physical, then it is too much. (Lily, 20, chose to not define her sexual orientation, trans Buddhist)[3]

Fahima, a 21-year-old heterosexual Muslim, converted to Islam halfway through her secondary school:

> I used to come into school dressed in really provocative clothing... But then I fell off that, so nobody really wanted to know and people couldn't understand it either, because even though I wasn't wearing a headscarf, I covered up, as they like to call it. I started wearing jumpers ... and everyone freaked out... I had friends, but a lot of my friends left me when I became a Muslim. They all thought I was crazy and I didn't go to the parties any more ... I fell off like the cool crew, as they would like to think – nobody wanted to know.

Fahima's conversion to Islam prompted a backlash from former friends, who could not accept and reconcile her new religious identity with her former identity. Fahima's bodily practices no longer complemented the group identity of the 'cool crew' with whom she had been associated. Her body thus became stigmatised and had to be expelled from the group in order for the group to retain its validity (Goffman 1963).

Meanwhile, Isma used school as a space for resourcefulness. Raised in a family who supported traditional gender roles, she used the school to participate in a group who were challenging gendered expectations. Isma emphasised the importance of following Islam and contrasted her own highly religious faith position with what she described as the 'moderately religious' stance taken by her family. However, she felt that many cultural impediments that went against Islam had been ratified in the culture and she used the space of the school as a means of debating the issues and promoting a religiously inspired, gender-equal approach:

> We used to sit at lunchtime and before school and after school, we would come early so we could have debates about what we like in the culture, what we don't like and what our parents are doing ... we used to encourage each other and say to each other, don't let your mum do such and such a thing... We don't want to get married at 16

where you have the whole world ahead of you ... we strongly argued for further education. (20, heterosexual Muslim)

School could be a space where religious identity was consolidated or denied. For some, as a space away from home and community, the school acted as a place of interaction and support, where injustices were challenged, confidence was gained, debates formulated, and faith could be strengthened.

The inclusion of sexuality

Formal level

A number of scholars have emphasised that school silences sexuality at an official level, as shown by the discomfort surrounding the attempt to discuss sexuality education in this space (Epstein et al. 2003; Kehily 2002). As Kehily notes, some teachers cannot reconcile the statistics which show high rates of sexual activity among the age group they are teaching with the pupils in front of them who 'look like children' (2002, 179). In the context of wider sexualised cultures, young people could perceive sex and relationship education[4] as irrelevant, since they already have access to information about sex from other sources such as magazines, television, and the Internet (Epstein et al. 2003; Regnerus 2007). Indeed, some of the young adults in the study dismissed the quality of such lessons. For instance, Fahima said, 'They just come in and they give everybody condoms... They might show a few pictures of STIs [Sexually Transmitted Illnesses], but they're not, they're doing it far too late.'

However, others used school as an opportunity to learn about sexuality, particularly in contexts where sexuality was not discussed at home. Jai, a 23-year-old heterosexual Hindu, said, 'Sex was never talked about at home ... so the only form of talk about sex, the realisation about it, actually comes from your peer group, and ... sex education at school.' In Jai's account, knowledge gained in class was complemented with knowledge gained through informal peer group interaction. This highlights the patchwork way in which young people find access to knowledge about sex, which may be fleeting and fragmentary (Rahman and Jackson 2010).

Meanwhile, Yasmin's mother had, in theory, opted for her withdrawal from sex education classes, but Yasmin chose to participate.[5] She said that sex was not discussed at home: 'Growing up was very sheltered; obviously you go to school and all of that is like left behind you. Everyone was like "vagina this, penis that"', leaving her feeling unprepared for the school culture. Instead, by opting herself to take part in sex education classes, Yasmin had subverted parental authority and used the school as a means of access to information about sex. Therefore, formally, school teaching could serve as a resource for gaining knowledge, especially in helping to give young people at least a cursory knowledge of sex that they could use to cope with the sexualised school cultures.[6]

Informal level

Of note at the informal level was the almost incessant discussion in peer and friendship groups around sexuality – what people were doing, with whom, and where, as the following quotes reflect:

> When we were about in Year 11, about to leave, everything was, you know, 'Did you have sex this weekend... Then there would be stories about 'Oh, he's lying, he hasn't really had sex', you know, 'Oh, she has slept with such and such.' (Parminder, 20, heterosexual Sikh woman)

> [The] devout Christians ... wouldn't have sex ... but I know that a lot of my year would go out and have sex every weekend or at any spare time ... it's scary of how much sex goes on. I mean there are people that have been caught in school having sex. (Craig, 18, gay Buddhist)

> Because when we were all 14, everyone went a bit mad ... because of the amount of damage caused in that short period... I was the person that had to pick up the pieces. I've had to take three of my friends to abortion clinics and things like that. (Rosie, 18, heterosexual Buddhist)

The gap between the formal processes of sexual learning in the school setting and the informal situation was enormous. While sex education was generally perceived as unsatisfactory for all but those who had little access to knowledge elsewhere, the actual lived reality of young people's lives was characterised by relationships, sexual activity, and problems associated with relationship breakdown and teenage pregnancy. Therefore, formal and informal school cultures did not appear to mesh in many cases.

As all the participants in our study self-identified as religious, many had developed a religiously inspired ethic of sexuality. A number of the religious young adults eschewed practices condoned by friends and peers, but interestingly, few felt ostracised or marginalised for not 'joining in'. Those who were in contexts of heightened sexual activity adopted four management strategies (which were not necessarily mutually exclusive): (1) agony aunt/uncle role; (2) finding a like-minded cohort; (3) specifically using religious scripts as a coping mechanism for maintaining alternative values; and (4) joining in. Rosie, cited above, hinted at the role she played in being the support mechanism to her peers when things went wrong. Similarly, Vishaal, who was studying for A-levels[7] at the time said:

> Dealing with [friends'] drama ... dealing with all their problems... Thank God no one became pregnant and stuff, but it was just scary ... I was counselling everyone. (21, heterosexual Hindu man)

By assuming a pragmatic observer role, Vishaal was able to assume the role of the agony uncle of the group, to whom people would go when things went wrong. Seeing the mistakes others made also consolidated his decision not to have sex.

Others developed networks with like-minded individuals. For example, Marissa, a 21-year-old bisexual Jew, attended a religious school where many also put a high value on virginity until marriage. Surjit, a 25-year-old heterosexual Sikh woman, was in a similar situation:

> I think going to an all girls' school almost helped and also having other Sikh children with similar ... a wider Sikh culture of dos and don'ts ... there was never sort of an issue of a relationship really, for me at that age.

Craig's comments quoted earlier also indicate that within predominantly sexualised school cultures, certain sub-groups create counter-cultural norms (in his case, the 'devout Christians') where other values are established and endorsed. Therefore, for him, it was not necessary for a unilateral culture of sexual restraint to be present in order for him to eschew over-sexualisation; pockets of resistance could form.

Meanwhile, Mark, a 22-year-old heterosexual Christian, used personalised religious resources, focusing on his relationship with God and the Bible as a strategy to maintain a different sexual ethic:

> At school it was, in your peer group growing up together ... you had this kind of period of time where everyone was exploring their sexuality... I found it very difficult to accept that other people were doing things that I didn't think were right... But I still clung to the Bible and to my faith and thought, 'actually it is ok; I've got to try and know that His plans are right.'

Others, however, endorsed the sexualised culture of school and used it as a site of experimentation, which contrasted sharply with the religious and home context, engaging in activities that were expressly disallowed, such as drinking, smoking, and sexual activity.

Counter-normative sexualities and heteronormativity
Formal level

A large number of participants recalled their schools as, if not explicitly homophobic, at least implicitly heteronormative. Heteronormativity refers to the 'numerous ways in which heterosexual privilege is woven into the fabric of social life, pervasively and insidiously ordering everyday existence' (Jackson 2006, 108). While it does not necessarily condemn other sexualities in any direct way, it creates a hierarchy where heterosexuality is foregrounded and privileged. For instance, Stephen, a 21-year-old gay Christian, said:

> [In] RE [Religious Education] lessons, I don't remember gay people ever being brought into it whatsoever; it was always about 'don't commit adultery, do not fornicate' and it was always about a man and a woman.

Heather, a 22-year-old heterosexual Christian, considered the curriculum to be inconsistent and confused, hegemonising different discourses, depending upon whether it was an RE lesson or a sex education class:

> We were told at one stage you should never have sex before marriage and we were told the benefits of contraception in the next class.

Schools that were specifically religious were viewed more often in a negative light in this respect; Erica, a 20-year-old lesbian Jew, who had attended a Jewish Orthodox school, recalled:

> In some cases they did do the whole kind of 'it is immoral, it is wrong, go to a Rabbi and talk it through'. In another class they informed them [homosexuality] was as bad as bestiality... I was just quite lucky with my friends.

Erica used her friendship network as a support mechanism for coping with the formal school culture, where there appeared to be an official consensus that homosexuality was wrong. Meanwhile, Helen, a 23-year-old lesbian Christian, was one of the few who had a very positive experience:

> Actually a very acceptable school, even though it's quite a rough area; it's just a bog-standard comprehensive. I don't know how it was for guys but for girls, as I said, it was almost fashionable to experiment and there were two lesbian couples in our sixth form; there were openly gay teachers… It was just a very accepting place and I guess that outweighed … home – my dad is very traditional.

In this school context, Helen was able to use the formal school culture as a means of coping with her father's traditional views and she carried this positivity through to later years.

Informal level

While at a formal level, schools were not perceived as particularly welcoming to counter-normative sexualities, the informal school culture also reinforced a heteronormative culture. Indeed, LGB participants either cited concerns about 'coming out' or experienced a culture of homonegativity:

> I do remember though there being a big deal made out of a girl who decided to get a girlfriend and there were no 'out' gay people in my school at all, so that suggests there was a bit of a problem. (Charlotte, 24, Buddhist, who chose to not define her sexual orientation)

Some participants admitted that at school, they had either participated, or been complicit, in the culture of homonegativity:

> When I was younger, I used to think that [being gay] was really, really wrong … at school, if somebody said to me, 'so and so is gay', I'd be like 'ooh my god, wait until I get home and tell my mum. Oh my god, they're such a bad Muslim.' (Adala, 25, heterosexual Muslim woman)

Adala constructed this time in her life as a moment of childishness and ignorance. In her narrative, she sought to emphasise personal growth and a movement from intolerance to tolerance.

Some participants had managed to be openly gay or lesbian in a relatively supportive environment. In the following quote, Jacob, a 23-year-old homosexual Jew, related how he accidentally 'came out' at a school sleepover:

> It therefore got out to the rest of the school and actually, despite my worst fears again, pretty much everyone was like ok. There were a couple of people who were like, 'stay away', like 'won't turn my back on you'.

Meanwhile, others experienced bullying because of their sexuality, as articulated in the following interview extracts:

> When I was growing up, I was called names like 'pineapple', because it's a type of fruit, and 'Pocahontas' – actually I have to admire how refined the bullying was, but I mean it was never extreme, I was never physically attacked … all the way through I've always felt that I was alone in terms of my sexuality. (Stephen, 21, gay Christian)

I was outed at school as being bisexual when I was 15 ... which went down pretty badly. And I was kind of bullied quite a lot because of that... My group of friends pretty much ditched me because I was outed as being bisexual. And I was viewed as an outsider by them from that point on. They stopped inviting me to stuff and stopped hanging around with me so much at school. (Stuart, 24, bisexual Christian)

A number of LGB participants concealed their sexual orientation in the school context and only 'came out' years later. Much research highlights that schools remain stubbornly heteronormative, leading to bullying and harassment of sexual minorities (e.g. Buston and Hart 2001; Hunt and Jensen 2007; Plummer 2001; Taylor 2007; Warwick et al. 2001). Nonetheless, the most recent research into school cultures in the UK highlights a positive step change in attitude (McCormack 2011; McCormack and Anderson 2010) where 'male-to-male physical and emotional expressions of affection were an integral and daily part of school life ... [with an] absence of overt homophobia' (McCormack and Anderson 2010, 855). However, this research captured data from only a small number of schools. It is conceivable that different school cultures operate in different settings, with young adults in this study recalling negativity as well as more positive, pro-LGB environments. However, McCormack and Anderson (2010) still highlight the presence of heteronormative assumptions, even in spaces where there is an absence of anti-gay rhetoric. Thus they advocate focusing on how heteronormativity is managed and promoted, even where there is an absence of overt homonegativity.

Concluding remarks

For many young adults recounting the past, schooling acted as a memory flashpoint of significance, where meanings about sexual and religious acceptance and difference were generated and experiences were forged. Schools were spaces of both constraint and enablement, with differences arising depending on the school culture and the way this was facilitated at formal and informal levels. Sometimes, formal and informal cultures were mutually reinforcing. But the salience of schooling in the formulation of religious and sexual identities continued to resonate in the lives of the young adults in our study, through the life narratives they recounted. As we have shown through the discussion of the empirical themes, our study corroborates the findings of previous research to a great extent. However, this research is also distinctive because of its multi-faith perspective and its focus on young adults of diverse sexual identities.

Notes

1. The project, entitled 'Religion, Youth and Sexuality: A Multi-faith Exploration' (AH/G014051/1), was funded by the Religion and Society Programme of the Arts and Humanities Research Council (AHRC) and Economic and Social Research Council (ESRC). The research team consisted of Prof. Andrew Kam-Tuck Yip (Principal Investigator), Dr. Michael Keenan (Co-investigator), and Dr. Sarah-Jane Page (Research Fellow). More details about the project can be found at www.nottingham.ac.uk/sociology/rys. The research team is grateful for the funding as well as the invaluable contribution of the respondents, individuals, and groups who helped with the recruitment of the sample and of the members of the advisory committee.
2. Year 7 is typically the first year of secondary school, commencing at age 11.
3. Transgenderism includes a variety of identities, subjectivities, and experiences that challenge the dualistic construction of gender and rigid association between gender and sex.

4. 'Trans' is the preferred term of members of this community. In the case of this participant, she defines herself as such to emphasise her resistance to rigid binary gender categories.
4. Despite the new terminological shift to sex and *relationship* education, historically, most Anglophone countries have taken a biological approach to sex education, with much criticism that this is not placed in a wider framework of emotions and relationships (Allen 2005; Bragg and Buckingham 2009).
5. Parents have the right to remove their children from sex education classes. Recently, in England, this right was reduced to pupils under the age of 15, but at the time that the young people in our study experienced schooling, the parental right to opt out extended to age 19.
6. However, this is not to imply that superficial and fragmentary education pertaining to sexuality is acceptable. As Epstein et al. (2003) have indicated, poorly delivered sex education can result in great confusion and anxiety for pupils.
7. A-levels are academic qualifications that pupils in England, Wales, and Northern Ireland undertake prior to attending university.

References

Allen, L. 2005. *Sexual subjects*. Basingstoke: Palgrave Macmillan.
Allen, L. 2009. 'Caught in the act': Ethics committee review and researching the sexual cultures of schools. *Qualitative Research* 9, no. 4: 395–410.
Bragg, S., and D. Buckingham. 2009. Too much too young? Young people, sexual media and learning. In *Mainstreaming sex*, ed. F. Attwood, 129–46. London: I.B. Tauris.
Buston, K., and G. Hart. 2001. Heterosexism and homophobia in Scottish school sex education: Exploring the nature of the problem. *Journal of Adolescence* 24, no. 1: 95–109.
Epstein, D., S. O'Flynn, and D. Telford. 2003. *Silenced sexualities in schools and universities*. Stoke on Trent: Trentham Books.
Goffman, E. 1963. *Stigma*. London: Penguin Books.
Halbwachs, M. 1992. *On collective memory*. Chicago, IL: University of Chicago Press.
Hunt, R., and J. Jensen. 2007. *The experiences of young gay people in Britain's schools*. London: Stonewall.
Jackson, S. 2006. Interchanges: Gender, sexuality and heterosexuality. The complexity (and limits) of heteronormativity. *Feminist Theory* 7, no. 1: 105–21.
Kehily, M.J. 2002. *Sexuality, gender and schooling*. London: Routledge.
Lawler, S. 2002. Narrative in social research. In *Qualitative research in action*, ed. T. May, 242–58. London: Sage.
Lawler, S. 2008. *Identity*. Cambridge: Polity Press.
Massey, D. 2005. *For space*. London: Sage.
McCormack, M. 2011. The declining significance of homohysteria for male students in three sixth forms in the south of England. *British Educational Research Journal* 37, no. 2: 337–53.
McCormack, M., and E. Anderson. 2010. 'It's just not acceptable any more': The erosion of homophobia and the softening of masculinity at an English sixth form. *Sociology* 44, no. 5: 843–59.
Plummer, D.C. 2001. The quest for modern manhood: Masculine stereotypes, peer culture and the social significance of homophobia. *Journal of Adolescence* 24, no. 1: 15–23.
Rahman, M., and S. Jackson. 2010. *Gender and sexuality*. Cambridge: Polity Press.
Regnerus, M.D. 2007. *Forbidden fruit*. Oxford: Oxford University Press.
Taylor, Y. 2007. Brushed behind the bike shed: Working-class lesbians' experiences of school. *British Journal of Sociology of Education* 28, no. 3: 349–62.
Warwick, I., P. Aggleton, and N. Douglas. 2001. Playing it safe: Addressing the emotional and physical health of lesbian and gay pupils in the U.K. *Journal of Adolescence* 24, no. 1: 129–40.
Weeks, J. 2007. *The world we have won*. Abingdon: Routledge.
Wilkinson, L., and J. Pearson. 2009. School culture and the wellbeing of same-sex-attracted youth. *Gender and Society* 23, no. 4: 542–68.

Yip, A.K.-T., M. Keenan, and S. Page. 2011. *Religion, youth and sexuality*. Nottingham: University of Nottingham.
Yip, A.K.-T., and S. Page. forthcoming. *Religious and sexual identities*. Farnham: Ashgate.

Index

Page numbers in **bold** type refer to figures
Page numbers in *italic* type refer to tables
Page numbers followed by 'n' refer to notes

Abbas, T. 127
Academies Act (2010) 8
Addison, J.: Rosensohn, M. and Spilka, B.P. 48–9
adults: educational initiatives 1; emerging 137
aesthetic judgements 84
affiliation: religious 35, 55
African Christian 20
aggression: youth 29
Aldenmyr, S.I. 102; and Furedi, F. 95
Alexander, C. 121
Allen, L. 152
Allport, G.W.: and Ross, J.M. 46
altruistic behaviour 45–6
Anderson, E.: and McCormack, M. 159
Anglicanism 72
Anwar, M. 121
Archive for the Psychology of Religion 32
Argyle, M. 32; and Beit-Hallahmi, B. 32, 36; *Religious behaviour* 32
Arts and Humanities Research Council (AHRC) 1, 5, 13, 27, 42, 62
Association of University Lecturers in Religious Education (AULRE) 5
Astley–Francis Scale of Attitude toward Theistic Faith 34–5, 41
Aston University 151
atheism 15, 148
Attitude toward Muslim Proximity Index 35
Attitude toward Religious Diversity Index (ARDI) *40*
Attitudes toward Religion Project 33, 35–6

Ballard, R. 121, 122
Banks, M.: and Morphy, H. 84
Batson, C.D. 46; and Darley, J. 46; and Gray, P.A. 46
Battaglia, D. 84
Baudrillard, J. 61, 71, 73; and Noailles, E.V. 71
Baumfield, V. 62–3, 96; Conroy, J. and Lundie, D. 9, 61–75, 77–80, 81

behaviour: altruistic 45–6; helping 46; pro-social 46–7
Beit-Hallahmi, B.: and Argyle, M. 32, 36
belief: paranormal 34; Post-Critical Belief Scale 47
believing without belonging 135
Bell, J. 140
Bend it like Beckham (Chadha) 120
Benson, P.L.: and Spilka, B.P. 48–51
Berger, P. 82
Berglund, J. 9, 109–18
Bhangra 120
Biggar, N.: and Hogan, L. 18
Boal, A. 81, 84–5
Bornstein, E. 74, 84
Boy with the topknot, The (Sanghera) 121, 131n
Boys' Brigade 19
Brah, A. 121
Brierley, D. 137–8
British Asian communities 121
British Association for the Study of Religions (BASR) 5
British Sikhs 119–32
British Social Attitudes Survey (BSA) 38
British society 24
Brockett, A.: Village, A. and Francis, L.J. 35
Buchardt, M. 78
Buddhists 34, 153–4, 156, 158
buddy teachers 112
Buri, J.R.: and Mueller, R.A. 48

Cartledge, M.J. 33
caste 122, 130
Catholicism 22, 72, 89
cell group: youth work 134, 137–8, 144, 147
Chadha, G. 120
Chartier, M.R.: and Goehner, L.A. 48–9
child slavery 88
child-centred learning 104, 138
childhood spirituality 87
choice: and voice 140, 143–4, 148–9
Christian: African 20

INDEX

Christian chain of memory 135–6, 148
Christian Churches 133
Christian consciousness 135
Christianity 24, 34, 82, 148; education 138; Francis Scale of Attitude toward 34, 47; negative connotations of word 'religious' 16; positive church experiences 142–3; in Religious Education (RE) 14; teaching about 24
Christians 15, 17–19, 21–4, 52, 140, 157–9; African 20; Catholicism 22, 72, 89; commonalities of belief with Islam 22; Protestant 18, 22, 89; youth work 133–50
Church of England 19, 133
Church of Scotland 18, 89
Church of Sweden 117n
circle time 103
cities: Muslim areas 19
coalition: Conservative–Liberal Democrat 2, 6
Collins-Mayo, S.: et al. 133–9, 141–2, 144, 147–9
Committee of Ministers 7
communities: religious 3; socio-religious 82
community cohesion 23
conflict: epistemic and ethical 63, 79
Conroy, J. 5, 63, 71, 85; and Lundie, D. 9, 81–94; Lundie, D.; and Baumfield, V. 9, 61–75, 77–80, 81
consciousness: ethical 90
consequential faith 136
conservative Protestantism 18
Conservative–Liberal Democrat coalition 2, 6
consistency theory 55
consumerism 139
controversy 90
conversation: inter-generational 104
Cooling, T. 96
Coopersmith Self-Esteem Inventory 48
Copley, T. 87, 96, 103–4
Corrymeela Community 22
Corulla, W.J. 37, 49–51
Council of Europe 6–9; tripartite aims 7
Croft, J.S.: et al. 31–44; Pyke, A. and Francis, L.J. 45–59
Crowne, R. 136
cultural difference 22
cultural relativism 137
culture: teenage 17

Daly, J.A.: and Kreiser, P.O. 102
Darley, J.: and Batson, C.D. 46
Davie, G. 133, 135–6, 139
Davis, M.H. 46, 47
Davis, R.: and O'Hagan, F. 71
Dawkinsmania 15, 25n
Dean, K.C. 136, 139

decline of religion 15
defining education 82
deism: moralistic therapeutic 135–6
Delphi method 62, 68
Delphi seminar 70, 73, 74n
Democracy and Tradition (Stout) 23
deniability: plausible 73
Denton, M.L.: and Smith, C. 120, 135
Department for Children, Schools and Families (DCSF) 27
DeVellis, R.F. 40, 52
differences: individual 32, 45
disorders: psychosomatic 37; psychotic 37
diversity: religious 45–59
Does Religious Education Work? (Project) 5, 9, 62, 77, 81
Drury, B. 129
Duriez, B. 46–7

Easting, G.: Pearson, P.R. and Eysenck, S.B. G. 47, 49, 51
Economic and Social Research Council (ESRC) 1, 5, 13, 27, 42, 62
educational ethnography 83
emerging adults 137
Emery-Wright, S. 137, 139
emotional connotations of words 27–8
emotional empathy: Questionnaire Measure 46, 49
empathy 45–59; Hogan Scale 46, 49; and religion 47
empirical theology 31–44, 46–7, 55
Empirical Theology in Texts and Tables: Qualitative, Quantitative and Comparative Perspectives (Francis, Robbins and Astley) 33
Engelke, M.: and Tomlinson, M. 73, 83
English Baccalaureate 2, 8
English cities: Muslim areas 19
Epstein, D., et al. 160n
Epstein, N.: and Mehrabian, A. 46, 49, 51
Erricker, C. 101
ethical consciousness 90
ethnography: educational 83
Eucharist 18
European Union (EU) 6
European Wergeland Centre 6–8
Everington, J. 9, 95–107; and Sikes, P. 95–6, 100, 104
examination encouragement **70**
examination success: RE 86
existential reflection 79
exotic religions 91
extraversion 36–7, 41, 50–2
Eysenck, H.J.: and Eysenck, S.B.G. 37, 49–50
Eysenck Personality Questionnaire 37, 50; Junior 37, 41, 50–1; Junior Eysenck

INDEX

Impulsiveness Questionnaire (JIVE) 45, 47, 49, 51; Revised 37, 50
Eysenck, S.B.G. 49–50; Easting, G. and Pearson, P.R. 47, 49, 51; and Eysenck, H.J. 37, 49–50; and Saklofske, D.H. 49
Eysenckian model of personality 36–8, 50; and religiosity 36

failures: of meaning in RE 61–75, 77, 79–80, 91
faith: consequential 136; immanent 138; non-Christian 23; schools 6
families: migration 112, 118n
Fitts, W.H. 48
food: Sikh 125
forum theatre approach 9, 81–94
Francis, L.J. 9, 33–4, 37–8, 42, 47–51, 55; Brockett, A. and Village, A. 35; Croft, J.S. and Pyke, A. 45–59; et al. 31–44; Gibson, H.M. and Robbins, M. 48–50; and Kay, W. K. 33, 34, 50; and Pearson, P.R. 46–7, 50; and Robbins, M. 33; and Sahin, A. 34; and Village, A. 33; and Ziebertz, H-G. 33
Francis Scale of Attitude toward Christianity 34, 47
Frelin, A. 111, 116–17
Furedi, F. 96, 103–5; and Aldenmyr, S.I. 95
Furrow, L.J.: King, P.E. and White, K. 46–7

Gerhart, M. 90
Gibson, H.M.: Francis, L.J. and Robbins, M. 48–50
Gilchrist, J. 89
Girls' Brigade 19
Glasgow University 5, 81
God images 33–4, 41, 45–59; of justice 33; of mercy 33, 55; New Index 50–1, 53
Goehner, L.A.: and Chartier, M.R. 48–9
Goffman, E. 154
Golden Temple 122
Good Samaritan Experiments 46
Gorsuch, R.L. 48; and Venable, V.D. 47
Gospel narrative 87
Gray, P.A.: and Batson, C.D. 46
Greene, M. 136
Grimmitt, M. 63, 77, 104
Grossman, P.: and McDonald, M. 117
Guba, E.G.: and Lincoln, Y.S. 97
gurdwara 119–20, 122, 124, 126, 128–31
Guru Granth Sahib 122, 124–5, 130
Gurus 119, 124–5

Habermas, J. 23
Habib, F.: Khan, Z.H. and Watson, P.J. 46–7
happy midi-narrative 135–6
Haredi Jews 14, 16
Hegy, P. 33

helping behaviour 46
Hervieu-Léger, D.L. 127, 135
heteronormativity 152, 157, 159
Heubner, D. 82
higher education (HE) 1
hijab 35
Hinduism: Santosh–Francis Scale 34
Hindus 17, 34, 155–6
History for all: History in English schools 2007–10 (Ofsted) 74n
Hogan Empathy Scale 46, 49
Hogan, L.: and Biggar, N. 18
homonegativity 158–9
homophobia 159
Hull, J. 91
Hyde, L. 85, 92

iconography: Sikh 124–5
identity: religious 39, 151; sexual 151; teacher 104–5
images: of God 33–4, 41, 45–59; teacher 102
Imagining God: Empirical explanations from an international perspective (Ziebertz) 33
immanent faith 138
impulsiveness: Junior Eysenck Questionnaire (JIVE) 45, 47, 49, 51
individualism 135, 138
inter-generational conversation 104
Intercultural Education and Challenge of Religious Diversity and Dialogue in Europe 7
International Journal of Practical Theology 33
International Journal for Psychology of Religion 32
International Society of Empirical Theology 33
Interpersonal Reactivity Index 46–7
Ipgrave, J. 9, 13–25, 27–30
Islam 6, 34, 65, 100, 111; commonalities of belief with Christianity 22; Sahin–Francis Scale of Attitude 34; traditions 116
Islamophobia 115

Jackson, R. 5–7, 9, 27, 29, 31, 42, 45, 63, 82; et al. 128; and Nesbitt, E. 121, 125
Jackson, S. 157
Jews 34, 157–8; Haredi 14, 16
Jhutti-Johal, J. 123
Johannine literature 55
Journal of Beliefs and Values 33
Journal of Empirical Theology 33
Journal of Psychology and Theology 33
Judaism: Katz–Francis Scale of Attitude 34
judgements: aesthetic 84
Junior Eysenck Impulsiveness Questionnaire (JIVE) 45, 47, 49, 51
justice: God of 33

INDEX

Kandiah, K. 139
Karlstad University 77
Katz–Francis Scale of Attitude toward Judaism 34
Kay, W.K.: and Francis, L.J. 33, 34, 50; and Ziebertz, H-G. 13, 28
Kehily, M.J. 152, 155
Khalsa code 126
Khan, Z.H.: Watson, P.J. and Habib, F. 46–7
King, P.E.: White, K. and Furrow, L.J. 46–7
knowledge: defining 96–7; teachers' life 95–106
Kozyrev, F.: and Valk, P. 28
Kreiser, P.O.: and Daly, J.A. 102

language: religious 71, 88–9; symbolic 88
late industrial societies 61, 73
Lawler, S. 152–3
learning: child-centred 104, 138
Leeds University 128
Lefstein, A.: and Snell, J. 83
LGB students 151, 158–9
liberal education tradition 70
lie scale 37–8, 41, 52
Liguori, A. 82
Likert, R. 36
Likert scale 36, 39, 50
Lincoln, Y.S.: and Denzin, N. 97; and Guba, E.G. 97
Liverpool Hope University 61, 81
Local Authorities (LAs) 2
Loughran, J. 105; and Northfield, J.R. 97
Loukes, H. 104
Loving and Controlling God Scales 49
Luhr, E. 139
Lundie, D.: Baumfield, V. and Conroy, J.C. 9, 61–75, 77–80, 81; and Conroy, J.C. 9, 81–94

McCormack, M.: and Anderson, E. 159
McCroskey, J.C.: and Richmond, V.P. 102
McDonald, M.: and Grossman, P. 117
Manion, L.: and Cohen, L. 97
marginalisation 8
Marion, J-L. 90
Maritain, J. 70
Markstrom, C.A.: et al. 46–7
Massey, D. 151–2
maths education 68–9
Mazabane, N. 136
meaning: making 61–2, 71, 73–4, 87; search 61
media: Sikhs portrayal 120
Mehrabian, A.: and Epstein, N. 46, 49, 51
memory: Christian chain 135–6, 148
Mental Health Religion and Culture 32
mercy: God of 33, 55

metaphysics 82, 87
migration: families 112, 118n; history 122, 130
Milner, D.: and Sinclair, J. 127
mixed method research 28, 31, 45
modernisation: Western 135
moral integrity 21
moralistic therapeutic deism 135–6
Morphy, H.: and Banks, M. 84
Moses 88
Mott-Thompson, K. 82
Moving English Forward: Action to raise standards in English (Ofsted) 62
Mueller, R.A.: and Buri, J.R. 48
Mujis, D.: and Reynolds, D. 96, 102
multi-dimensional nature of religion 34
multi-faith Religious Education (RE) 13, 24, 28–9, 96
multicultural education 29
Muslim areas: of English cities 19
Muslims 16–17, 20, 22–3, 52, 100–1, 153–5, 158; pupil and teacher relationship 109–18; Swedish 109–17
myths and parables 88

National Association of Teachers of Religious Education (NATRE) 5, 8
National Study of Youth Religion 135–6
nature-nurture debate 114
neo-individualism 71
Nesbitt, E. 97, 122, 124, 126, 128, 130; and Arweck, E. 78; and Jackson, R. 121, 125
neurotic disorders 37
neuroticism 36–7, 41, 50–2
New Index of God Images (NIGI) 50–1, 53
New Labour government 2, 6
New Testament 55
Noailles, E.V.: and Baudrillard, J. 71
non-Christian faiths 23
Northfield, J.R.: and Loughran, J. 97
Nottingham University 151

objects: religious 84, 91
Ofsted (Office for Standards in Education) 9, 13, 24, 61–3, 87
O'Hagan, F.: and Davis, R. 71
Ohrlander, G. 111
Organisation for Security and Co-operation in Europe (OSCE) 6, 8; Office for Democratic Institutions and Human Rights (ODIHR) 8
Osbeck, C. 9, 77–80
Outgroup Prejudice Project 33, 35–6
Owen, R. 70

Paek, E. 46–7
Page, S-J.: and Yip, A.K-T. 10, 151–61

INDEX

Parable of Good Samaritan 46
parables 88
paranormal beliefs 34
Pearson, P.R.: Eysenck, S.B.G. and Easting, G. 47, 49, 51; and Francis, L.J. 46–7, 50
Penner, L.A.: et al. 47
personal life knowledge: teachers 95–107
personality 36–8; Eysenckian model 36–8, 50; Prosocial Personality Battery 47
Peters, R. 70
PGCE (Post-Graduate Certificate in Education): RE places 8
Pimlott, J.: and Pimlott, N. 133, 136, 139
Pinker, S. 73
Plato 68
plausible deniability 73
Pollock, D. 83
Post-Critical Belief Scale 47
post-secular debates 6
pregnancy: teenage 156
pro-social behaviour 46–7
Prosocial Personality Battery 47
Protestant Christians 22, 89
Protestantism: conservative 18
Protestants 18, 22, 89
psychology: of individual differences 32, 45; of religion 31–2, 34, 45–6, 51, 55; social 31–44
Psychology of Religion and Spirituality 32
psychosomatic disorders 37
psychotic disorders 37
psychoticism 36–7, 41, 50–2
public arena 6, 23
Public Significance of Religion, The (Francis and Ziebertz) 33
Punjabi 119, 121–2, 126–30
pupil–teacher relationship: and Muslims 109–18
pupils: confidence in teachers 111; opinions 64–5, 66–8, 72–3
Putnam, R. 22
Pyke, A.: et al. 31–44; Francis, L.J. and Croft, J.S. 45–59

Questionnaire Measure of Emotional Empathy 46, 49
Qur'an 20, 23, 100, 115

reactivity: Interpersonal Index 46–7
REDCo (Religion, Education, Dialogue, Conflict) Project 6, 8–9, 10n, 13–14, 19, 27–8
reflection: existential 79
relationships: and sex 87
relativism: cultural 137
Religion in Education: Findings from the Religion and Society Programme 5

Religion Inside and Outside Traditional Institutions (Streib) 33
Religion and Society Programme 1, 5–11, 9, 13, 27, 62
religiosity: and Eysenckian model of personality 36
religious affiliation 35, 55
Religious behaviour (Argyle) 32
religious communities 3
religious diversity 45–59
Religious Education Council (REC) of England and Wales 5
Religious Education (RE): Christianity in 14; curriculum changes 103; multi-faith 13, 24, 28–9, 96; in Sweden 77; young people's attitudes 23–4
Religious Education (RE) in schools 1, 85; avoiding difficult questions 89–91; educational aims 61, 63; epistemic and ethical conflict 63, 79; examination success 86; marginalisation 8; meaning failures 61–75, 77, 79–80, 91; non-statutory guidance 2; opinion forming and expressing 68, 79; publicly funded schools 6–9; pupil opinions 64–5, 66–8, 72–3; purpose and context 2, 62–73; role in society 24; sex and relationships 87; Sunday School model 91; teachers' personal life knowledge 95–107; teaching about Christianity 24
religious identity *39*, 151
religious language 71, 88–9
religious literacy 24, 29
religious objects 84, 91
religious socialisation 1, 130, 137
religious traditions 45–6
Review of Religious Research 33
Reynolds, D.: and Mujis, D. 96, 102
Richmond, V.P.: and McCroskey, J.C. 102
Ricoeur, P. 65
Riegel, U.: and Ziebertz, H.G. 82
Robbins, M.: et al. 31–44; and Francis, L.J. 33; Francis, L.J. and Gibson, H.M. 48–50
Roberts, K.A.: and Yamane, D.A. 120, 125, 130
Rosensohn, M.: Spilka, B.P. and Addison, J. 48–9
Ross, J.M.: and Allport, G.W. 46

Sabbath-Day observance 19
Sahin, A.: and Francis, L.J. 34
Sahin–Francis Scale of Attitude toward Islam 34
Saklofske, D.H.: and Eysenck, S.B.G. 49
Sanghera, S. 121, 126, 131n
Santosh–Francis Scale toward Hinduism 34
Sants (charismatic individuals) 121, 128
Savage, S.: et al. 135–6

INDEX

Schihalejev, O. 9, 27–30
schools: culture 29, 152; publicly funded 6–9; sexual and religious cultures 151–61; Sikhs 126–8, *see also* Religious Education (RE) in schools
Schweitzer, F. 77
Scottish Reformed tradition 18
Scottish Religious and Moral Education (RME) 14
Scripture Union (SU) 21–2
search for meaning/truth 61
Seer, The (Smith) 85
Selander, S-Å. 77
self-esteem 55–6
Sennett, R. 102
sex: outside marriage 17; and relationships 87
sexual identity 151
sexual and religious cultures in school 151–61; formal level 153–4, 155, 157–8; informal level 154–5, 155–7, 158–9
sexuality education 155–6
Shepherd, N. 137
Sikes, P.: and Everington, J. 95–6, 100, 104
Sikhism 34
Sikhs 16, 23, 101, 154, 156; British 119–32; food 125; history 129; iconography 124–5; media portrayal 120; school 126–8; stories 125–6
Sinclair, J.: and Milner, D. 127
Singh, G.: and Tatla, D.S. 121–2, 128
Singh, J. 9–10, 119–32
slavery: child 88
Smith, A. 85
Smith, C.: and Denton, M.L. 120, 135; and Snell, P. 136–7
Snell, J.: and Lefstein, A. 83
Snell, P.: and Smith, C. 136–7
Snyder-Young, D. 83
social club: youth work 134, 138, 147
social psychology 31–44
social sciences 32, 36
socialisation: religious 1, 130, 137
socio-religious communities 82
Socratic engagement 68
Södertörn University 109
Spilka, B.P.: Addison, J. and Rosensohn, M. 48–9; and Benson, P.L. 48–51
spirituality: childhood 87; in Religious Education (RE) 87
Standing Advisory Council for Religious Education (SACRE) 2, 8
Stanton, N. 9, 133–50, 138
stories: Sikhs 125–6
Stout, J. 23
Sunday School 18–19; model 91
Sunday service: youth work 134
suppression: of religious voices 23

Sutcliffe, J. 136, 138
Sweden: Religious Education (RE) 77
Swedish Muslims 109–17
symbolic language 88

Takhar, O.K. 122
Tartu University 27
Tatla, D.S.: and Singh, G. 121–2, 128
teacher–pupil relationship 109, 113; distance 100; openness 101–4
teachers: biographies 96; buddy 112; identity 104–5; image 102; life knowledge 95–106; neutrality debate 96; personal life knowledge 95–107; pupil confidence 111; training 114–17
teaching: about Christianity 24
teenage culture 17
teenage interaction 23
teenage pregnancy 156
Teenage Religion and Values (Francis and Kay) 33
Teenage Religion and Values Project 33–4, 36
Teenagers and the Church (Francis) 33
Tennessee Self Concept Scale 48
theology: empirical 31–44, 46–7, 55
Toledo guiding principles on teaching about religions and beliefs in public schools, The (OSCE) 8
Tomlinson, M.: and Engelke, M. 73, 83
Tony Blair Faith Foundation 5
traditions: religious 45–6
training: teacher 114–17
Transforming RE: Religious education in schools 2006–09 (Ofsted) 13, 62–3, 78
truth: questions 99; search 61
Turner, V. 89

universities: Glasgow 5, 81; Leeds 128; Religious Studies 6; St Thomas 48; Warwick 5, 13, 29, 31, 45
Urban Hope and Spiritual Health: The adolescent voice (Francis and Robbins) 33

Valhalla 88
Valk, P.: and Kozyrev, F. 28
Values Debate: A voice from the pupils, The (Francis) 33
Ven, H. van der 32
Venable, V.D.: and Gorsuch, R. L. 47
vicarious religion 133–6, 142
Village, A. 35; and Francis, L.J. 33; Francis, L.J. and Brockett, A. 35
voice: and choice 140, 143–4, 148–9; suppression 23

Ward, P. 138–9
Warwick, I.: et al. 152

INDEX

Warwick University 5, 13, 29, 31, 45; Warwick Religions and Education Research Unit (WRERU) 5–6, 13–14, 27–9, 31, 33, 42, 45, 95
Watson, P.J.: et al. 46–7; Habib, F. and Khan, Z.H. 46–7
Weeks, J. 151
Werbner, P. 120
Western modernisation 135
Westminster Faith Debates 3
What do we Imagine God to be? The function of 'God images' in our lives (Hegy) 33
White, K.: Furrow, L.J. and King, P.E. 46–7
Who wants to be a Millionaire? 86–7, 91
Woodhead, L. 5
words: emotional connotations 27–8
world religions: six major 3, 34, 103

Yamane, D.A.: and Roberts, K.A. 120, 125, 130
Yip, A.K-T.: and Page, S-J. 10, 151–61
York St John University 35
young people's attitudes 13–25; abnormality/normality of religion 14–18, 18–23; contextuality 27–30; defining religion 15–16, 19–20; impact on religious students 17–18, 21–3; implications for Religious Education (RE) 23–4; relating to religious peers 16–17, 20–1
Young People's Attitudes to Religious Diversity (project) 9, 31, 45, 51; instruments of measurement 36; levels of measurement 35–6; multi-dimensional nature of religion 34; quantitative approaches 31–44, 45
Youth 4 Christ 136
youth aggression 29
Youth in Transit: A profile of 16–25 year olds (Francis) 33
youth work 133–50; cell group 134, 137–8, 144, 147; Christian 133–50; social club 134, 138, 147; Sunday service 134; three domain model 146–9

Ziebertz, H-G. 33; and Kay, W. 13, 28; and Riegel, U. 82
Zuckerman, P. 120

www.routledge.com/9780415713054

Related titles from Routledge

Religion, Religious Organisations and Development
Scrutinising religious perceptions and organisations
Edited by Carole Rakodi

This collection adds to a burgeoning literature concerned with the roles played by religions in development. The authors do not assume that religion and religious organisations can be 'used' to achieve development objectives, or that religiously inspired development work is more holistic, transformative and authentic. Instead, they subject such assumptions to critical and (as far as possible) objective scrutiny, focusing on how adherents of several religious traditions and a variety of organisations affiliated with different religions perceive the idea of development and attempt to contribute to its objectives. Geographically, chapters in the volume encompass Africa, South Asia and the Asia-Pacific.

This book was published as a special double issue of *Development in Practice*.

Carole Rakodi is an Emeritus Professor in the International Development Department, School of Government and Society, University of Birmingham, UK.

September 2013: 246 x 174: 288pp
Hb: 978-0-415-71305-4
£85 / $145

For more information and to order a copy visit
www.routledge.com/9780415713054

Available from all good bookshops

www.routledge.com/9780415783040

Related titles from Routledge

Sexuality, Religion & the Sacred
Bisexual, Pansexual & Polysexual Perspectives

Edited by Loraine Hutchins & H. Sharif Williams

This thoughtful collection of bisexual, polysexual and pansexual scholarship on religion and spirituality examines how religious and spiritual traditions address sexuality, whilst also exploring the ways in which bisexually-, polysexually-, and pansexually-active people embrace religious and spiritual practice. It offers an accessible yet scholarly treatment of these topics through a collection of critical essays by academics of theology, humanities, cultural studies and social sciences, as well as sexology professionals and clergy from various faith and spiritual traditions. It gives readers an insight into the intersection of sexualities and spiritualities, and attempts to disrupt this very dichotomy through its careful consideration of a wide variety of discourses.

This book was originally published as a special issue of the *Journal of Bisexuality*.

December 2011: 246 x 174: 240pp
Hb: 978-0-415-78304-0
£85 / $145

For more information and to order a copy visit
www.routledge.com/9780415783040

Available from all good bookshops